Wearing the
Coat of Change

Wearing the Coat of Change

Handbook for Personal Survival and Prosperity in the Unpredictable World of Work

Tim Drake

ORION
BUSINESS
BOOKS

The right of Tim Drake to be identified as the author
of this work has been asserted by him in accordance
with the Copyright, Designs and Patents Act 1988.

First published in Great Britain in 1998 by
Orion Business
An imprint of The Orion Publishing Group Ltd
Orion House, 5 Upper St Martin's Lane, London WC2H 9EA

A CIP catalogue record for this book
is available from the British Library.

ISBN: 0 75281 246 7

Typeset by Deltatype Ltd, Birkenhead, Merseyside

Printed in Great Britain by
Clays Ltd, St Ives plc.

This book is dedicated to Lizzie and our two daughters Tansy and Lettice, with thanks for their love and humour

Acknowledgements

MY WIFE LIZZIE, for her tireless support in reading, and suggesting enhancements.

Simon Trewin, the literary agent who midwifed the book, for his positive support, and patient teaching, throughout the process of writing it.

John Jones, CEO of Promar, the strategic consultancy with whom I work from time to time, for his unwitting support for this book, and for his sharing the fruits of an outstanding brain and a dry sense of homour.

Martin Liu, my publisher, for his patience and skilful guidance.

Contents

A Personal Note

Towards the end of 1990 our bankers valued my share of Cobra Sports at £5 million. This, they said, was a conservative valuation. The recession seemed to be over; we had weathered it well; the future looked bright. Two years later, for reasons I'll touch on later, we had to sell the business for the equivalent of 5 pence.

After fourteen years of building, with a partner, an excellent team, and an excellent business, which was to have been our life work – and our pension! – I found myself without a partner, without a company and, apparently, without a future. I was forty-eight, had lost two stone in weight while losing the company, and had some thinking to do.

I did, however, have some assets. The first was a wonderfully supportive wife, and children aged ten and six (the price on the Mad Hatter's hat) who were a constant source of joy. They would, however, for the foreseeable future, need feeding, clothing and educating. So sitting around feeling sorry for myself wasn't an option.

I also had some marketing skills built over the years from my advertising and retailing background. In addition, and very importantly for me, I had the peace of mind of knowing that, however difficult and traumatic the last year or so had been at Cobra, the final resolution had been a good one for the company we had built. Indeed, the company is now almost twice the size, and is run by the same management we had recruited and trained over the fourteen years it had taken us to grow from our one shop in the King's Road to forty-two nationwide.

But I still had quite a large hole in my world – and my pay packet. So I had to do something. But what? Fortunately I had a short period of consultancy from Cobra, which helped, but after that, school fees and supermarket bills stretched endlessly into the distance.

Following the old adage that failure is but a stepping stone to success, after much reflection I put together a new and original retail package and took it to a couple of merchant banks. Both were extremely complimentary, but were turned down by their management committees. Both later privately admitted that, while they personally felt the recession was coming to an end, the corporate position was that retailing was still firmly off-limits as an investment area. A retail concept almost identical to the one I had put forward was launched by an existing retailer some two years later in Liverpool, with great success. Ho-hum.

It could be argued that I am not a true entrepreneur, for had I been I would have found the money somewhere – from mortgaging the part of the house the building society did not already own, borrowing from friends, etc. However, having stood so recently on the very brink of financial ruin (personal guarantees to banks, landlords, etc.) the idea didn't appeal.

So I chose a different course. I became an **IBG** (an **Independent Business Generator**). This meant developing my own income streams – as many and as different as possible – in order to have some protection against any drying up of these individual sources. If security of income no longer exists – and it doesn't – let's dig as many wells as possible. If we can't have security, let's at least try for independence.

One of these income streams turned out to be the writing of heavyweight tomes for the clients of an esteemed management consultancy (who pretended I worked for them). These works, which involved the analysis of trends (consumer, economic, technological, etc.) and the evolution of strategies to cope with, and capitalise on, these trends, sold well around Europe. My specific area of specialisation was the strategic implications of future changes on how people will feel about shopping, and how, and where, they will shop.

The researching and writing for these works led me to think further about what changes have taken place in society in general, what sort of changes are likely to take place in the future, and how, in a world where income for most people will be less stable and more uncertain, we can prepare and equip ourselves for the resulting challenges.

My personal experience forms a part of the book, to show I've walked the talk.

My life is not a blueprint for yours. Your talents will be different, and in many cases, larger, than mine. By weaving my experience into a wider context, and looking at why and how we'll adapt to change, I hope to convince you that you *will* survive and even flourish – whatever challenges you have been going through. I also hope to convince you that you may find the journey of personal discovery unexpectedly enjoyable and fulfilling.

Before You Start

Dig the well before you need the water
Chinese proverb

BEFORE YOU START the book, focus your mind on one thing, and tuck it away for your subconscious to mull over for the next few hours, weeks and months. That one thing is survival – personal (and family) survival – in a world where your current income stream may suddenly slow to a trickle, or dry up completely. The question you should be asking yourself, consistently and persistently, is:

Assuming I'll be out of a job within twelve months, how do I start preparing myself with some options – now?

Remember the definition of worry: interest paid on a debt not yet due. Look at it not as a source of anxiety, but as an opportunity to organise your life better. This exercise is just some pre-course preparation before you get into the meat of the book. The intention is to help you look for the good that always comes out of the bad.

ONE

The Coat's Many Colours: Themes Developed in the Book

IT WAS ON the eleventh day of the eleventh month – memorable because it was the same date on which the Armistice was signed to end the First World War – in 1992 that I signed the documentation that ended my ownership of shares in Cobra Sports.

I owned just over a third, my partner the same, and the remainder was split between others who worked for or with the company. It was bought by the family trust of a member of the board, who invested substantial sums to refinance it, and turned it once more into a successful and growing retail operation. The company and its culture had been saved. We as individuals had been saved.

Personal bankruptcy had been avoided, but we were left with a massive sense of loss. Fourteen enjoyable years of building a multi-million-pound retail business, which had an unusual degree of customer loyalty, and developing a management team, most of whom had grown with us over more than a decade, was over. The hole in my life was a profound one, and to make the situation worse, I had no idea what to do next. In most business situations you plan fall-back positions, but when you are applying all your mental and physical efforts to saving a company, there is no time or space to plan exit routes. Moreover, to do so would involve admitting to yourself that the situation could not be reversed.

So on 12 November I found myself with no company, and professionally alone – my partner had decided to go his own way. How it came about is not important, although I'll touch on it briefly later. For now, my personal challenges in 1992 are mentioned merely to show that the messages in this book come from someone who has lived amongst the muck and bullets.

I emphasise this for a good reason, which is that if you've been close to the bottom of a very unpleasant pit, you know that it is extremely black and unattractive. Well-meaning advice from friends and business associates tends to sound shallow and glib. However kindly intentioned they may be, they are faintly embarrassed talking to you. Like someone attending a funeral, they are not sure what to say. They end up dispensing platitudes to the bereaved, and both donors and recipients know that what is being said is inadequate.

What I will be saying in this book may run the danger – for someone in the middle of a period of private hell – of sounding somewhat easy, even facile. That is not the intention. I hope that the fact that I have been there myself will give you some reassurance that the solutions I put forward have been tried in the fire, and found to work for me. At times, this has not been without considerable difficulty. When you're in the shite, you're in the shite. No amount of clever ideas or advice will change it. What this book sets out to do is to try to help you cope a whole lot better. The ability to *fight the shite* is, indeed, one of the themes of the book.

The overall theme, if we can lift our view from the pit to the mountain, is *that we are now at a turning point*. The turning point applies both to individuals and to society as a whole. On a world scale, states are embracing the capitalist system of economics, and on a European scale states are tending to adopt the Anglo-Saxon model of economics, rather than the Bonn model. In essence, the Anglo-Saxon model is based on the belief that economies are more efficient – and thus in the long term more effective in protecting their citizens – if capital and labour are flexible, and left to find their own level. This means little protection for individuals, as redundancy, temporary or part-time working, and low-paid jobs, are all part of the economy finding its own level.

The Bonn economic model, on the other hand, is built on social justice and minimum wages that are life-supporting. The downside to this model is higher taxes for both business and individuals and, quite often, higher unemployment, because companies are unwilling to take on staff who are expensive (high minimum wages, plus a large tax bill to employ them). This model is at its most effective in strong economies that are also successful in remaining clear of recession for the majority of the time.

If social justice becomes unaffordable, the devil takes more of the hindmost

The movement towards the Anglo-Saxon economic model, as we shall see later, is not because politicians are becoming more cynical or less caring (although at times it appears to be the case), but because, for a number of reasons, the welfare state is no longer affordable. Once the welfare state becomes unaffordable, difficult choices have to be made as to who gets what money there is. More cracks in support appear, and more people fall down them. Social justice comes under severe pressure, because there are more and more deserving cases that are not being coped with by the system.

It's not only the hindmost who are in trouble

Global competition and technological advances are also hitting society from the other end. As companies react to the increasingly intense commercial environment by taking out any surplus management left after previous culls, their overriding need is for flexibility. All costs that are non-core are contracted out, making them variable, rather than fixed.

One major cost that is moving fast from being a fixed cost to a variable cost is labour. The direct result is the rapid increase in part-time working, temporary working, short-term contracts, and wholesale contracting out of departments to employment agencies. There is already a merchant bank in the City of London that only employs 6 per cent of its staff on full-time contracts of employment. Everybody else is hired in from outside.

As the core workers and core management get fewer and fewer in number, the direct result is that more and more of the workforce are losing even the pretence of security of employment. So-called Knowledge workers are reasonably secure in the labour market overall, because their skills are much in demand. For the majority of workers, however, supply exceeds demand. Enforced early retirement may be better than redundancy, but as pension provision gets thinner and thinner, it can still be distinctly uncomfortable, especially if the family is still consuming more money than is coming into the household each month.

Employment is returning to being a concept without meaning. Before the Industrial Revolution, jobs hardly existed. Labourers were hired as needed and, apart from those in service, who had little or no protection from the whims of employers (see *droit de seigneur*), most people were what we would nowadays call self-employed.

Because of the imbalance in supply and demand, the fragmentation of the concept of employment has all been employer-driven. Nil Hours Working – a contract that allows an employer to call on the services of an employee from anything between nil and forty or so hours a week – is a practice constructed purely for the convenience of the employer, and would not exist if demand for labour exceeded supply.

As the availability of a job – particularly a job for life – continues to dissolve, more and more people go to bed at night with a feeling of angst. This feeling is often justified, because their income stream is not secure. The angst is made worse by the fact that they are aware that in the event of redundancy, getting another job at a similar income level would be extremely challenging.

Full employment and the welfare state were very comfortable, but what now?

So we are now at a turning-point. Companies are embracing technology, and gearing themselves to face global competition. As a result they need smaller, more flexible, workforces with new and different sets of skill. Employment, even for High-flyers, is insecure and essentially temporary.

States are finding welfare budgets unfundable at any level close to that which their people have become accustomed to. To make matters worse, hidden taxation – leaving the better off to fund their own private health, education, pensions, etc. – doesn't make up the shortfall. The dilemma is that, just as conditions begin to deteriorate, and we need help, our two lifelong crutches – security of employment, and the welfare state – are no longer strong enough to support us. To make matters worse, these two crutches have, without our realising it, *reduced our comfort zone*.

Whatever happened, either a job, or unemployment benefit till the next job, were there to protect us. Our health was looked after, our children educated, there were homes and pensions for the elderly. Now the cold winds blow, and we seem to stand there feeling more exposed. We are not comfortable. This feeling of discomfort is heightened by our not being *used* to feeling vulnerable, and somewhat at a loss. Our comfort zone is minute. Job insecurity, job loss, company loss, loss of home, now touch us all. If it hasn't happened to us, we know someone to whom it has happened. We're outside our comfort zone, and it's no fun.

The two major themes of this book evolve directly from these new conditions:

   1. *Each of us needs to be able to cope with the new circumstances on our own.*

2. We also need to shoulder the mantle (part of the coat) of social responsibility.

The second point is a logical extension of the first. If the state is no longer able to look after us comprehensively, and we no longer have a guaranteed income stream sufficient to cope with our needs, it automatically means that there will be others who are also in a similar, and possibly worse, situation, and in need of help.

This awakening of social responsibility will be slow. Responsibility to ourselves, to our families – near and extended – and to the societies we live in, is forced upon us by the new situation. Part of this sense of responsibility will be born of enlightened self-interest. One example will be care of the aged. As state provision of care for the aged declines, families will increasingly step into the breach. This will partly be through love and regard for the elderly relative, and partly as a strong example to younger members of the family to follow. If children watch their parents abandon their grandparents, when their turn comes to look after the aged parents, the example will have been set. Both generations of aged parents will have been abandoned to whatever state support exists for those who have no resources.

We are thus talking on both an individual and social level about responsibility, and how we cope with it. The specific themes of the book address both of these aspects directly. Let's first touch on the themes addressing how we grow into enjoying our individual responsibility to get on the front foot in dealing with what life is going to throw at us.

Get fitted for the Coat of Change – take a STOC Check, create an IBG Action Plan

Taking a **STOC Check** involves taking an objective but fair look at where you stand now. It stands for **S**trengths, **T**alents and blessings, **O**pportunities, and **C**hallenges. This requires some concentrated thought, as well as some writing and rewriting, but is well worth the effort.

It is very different from writing a curriculum vitae. For a start, it's honest! This is not to imply that cvs are anything less than honest – merely that they tend to edit the truth. A STOC Check is a very frank and personal statement of your strengths, and the challenges presented by the weaknesses. Working out a balance sheet of strengths, talents and blessings can be quite surprising. You take so many of them for granted, that writing them down on a list can evoke a sense of wonder that one individual could have so many talents and blessings! The fact is that they are all true, and can bring a much-needed sense of balance, if the world is looking particularly black.

The **IBG Action Plan** resulting from the STOC Check gives you a clear path to follow in developing the assets and talents you have as an individual. By clearly articulating your strengths and talents, and where they might lead you, a sense of self-worth is restored. The inclusion of blessings, in particular, because it will include such things as family, sense of humour, and friends, will help to reorientate thinking to a more optimistic view of the situation.

Go for CZG. Every day.

A business leader who had been appointed to run a recently privatised utility in the United Kingdom, was asked what he thought about the ethics of operating a monopoly. His reply was that running a monopoly was a bit like having a baby. It might not be very attractive, but it looked a lot better if it was your own.

I'm not a great lover of acronyms but, like a monopoly, they're more attractive if they're your own. **CZG** stands for Comfort Zone Growth. Our comfort zone – by which I mean that area of activity in which we feel totally at home operating – can become minute if we get too used to working for a large company, where secretaries, messengers and other infrastructure are constantly on hand to provide support, and remove the need for individual action. Real life seldom encroaches.

Recalling the challenge that precedes this chapter, and imagining yourself without a job in a year's time, you could find yourself without a comfort zone to slip back into. Losing a job and a consistent income is bad enough. If you are like the majority of people, you *will also lose your compass point on the map of society*. Trade, profession, seniority, and even income, define who we are and where we fit in. Take that away, and we are floating. We not only have the challenges of uncertain income, but of *uncertainty in how our worth is measured, both by ourselves and others*.

It therefore makes sense to spend time outside your comfort zone, in order to acclimatise yourself. Comfort Zone Growth is vital at all stages. Very few people have a comfort zone that is big enough. I certainly don't, and I've been working hard on it for some time. But the more times you stretch yourself to cope in new, unfamiliar, or even threatening situations, the better you feel, and are able to cope, next time.

CZG covers many areas. One important area for IBGs is talking to people. All sorts of people. It is about initiating conversations, when your comfort zone tells you it would be easier to hold your counsel, and say nothing. The importance of talking to people is fundamental on two levels. Firstly, in order to live in a society where even the basics are no longer guaranteed, it is important to engage at as many levels as possible. The cocoon of income and *status* no longer exists. You're down there with everyone else, and you have to operate and survive at that level.

Secondly, you have to talk to people to create income. All sorts of people. And practice makes perfect. The reason for this is that, unless you are incredibly lucky, the world will not beat a path to your door with offers of work. This is for many reasons. Partly it is because people are genuinely too busy to think about you, and create work for you. Partly it is because people like to associate with winners, and however well you may have performed in the period leading up to your departure from your job, and however much the out-turn may have been outside your control, you are not seen as a winner. It is also partly because people, probably rightly, feel you need some space to sort out what you want to do with your life.

Whatever the reason, experience seems to indicate that it takes at least six months longer than you anticipated to generate the sort of income you thought you would, from the project or projects you decide upon (including the option of another job). The earlier you start on CZG, the sooner you will feel confident talking to anyone, and the sooner you'll feel you're talking as a relaxed equal, rather than as a supplicant.

Be an IBG – even when you're working for a company or organisation

An IBG, as we have seen, is an Independent Business Generator. The terminology is intentionally mechanistic. The soft, human issues do not come into it. Being an IBG is about programming yourself to create income. It is about a totally commercial approach to income generation that admits no excuses. It is about throwing enough things against the wall till eventually something sticks. It is about maintaining discipline and a work ethic, no matter what.

It is also concerned with marketing the assets identified in the STOC

Check. Being an IBG means treating yourself as a business enterprise, with a brand or brands that are there to be marketed. This includes the relaunches and re-presentation of existing brands, and the development of new products and services. It also involves rethinking what market you are in, and whether you should be moving to different markets, or even developing new ones.

Becoming an IBG is an explicit acknowledgement that the **Incomes Revolution** has taken over from the Industrial Revolution, and that you now looking for **a core income stream**, supported by **alternative income streams**, and beyond that **secondary income streams**.

Being an IBG gets to the heart of how we should think of ourselves in the new situation in which we find ourselves. My children have great difficulty in explaining to their friends what Daddy does. I have great difficulty explaining to their parents what Daddy does. Giving ourselves new labels, such as being an IBG, will be a useful step towards helping us, and others, *to understand and define what we do*. It will also help us to cope more effectively with what will remain a dynamically evolving marketplace, in which individuals create, and trade, in goods and services in new, and excitingly different, ways.

Be an ASC – for rocket-powered CZG!

An **ASC** is an **Active Social Contributor**. If becoming an IBG is the first step in coping with the changes that are taking place in the field of work, the next, bigger and more important step is to become a contributor to the cohesion of society as a whole. As the welfare state retreats, a whole load of human detritus will be left behind.

Individual members of society will need to be involved in a wider, more holistic view of that society, and the contributions they can make to it. And we should start by taking a more holistic view of ourselves. We need to look at ourselves as humans, not as workers (professional, unskilled, businessman, soldier, etc.), or unemployed, but as human beings fitting actively into the social dimension. We need to feel involved, wanted, and valued. Ask an ASC and help is at hand.

Importantly, it will not be necessary to be an IBG to be an ASC. Looking at where technology replaces jobs, unskilled manual workers will continue to be in the firing line. It will be more difficult, though not impossible, for them to become IBGs, as their education and training will tend to give them fewer options. As a result, not only will they suffer from lack of employment in the historical sense, they will also have more of a challenge in creating income from other sources.

Being an Active Social Contributor may be personally directed – in the sense that the individual chooses where to commit his or her resources. Or it may be centrally directed, with some central or local coordinating body focusing resource where it is most needed. A wider frame of reference would enable help to be directed to where it was most needed – elderly care, child care for single mothers to get them back into society, education of prisoners, drug rehabilitation, etc.

Being an Active Social Contributor will give a point of reference in society. It will make individual challenges less overpowering and less unique and, in comparison to those being helped, quite minor. Becoming an ASC will, by definition, mean that you become a Team Member within the **Team Sector**. This is perhaps a more helpful description of the social, or third, sector. It is more useful because it broadens the concept to include all members – the individuals and government agencies that give the help, *as well as most of those that receive it*. As we shall see, there is mutual self-interest involved, as well as recognition of the genuine satisfaction enjoyed by both parties.

The Team Sector will need thinking about – as well as funding – and will be looked at in more detail later. Looking at it as the Team Sector, rather than the third, or social sector, means that there is *a real chance of the state avoiding having to pick up the tab as the employer of last resort*.

I have a friend with a relatively young family who took early retirement from a successful corporate career, and now works in a citizens' advice bureau. It's stressful, he's hard up, and he wishes he'd done it years ago. The challenge will be to make the rest of society see him as an ASC, rather than as an ass. It is achievable. It will need new thinking not only in individual growth and development, but in societal growth and development.

And a great deal of Comfort Zone Growth for both.

Become a SAT, and really start developing

This is a tricky one. **SAT** stands for Seeker After Truth. It relates to the area that most people, including myself, are wary of discussing openly, for fear of being laughed at.

I was an atheist, and am now agnostic. Perhaps this is because death is that much closer; perhaps it is because I've seen and experienced enough to believe that human beings can, from time to time, operate at levels that are outside conventional analysis.

When I was getting married, we had decided on the church we wanted to get married in, but we faced a tricky conversation with the vicar, as neither of us were practising Christians. The vicar probed quite firmly on the question of our religious beliefs. We obviously couldn't tell an untruth – particularly to a vicar – so I found myself saying that although I had no religion, I was religious. My wife-to-be snorted audibly, and the vicar looked baffled.

It was, however, the truth. Although rationally I cannot accept the existence of a god or gods, I have always had a sense of what I would term positive open-mindedness. I am also aware that people far more intelligent than I am are strong believers. Thomas Hardy wrote a short poem about a local folk tale that told how each year, on Christmas Eve, at a certain farm in the district, the oxen would kneel, in some atavistic memory of the birth of Christ centuries before. The poet knew it to be a old wives' tale, but he ends the poem by saying:

> Yet I feel
> If someone said on Christmas Eve,
> 'Come; see the oxen kneel
>
> In the lonely barton by yonder comb
> Our childhood used to know,'
> I should go with him, in the gloom,
> Hoping it might be so.

This very much sums up my feelings. While I have yet to make the final step towards religious belief, and may never make it, I am, as I said, religious. By this I mean that I am profoundly aware of things like the ability of exceptional individuals to achieve things beyond the range of most human beings. This stretches from religious martyrs, who endure torture and death gladly from a faith that transcends conventional logic, through to leaders such as Abraham Lincoln and Nelson Mandela, who go through years of rejection and suffering and still emerge as human beings with huge vision and generosity.

There is clearly something at work here that is larger and more significant than day-to-day self-interest and existence. I am sure such things could be explained by some psychological label, but I feel there is something more important going on. These individuals all shared one thing in common. They all had a belief – you could say an unreasonable belief – that what they believed in was bigger than themselves, and worth sacrificing everything for. Suffering merely tempered the steel, rather than creating a lust for revenge.

All of us, at times, have a sense that there is a wider frame of reference. Whether this is moral or religious is not really the point. We have a sense of what integrity means, and where it starts and ends for us individually. Whether we acknowledge it or not, we have consciences. We also know that moral complexity insists, and that there are no easy answers. But in acknowledging moral complexity we also acknowledge there is right and wrong.

Becoming a Seeker After Truth merely means that we believe there is a wider frame of reference for our actions, and that we are aware that integrity and conscience are issues to be thought about seriously. Spirituality and religion may, or may not, come into it. It links directly into responsibility for self and others, and unifies all the issues we have been talking about.

You can be an IBG without being an ASC. You can be an ASC without being a SAT. It's difficult to be a SAT without being an ASC, though you could be, without being an IBG. I hope that's CLEAR.

The most important initials in the coat read DPD – Daily Personal Development

The underpinning to all the new roles and focused approaches to life that I am suggesting above is personal development. Without personal growth, some of the challenges that lie ahead will be daunting, and are likely to cause the shrinking of an individual's sense of self-esteem and self-worth.

What is personal development, and how do you achieve personal growth? *Put succinctly, personal growth is about getting more enjoyment out of life by being able to fight the shite more effectively.*

Three chapters are devoted to this. They will cover areas such as managing priorities, working with the subconscious, and positive thinking. I used to think books on such subjects were extremely naff. They were for people who were inadequate in some way. Moreover, books with titles like *How to Win Friends and Influence People*, or *How I Raised Myself from Failure to Success in Sellling* were at best inane, and at worst, manipulative. Certainly they did not warrant serious considera-tion.

I had, of course, not read any of the books of which I was so contemptuous. And I was profoundly wrong. They work for the strong as well as the temporarily weak. I will explain at some length the learning curve that I encountered, and the joys, the pitfalls, and the benefits of such books. The quality of writing of these books isn't always sumptuous, but the quality of the advice and the insights are frequently rich beyond measure.

Unfortunately, personal growth, and particularly the positive enjoyment of life as it is lived day to day, is just like personal fitness – hard to gain and quick to lose. The parallels go beyond that. I find that as an ex-rugby player if I don't keep up a minimum level of exercise, I begin to feel dreadful. It's like a toilet – if I don't flush my body with exercise, the build-up of noxious substances is less than pleasant. A positive mental outlook is just the same. If you don't regularly flush the negative self-doubts out by consistent positive re-enforcement, there is a rapid spiral downwards. Life becomes more challenging, and less enjoyable. Same life, just a different approach to it.

The development of **Mind Leadership** develops naturally from personal growth. The various tools that go along with it, like **Values** and **Missions statements** to clarify where we're going and why it's important to us to get there, all contribute to a growing and resilient sense of self-worth. This sense of self-worth in turn provides a well-based self-confidence that makes us more effective in all our activities.

Watch out for recidivism, and always apply the Cobblers Test

Nothing is easier than to start out along the path with good intentions of becoming an IBG – diversifying income streams, and spreading risk – only to find that, a few months into the application of the new strategy, things are going rather well, thank you. A project may be going faster than anticipated, bringing in good money. A client may want your services almost full-time. Or you may even have a new job.

This is a dangerous time. There is a massive temptation to slip back into the old comfort zone (now very slightly enlarged), and pull up the covers. This should be resisted at all costs. Recovering a second time from a subsequent setback is harder. Not only will many of your escape routes be closed, because you haven't kept them open, but restarting will take longer, as you will be back as a supplicant rather than an active IBG. Worse, you will be a supplicant in your *own* eyes, as well as the people you are talking to, because you will have let your personal growth plan slip, and you will find it a whole lot harder to cope with the reverse and the consequences.

The same applies to letting slip your work as an ASC. Back temporarily in your old comfort zone, you find you have neither the time nor the inclination to carry on with the work you had previously felt so worthwhile. Getting back into the work as an ASC will be even more difficult. You will start to have doubts about your motivation the first time around, and this will further dent your sense of self-worth, at a time when you need it least.

The Cobblers Test is for application to all suggestions that purport to sort your life out at a stroke. It should be applied stringently to the ideas in this book. You may have already applied it, and found some of the ideas a load of the said cobblers.

If so – good. It means that you have a healthy scepticism, and therefore will need convincing that the concepts have legs and can be effective in the new environment. The purpose of the book is to open the discussion on the likely nature of some of the economic and social developments facing us, to examine the possibility of enjoying, and benefiting from them, and to explore some of the ideas that have helped me in the early stages of what could be quite profound changes. Bring an open but sceptical mind, and enjoy the journey.

TWO

Change? We've Already Got the T-shirt! Or Have We?

WHEN I STARTED working in the late 1960s and early '70s I was the proud owner of a slide rule. It was a low-mileage model, as I only knew how to work out percentages on it, but even that was better than some of my colleagues, who were struggling with long multiplication or logarithms to do the same work.

The point is that it's only three decades ago, and the pocket calculator had still not been invented.

I remember, in the early 1970s, sitting in a meeting in the viewing room of the advertising agency I worked for, taking part in a discussion with our client, Procter and Gamble, on whether the commercial which had just been approved should be shot in black-and-white, or colour. The discussion, as with most discussions with that client, was long and carefully articulated on both sides. The agency, of course, looked to the future, and argued strongly for colour. We were finally overruled, on the grounds that there were still too few colour sets in existence for it to be worth the extra investment in colour film.

At the same period, I recall the excitement of the company's first computer being delivered. The accounts' office window was temporarily removed, while the computer was swung into place by a crane especially hired for the purpose. The computing power was probably less than a Psion Personal Organiser.

Not only was colour television a rarity, and the personal computer still some way off, other everyday objects had still to be invented, like the digital watch or the camcorder. How we existed without such basic everyday tools I now find hard to imagine.

Take the digital watch. We can shower in it, and drop it without worrying. We don't need to wind it. It's a stopwatch and an alarm. If we lose it we can replace it for less than ten pounds, and if we need to change the time because the clocks are going forward for Summer Time, or back for Winter Time, all we need is a helpful ten-year-old to do it for us.

How *did* we exist without it? And where would we be without the massive choice of entertainment, and breadth of news coverage? Multiple TV channels, PC games, multiplex cinemas, on-the-spot live TV news coverage from the middle of war zones – we accept them all without a second thought.

The truth is that we and our parents and grandparents before us – and their forebears before them stretching back over the past two centuries – have seen and accommodated huge technical advances and social changes. Many of these changes have not only been big – they've been fast.

Inventions that changed people's lives

Most would agree that the world in the next century will be faster, smaller, and tougher. And possibly more dangerous. But the fact is, human beings have coped with far bigger changes in the past. Let's look at a few.

Despite my children's perception of my age, I personally was not around when the train was emerging as a revolutionary method of transport in the early part of the last century. As the train took over from the horse as the fastest and most efficient method of covering distance, it brought with it a complete change in the rules. Distances could be covered at speeds – and in a degree of comfort and security – that were previously unimaginable. People could suddenly travel en masse – to the town, to the seaside, to visit relatives. Fresh food could find new markets. Market gardens no longer needed to be located so close to major towns. Heavy goods could be moved more quickly than by canal. The railways – both in Europe and North America – brought with them almost a sense of glee. At last we were beginning to conquer our environment, to add whole new dimensions to life. Breakthroughs in engineering and science were bringing justified pride in achievement, and confidence in our ability to rethink what was possible.

The telegraph, like the train, radically changed our ability to cope with distance. It was slow initially to evolve, and what really supercharged its development was the need to move information rapidly during the American Civil War. It was said that the Rothschild family fortune was based on their having carrier pigeons at the Battle of Waterloo. These early versions of fax and e-mail brought early news of the result to the Rothschild operatives on the Stock Exchange, which enabled them to make a financial killing. In the same way, information – particularly early information – could provide significant competitive advantage in a brutally intense civil war.

The lightbulb, pioneered by Sir Joseph Wilson Swan, and developed to effectiveness by Edison in the 1870s (after 10,000 unsuccessful experiments) again ultimately transformed man's control over his environment. The journey from Edison's workbench, through to power infrastructures (backed by J.P. Morgan and the Vanderbildts), use in paddle steamers, hotels, theatres, stores and finally houses, was a long one. But what a transformation it brought to everyday life.

Instant light and visibility is a gift of almost primitive desirability. However attractive in the future may be the gifts that computerised virtual reality may bring, they will not compare with the ability to flick on an electric light switch in a dark house, and instantly banish the dark – and with it, all the demons that may lurk there. Those of us with children know how important it is for a child to have the reassurance that he or she can reach out to switch on the bedroom light. Just in case.

The telephone, the motor car, the aeroplane, moving pictures, radio, television, the fax, the mobile phone, tele-conferencing – the list goes on and on – have all helped us to communicate more easily and more frequently with each other.

There have been larger changes, with more profound effects

The development of **universal education** was one of these large changes. During the 1870s and '80s most governments in western Europe began to provide universal public schooling. This involved required attendance, at least until the age of ten or eleven. The basic skills of literacy and numeracy were taught. Governments' motives in the provision of this education were not entirely altruistic. Literature and history courses were skewed heavily to develop nationalism, and thus loyalty to the government, producing a relatively docile and coherent workforce, which in turn would pay its taxes and play its part in what was presented as the natural and desirable way of things.

In countries like France, the opportunity was taken to create still more unity by enforcing the use of French as the first language. Up till then, many French people were unable to speak French. Particularly in the south, and in Brittany, the local patois was spoken in daily life well into the twentieth century, confirming for them their difference and individuality.

For countries like France and Italy, the advent of universal education was especially profound. As Catholic countries, much of the education they had was in the hands of the Church. Religious rites were all in Latin, further confirming the Church as the source of all knowledge and wisdom, both secular and divine.

Imagine the surge of freedom that must have come with being able to read and write! The ability to read letters from friends or family, knowing, for the first time, that they were being read as written, and not edited and changed by intermediaries, well-meaning or not. To understand, with certainty, what contracts said. To be able to read notices, signposts, directions, and books. To be able to write a letter, knowing it was an accurate transcription of what you said. To be able to write a diary, or something as simple as a shopping list.

The achievement of basic literacy and numeracy across millions of people is a profound change. Far greater than the acquisition of computer literacy, or the ability to surf the Internet, both of which are merely relatively insignificant extensions of the world-changing ability of being able to read and write.

Often, whole communities were shattered

We read about the great events of the past couple of centuries, and they are both exciting as stories, and portentous in the way they throw their shadows forward onto the events that followed: the Enclosures and the Industrial Revolution in Britain, the Civil War in America, and two world wars that caused massive destruction and human suffering across Europe, and in the latter case, the world. Take the Irish Potato Famine as a more localised example. As the potato crops failed, the landlords, often absentee English Protestants, behaved with breathtaking callousness. With no income, the tenant farmers and their workers could not pay their rents. They were summarily evicted, and their cottages knocked down to prevent the desperate and starving families from moving back in. Starvation and fever killed over a million people, and by the late 1840s over a million and a half more emigrated, mainly to the United States.

Not that destitution and emigration were confined to Ireland. The nine million people that emigrated from Britain between 1850 and 1914 (from a country with an average population of 34 million) testify to how many of that population were surplus to requirements. Some left to seek fame and fortune. The very high numbers indicate the truth of the matter: most left to escape something much darker.

Such events left families and societies shattered. Yet in each case, somehow the human spirit enabled those societies to reform, and rise phoenix-like from the ashes. Sometimes this healing, or rebirth, took place within a generation; sometimes it took longer.

The Berlin Wall falls; and the French eat McDonald's.

None of my generation believed that they would live to see a united Germany. There was no way the Russians would release their colonies – and that included East Germany – and yet, in the blink of an eye, glasnost arrived, and they began to withdraw. The end of Apartheid was similar. Intractable as a problem, and seemingly incapable of positive resolution, yet the system crumbled overnight.

On a lighter note, but no less unthinkable in the relatively recent past, is the thought of the French eating hamburgers. But yet, in the very home of the Serious Lunch, we see many hundreds of McDonald's springing up. And they are full of French people, not tourists. These changes have happened, and at a speed that at times has left us blinking in disbelief. Ideas, culture, money and people are flowing around the world at a faster and faster pace, supercharging changes of all sorts.

Worldwide competition, along with improving technology, drives down costs and increases activity of all sorts. Take air travel as an example. The world itself has shrunk along with air fares. Worldwide, passengers *fly twice as many miles as ten years ago*. Communication, too, is easier and cheaper. We talk to people in foreign lands as easily as we did to friends in the same town. The volume of international telephone calls is doubling *every three or four years*.

As well as reducing air fares and phone charges, the forces of competition have meant that governments as well as corporations are now fighting in a global market. Just look at the figures. Since the 1970s world trade has more than trebled. Foreign direct investment has more than quintupled. And both have taken place against a background of world output only 80 per cent higher overall.

What is happening is that resources are being shuffled around the world to achieve optimum efficiency. The result is that historical national and cultural boundaries count for less and less. So we find British workers learning the principles of *kaizen* – continuous and relentless improvements in systems and processes – in UK factories run by Japanese managers. Thirty years ago we were still laughing at the Japanese for their ability to copy our goods. Now we are grateful to them for letting us help them make theirs.

More unsettling changes

For what now constitutes the majority of people in Europe *the loss of the certainties of religion* has also had a profound effect. This is not a worldwide phenomenon. Through many parts of Asia, North Africa and amongst some immigrant groups in southern Europe, religious fundamentalism is on the increase. In the USA religion is also thriving, with a growing majority of the population in some kind of active religious – mainly Christian – involvement. The reasons for this increase in fundamentalism (and much of the US Christianity is of the fundamentalist, born-again variety) are much debated. The most likely explanation has to lie not in a sudden flowering of new-found spirituality – although, as we will see later, this may form an important element within it – but in a primitive need for simple (though not necessarily easy) answers to increasingly deeply challenging and worrying situations.

Religious extremism – like any extremism from the right or the left in politics – offers apparently simple answers to what are normally complex problems. The prospect of a divine hand behind these disturbing and perplexing situations and events – and even the prospect of some divine intervention to resolve them – has a certain undeniable appeal. This divine reassurance is helpful in what has become a relatively secular world.

Imagine therefore, how traumatic it must have been for recent generations who have lost their faith. No longer is there a divine plan. No longer is there a chance to receive a reward in heaven for putting up with a grim situation on earth. The death of a new-born child, a spouse, or a close friend; illness or disease that cripples or incapacitates; a harvest or an industry that fails, bringing hardship and hunger; such individual or family tragedies had hitherto taken place against a framework of a divine providence – somehow, somewhere the plan would be revealed, and compensating rewards made. The solace religion offered was the ultimate weapon in fighting the shite. The loss of belief came slowly, over a couple of generations in the early years of this century. Its impact should not be underestimated.

Today, in what has become for most of us a relatively God-free world, the absence of divine underpinning is accepted, and therefore is less concerning. For the generations that lived through the mayhem of the Great War, the Depression of the 1920s and '30s, and the horrors of the Second World War, the loss of faith in some greater meaning and framework to life compounded a sense of powerlessness in the face of a cruel and random world.

At the same time these generations were experiencing something we touched on in chapter one. Something totally new, and equally unsettling: *the break-up of the extended family.*

For centuries the most effective, and for most people, only pension scheme had been to have as many children as possible. For those who could not have children, it was important that their brothers and sisters did, in order that someone, somewhere, would look after them when they could no longer look after themselves. The system still exists in many parts of the world today.

As we saw earlier, the reason the system works is that it is based on a very simple principle: enlightened self-interest. However it is dressed up, the implicit deal is: 'I look after my parents, and my children look after me. If I renege on my responsibilities to my parents, I thereby hand full permission to my children to renege on their responsibilities to care and look after me.'

Once the welfare state exists, this deal goes out of the window. The situation becomes: 'I've got a pension and healthcare. So have my parents. It's no longer my responsibility to look after them.' The extended family in northern Europe is largely a thing of the past (apart from immigrant families where the culture still exists). This is less the case in some southern European countries.

In the UK, the welfare state was introduced by the Liberal Government in 1906 and further measures, including rudimentary pensions and unemployment benefits, were introduced between then and 1911. It was not the state protecting its citizens from cradle to grave, as the post-Second World War Labour Government aimed to do, but it was a significant first step down the road. It did not instantly signify the end of the extended family, but it enabled the first cracks to appear, which widened to chasms after the Second World War, once the system became more comprehensive.

For the young, the definition of friends, as being God's apology for relations, suddenly became less relevant. If you lived with your parents in their house, and didn't like them, you could move out, and social security would provide in one form or another. If you lived with your parents, and it was your house, and you didn't like them, or they were inconvenient, you could put them into a home and, again, the state would provide. For many, greater affluence meant that both families and elderly parents had their own homes. For the elderly in this situation, when the time came that they could no longer look after themselves in their own homes, they found they were cut off without retreat. There was no way back into their children's homes.

Many brought it unwittingly on themselves. Not wanting to be a burden, as their parents had been to them, they volunteered to leave. The better-off families created a granny-flat that combined propinquity with independence. But even for these lucky few, there came a time when they could no longer cope, and with the daughter or daughter-in-law working at an often demanding job to support the family, the burden was considered too great to provide the full-time care required.

For the elderly who were the first to suffer the humiliation of being rejected by their children, it was devastating. They had fulfilled their part of the deal, and had looked after their parents. Now, just when they were at their most vulnerable, and needed the most help, the love and support were withdrawn. However many visits in the home for the elderly were promised by the children making the arrangements, the sense of loss of independence, and often with it, dignity, was profound.

There was also a resigned recognition by the people putting their relatives into homes, that their own time would come. A deal is a deal. If they do this to their parents, their own children in turn have full permission to despatch them to homes when the time comes. *This is not about relative wealth.* All that money can do for you is to buy you a better quality retirement home. It is no longer likely to buy you a home where you most want it: with your children, grandchildren, and even great-grandchildren.

Of course the extended family is a much wider concept than whether the elderly are allowed, or even welcomed, to hang around in the family unit after their sell-by date has passed. In a true extended family, aunts, uncles, brothers, sisters, and even in-laws all have a degree of responsibility for one another. What concerns us here, however, is how fundamental this change was, and how it has required a profound reappraisal of thought by all of us, in the quality of life we expect in our declining years.

The glass is half empty – the bigger picture

Later, I will be taking a more positive view of the current situation, but for now let us look cold-eyed at some other developments that lead me to the view that we are reaching some sort of a turning point.

Taking a world view, two trends are particularly concerning in terms of their current, and potential, impact on societies. The first is the 'victory' of capitalism over communism as a system for running societies effectively. The second is the break-up of empires (British, Russian, etc.) that has been one of the contributing factors behind the increase in civil, guerrilla wars.

Taking the second trend first, it is a disturbing fact that casualties of armed conflicts are now *90 per cent civilians*. This is the exact opposite of a hundred years ago, when 90 per cent were military. As states fragment into smaller and smaller entities, and more groups and subgroups fight for their sovereignty, civil wars multiply, and the rest of the world is virtually powerless to do anything about it. Nor can the more developed nations afford to be smug. Europe, for all its attempts to unify, economically and politically, was powerless to prevent the bloody break-up of Yugoslavia.

If instability and internecine local conflicts look like being with us for a generation or more yet, along with the resulting impact on the individual lives of innocent bystanders, the collapse of the Soviet empire has implications well beyond its former boundaries. The challenge comes from the incipient sense of quiet triumphalism of some right-wing parties. The unspoken message is: 'Capitalism has won, as a world system. We can now pull up the ladder.'

When there were two world powers, part of maintaining the balance was the social, rather than the military, imperative of presenting to the rest of the world a political system that was fairer to its peoples. Communism positioned itself as being a system run entirely for the benefit of its citizens. The capitalist system, having been manifestly uncaring in the 1930s, countered the new conditions of the Cold War in 1945 with the rapid development of welfare states. Much of this development was the result of genuine social concern, but it was also partly to counter the intellectual and social attractions of communism.

The sole remaining world power, the United States, is relatively benign as a military power. Its economy, however, has always inclined heavily towards the pioneering mentality of robust self-help. The deprivation and alienation of the inner cities is but one result of this, where citizens who feel excluded from the system find other methods of helping themselves. The concern must be that if more and more right-wing parties in the rest of the world gain power, they may decide to follow the United States paradigm, particularly in the light of the fact that controlled economies, run for the benefit of the majority of the people, have demonstrably failed to deliver as an economic and social system.

Once there is no external pressure for political and economic systems to be inclusive, and those in power can resist internal pressures on the ground of unaffordability, the outlook for large numbers of citizens could be extremely grim.

The glass is half empty – the smaller picture

One important change that has come upon us almost imperceptibly is the realisation that our societies are not as nice as we thought they were. The increasing openness of society – largely the result of the relentless, and often intrusive, scrutiny of the media – has exposed some dark secrets that had lain hidden for centuries. One particularly disquieting area is that of child abuse. When stories began to emerge on the scale and extent of the sexual and physical abuse of children, especially within families, I simply didn't believe it. It was so far from what I had experienced in my family, and those, as far as I knew, of my friends, that I found it inconceivable that people were behaving that way. The weight of evidence soon convinced me otherwise, but the slow dawning of the reality was like a loss of innocence.

The work of Amnesty International continually exposes disturbing examples of institutionalised torture and brutality. These stories, each individually heartrending, come from around the world. Even the United States and Europe are not exempt from sickening stories of abuse of human rights.

Add to this homelessness and poverty – and their very public manifestation on the streets of most western countries – and there emerges a sense that, despite the massive advances achieved by technology, we as human beings haven't yet evolved in any significant way. The very existence of bodies such as Amnesty International and the homeless charities to provide a positive response is, of course, encouraging. The fact that they are manifestly dealing only with the tip of a very unpleasant iceberg, is less so.

Time for a better T-shirt

The wider point from all this is that we are reaching a turning point at which all of us at some time need to make some decisions – even if only in the privacy of our own consciences. If the welfare state is becoming less affordable in economic terms, and less important, with the demise of communism, in political terms, then its power as a financial and emotional crutch begins to diminish.

The vulnerability of income for most people intensifies this sense of increasing nakedness in a hostile world. As a result, many people are spending more and more time outside their comfort zones, and are finding themselves lacking in skills to cope. As we have seen, both we and our forebears have dealt with massive change and disruption in the past, but for us, in a way, it is more difficult. Having lived through times when we thought we were developing successful, inclusive societies, that had growing welfare states that cared for its citizens from cradle to grave, we now seem to have lost the plot. Rude interruptions to comfortable lifestyles are happening to more and more of us, and with increasing frequency.

My own story is a very small, but typical, example of this. After fifteen years of building an excellent company, with some excellent people, my partner and I, through a combination of recession, fashion change, surfeit of new competition, and under-capitalisation, found ourselves, despite considerable energy and marketing ingenuity, trading at a level 40 per cent lower than we had been two years earlier. In spite of a vigorous attack on costs, including an across-the-board pay cut of 10 per cent, and the selling of all company cars, the inflexible fixed costs of too many over-rented properties proved unsustainable. The heartening aspect was the resolute and cheerful commitment of staff throughout, despite their knowledge of the difficulty of the situation. No key staff left, despite the pay cut and the austere conditions.

My situation is in no way unique. Companies have failed in the past, and they will fail in the future. People have lost jobs and careers in the past, and will do so again in the future. *In the past, however, it always happened to someone else.* More often than not, the people who lost jobs or companies seemed in some way to deserve it – either through laziness, or incompetence, or both. Now, the axe seems to fall randomly, on the deserving and undeserving alike.

Change is suddenly getting personal, and we're not comfortable with it. *Intellectually*, we've bought the T-shirt. *Emotionally*, we're still reading the book, and the film has yet to come out. The absence of world wars, and the comforting existence of both full employment and the welfare state, have meant that up till recently most of us have not had to face sudden deprivation at first hand. This book attempts to develop our ability to deal emotionally as well as intellectually with some of the changes we are facing, and will face. And to create a coat, rather than an ill-fitting and uncomfortable T-shirt, to give us some protection from the chill and capricious winds of change.

THREE

From the Industrial Revolution to the Incomes Revolution

SO THE UNPLEASANT shocks that used to affect other people now affect us. Few of us have not been touched on the shoulder lightly or, in some cases, heavily, by the hand of failure. A dozen or more years ago failure was for the untalented, or the unlucky. Today, no one is safe.

It is a strange irony that while changes in fortune are now more personal, other changes have become less so. Inventions are now corporate, rather than individual. We all could name the inventor of the telephone, the steam engine, the radio, and the jet engine. But who invented the fax?

We all accept inventions, innovations and improvements as part of life. But it was not always so. I recall a Bob Newhart monologue from the 1970s that, like his version of Sir Walter Raleigh's bringing tobacco from the New World to the Old, provided a fresh insight into things that we accept as commonplace. The monologue took place against the background of the American motor car industry being put under pressure by the importation of small, European cars, especially the rear-engined Volkswagen Beetle.

The scene he painted was a board meeting of the General Chariot Corporation in Rome. The board is discussing the threat from the smaller, more manoeuvrable, chariots of the Hun. Several improvements to the General Chariot Corporation's products are suggested. These include putting the horses at the back, to improve the view of those driving the chariot, and having a specially fitted rope, to prevent the toga from flying up in the wind.

As well as the intrinsic humour of the concept, the monologue serves to underline that product development as a process is a relatively new one. Invention, innovation, New Product Development, have now become mechanised within the processes of any business enterprise.

This, of course, applies to services as well as products. Constantly improving products and services is now an intrinsic part of staying in business.

There are many reasons for this. One, of course, is global competition. Another is the fact that there are more scientists alive today than ever lived in the history of the world. We have quantity, as well as quality, in the number of potential inventors and discoverers. Most of these scientists work directly, or indirectly, for corporations, as much university research is corporately funded.

This brings us to the twin drivers of modern macro-economics – the advance of technology, and the globalisation of business. One feeds off the other, as global reach, necessitated by the global forces of competition, facilitates the capacity of corporations to source technical expertise worldwide in order to gain competitive advantage.

Macro-economic trends and their unpleasant effects

The General Chariot Corporation of Rome may have been playing a familiar game of technology catch-up, but the by-product of their improved designs would not have been – as it would today – to put half the employees of the company's Roman division out of work.

We all know that technology is replacing jobs. This is for two reasons. Firstly, the elimination of labour obviously reduces costs. Second, the cost of computer-driven technology is falling, whereas the cost of skilled labour is stable, or rising. Lower capital equipment costs makes it even more advantageous to replace jobs with machinery.

This is compounded by global competition causing pressure on prices, which results in global companies searching out the cheapest reliable labour markets for the manufacture of the goods, and often for the provision of their support services.

This is leading to what I call the Incomes Revolution, not a terribly original name, but it does get to the heart of what this book is about. The central thrust of my message is that employment as a concept is on its last legs, and people should begin to think of themselves as income generators, not job holders. This has implications beyond the exchange of money for hours worked, as it includes all people *receiving as well as generating incomes*. This means that the unemployed, and those on welfare support, are included in the new way of considering how we will live in the future. It gives us the opportunity to create an inclusive framework that provides an opportunity for those who *traditionally have been seen as dependants, to become contributors.*

Before examining those wider issues, it is worth taking a look at a few figures to be able to begin to understand what is happening in our societies now, and thus get some insight into what might happen in the next few years. Let's start with the rapid and potentially devastating polarisation of incomes, and thus society, which has been brought about by the rigorous application of winner-takes-all capitalism as it is developing around the world.

This is a global phenomenon, with many of the world's billionaires (yes, people *individually worth a thousand million dollars*) coming from the explosive economies of South America and the Pacific Rim – countries which still have more than their share of very poor people. Looking globally, in the early 1990s there were 358 billionaires with a combined net worth of $760 billion. This equals the *combined net worth of the poorest 2.5 billion of the world's people.*

If the Anglo-Saxon model of modern capitalism seems to be winning the economic, if not social, argument wordwide, it is worth looking at the spiritual home of the model, the United States. Polarisation of income has been happening in the US for a considerable time. *Business Week* revealed that between 1980 and 1993, the Fortune 500 industrial firms reduced their workforces by almost 4.4 million people. This equated to more than 25 per cent of the previous number of total jobs. During the same period, their sales increased by 1.4 times, and assets by 2.3 times. While over four million people lost their jobs, the resulting sparkling financial performance enabled the firms' chief executive officers at the largest corporations to increase their salaries by 6.1 times, to $3.8 million a year.

Other sources reveal that the effect of global competition and technology replacing jobs, particularly lower skilled jobs, meant that between 1977 and 1989 the income of the top 1 per cent of US families *increased by 78 per cent*, while the income of the bottom 20 per cent of families *decreased by 10.4 per cent.* What is worse, those employed in 1989 were working longer hours than those employed in 1977. Furthermore, more families had two breadwinners, as more women entered the workforce. *During this period most of the bottom 60 per cent of US families could not keep up with the decline in wages, despite working longer hours and having an extra wage earner.*

Looking specifically at low-skilled men, the picture is even more miserable. Since 1979 real earnings of men with a minimal twelve years of schooling has *dropped by 20 per cent.* The initial wage for these workers, when they first enter the labour market, has *dropped by 30 per cent.*

The United Kingdom, whose economy is the closest in Europe to that of the United States, is also beginning to see a decline in spending power for the worst off. Real incomes for the bottom 20 per cent of the population have grown only 6 per cent since 1979. Taking account of fewer full-time jobs, and housing costs, which have risen in real terms, *incomes for couples and childless single people – those most likely to be in work – actually fell over the period.*

Defenders of the system claim that the picture of deprivation and relative poverty is exaggerated. As evidence, they point to the spending figures for poor households, which are higher than those of income received. The reason for this is cited as transfers between family members (the relatively better off helping the poorer), and income from the black economy. But even the defenders of the system can find no answer to the increased numbers of homeless and those in temporary shelter.

The Race to the Bottom

The downward trend in incomes for the worse off in our societies is distressing, particularly as it looks as if it is only just beginning to get into its stride. What makes it worse is that it is a global phenomenon, that creates an even more miserable effect in Third World countries.

As American, Japanese, and European companies continue to move more and more manufacturing and service support jobs to low-wage economies in distant parts of the world, this is often the start of a bartering system to achieve the lowest overall cost, by achieving the lowest labour costs. The massive surplus in world labour means there are always people prepared to go lower in price in order to win the orders. This has been called the **race to the bottom**. It involves underdeveloped countries fighting each other in seeing who can provide labour cheapest. This is often compounded by their governments paying development grants and subsidies, to encourage foreign firms to exploit their surplus labour force, rather than that of another country.

For workers in Third World countries the choice is simple. Either accept low wages, long hours, and poor working conditions – often with your children working in worse conditions – or starve, along with your family and extended family. Not much of a choice, and the decision is quickly made.

Because the suffering caused takes place a long way away, most corporations believe their public relations machines can take care of any fall-out from the ethical lobby. They comfort themselves with the thought that their customers are getting a good deal, so there are as many winners as there are losers.

The circle created is truly vicious

The knock-on effects are very unpleasant. Suppliers moving jobs abroad means more unemployed customers in their home markets. The pressure of international competition continues to reduce incomes of many of those in work in the home markets, which, combined with more people without jobs, or with low-paid, or near-jobs, means more and more customers are worse off. Being worse off, they are less able to pay for the goods and services in question. This puts pressure on prices, which in turn makes suppliers demand lower costs. And how are lower costs achieved? Yes – lower wages.

And so the circle goes on. One addition to the circle will be the search, through the ever more sophisticated use of technology, for *worker-free factories and computer-run service industries*. A start has been made in the latter in such areas as banking and insurance, where people who used to process and manage data are being replaced by technology that is more reliable, and does not need paid holidays or pension-funding.

Some good news: prices stabilise, and even go down

For most of our lives we have lived with inflation. It seems always to have been with us. When I was at university, there was something called the King Street Run. This was a disgusting undergraduate ritual that was enormous fun. It involved drinking a pint of beer in each of eight public houses in the street, and finishing the eight pints without resorting to physical relief of any kind along the way. Each person attempting the feat was accompanied by a whipper-in, who supervised strict adhesion to the rules. Any visit to the toilet was penalised by going back one pub, and adding an extra pint to the challenge.

The tie awarded to the contestants had an embroidered tankard, with a crown above it – for the king – and the appropriate number of silver or gold letter Ps (for pee or puke) collected along the way (I said it was disgusting). My pride in achieving a clean tie was considerably diminished by a slender girl undergraduate in the group, who not only achieved the same feat, but consumed a further pint of Guinness, before sauntering off to the toilet.

The reason for mentioning this far from salubrious episode in my life is that I clearly recall the cost of the evening's entertainment. At the start of the evening, one handed over a £1 note (they existed in those days) to the whipper-in. He would then purchase the eight pints of beer, several bags of crisps to help absorb the liquid, and would return about 2 shillings (10 pence in today's money) change at the end of the evening. Today, a pint of beer costs anything between £1.50 and £2.50, depending on the outlet.

An increase of at least fifteenfold in the price of a basic commodity such as beer gives an indication of the sort of inflation we have been living with in my lifetime. But it was not always so. For most of the last century, prices were stable or declined in the United Kingdom. From the early years of the last century to 1945, prices actually *fell* in fifty-seven of those years (they rose in sixty).

All the signs indicate that low inflation, price stability, or even deflation, are with us for the next few years. This, for the most part, is good news. No longer will governments be able to steal people's savings. In turning a myopic, if not blind, eye to inflation, in order to camouflage other ills in the economy, governments allowed the value of savings to be decimated. This tended to penalise the thrifty and reward the profligate (by reducing the value of debts owed).

Price stability, and particularly price declines, do, of course, have their downsides. They tend to slow consumption down, and thus the economy. In the recent past there was always an incentive to buy now, because next month, or next year, the product or service would be more expensive. Now, the opposite is likely to be true. The knowledge there will be more value tomorrow encourages delay in purchase, more shopping around, and thus even lower prices and margins.

But it doesn't look good for the welfare state

Welfare provision is coming under pressure in nearly all advanced societies. This is not because governments are hardhearted or irresponsible, although some of them tend to exhibit these characteristics. The pressure on welfare budgets is the direct result of demand being too high, and supply being too low. As populations age, the dependency ratios (the number of people supported against the number of people needing support) deteriorate. These trends vary country by country – with Japan having one of the fastest ageing populations in the developed world and the United States one of the slowest – but all developed nations are finding that they are increasingly having to support more dependent people from fewer working taxpayers.

At the same time, demand will continue to soar. There will be more elderly needing pensions, and more care, as they live longer, and demanding the ever-increasingly expensive treatments that advances in technology will continue to make available. This source of extra demand is widely recognised. What is less widely recognised is that the real challenge lies in the fact that welfare states were conceived at a time when the structure of society was entirely different.

Welfare states were conceived in periods of social stability, full employment, low crime, nuclear family units, and young workforces. On the last, state pension provision has been compared to pyramid selling. Those in first, when there were plenty of workers, and few people drawing pensions, did well. Those who came in later were caught in the trap of there being more people drawing out than paying in.

Nuclear families, in a time of full employment, meant one or more of the parents having a job, with a regular income coming into the home. Housing costs (rent, heating, lighting, etc.) were shared across four or more people, and there was only infrequent need of unemployment benefit, or income support.

Once families started to break up, costs soared. With parents separated, two homes required funding for rent, heating, lighting, etc. It is estimated that, in the United Kingdom, divorce costs the state £10,000 a year for each family. The breakdown in family unit, coupled with more unemployment, and the relative poverty of those not lucky enough to have skills that command levels of payment that at least stay in line with inflation, all tend to increase both dependency and crime.

Governments try to argue that higher levels of crime are not related to their economic or social programmes, but common sense would indicate a link between very low incomes, poor housing conditions, low family cohesion, an increasing sense of relative social disadvantage, and the tendency of, particularly young, people to lash out, and help themselves. Crime has high costs. These costs are financial, as well as human.

This was brought home to me on a recent holiday in France. We were at a godchild's fifth birthday party. We got talking to a local French couple, who seemed to have a large number of children attending the event. The father was a self-employed carpenter and the mother, who seemed to be the chief income earner, was a child carer. Two of the five children with her belonged to parents who could not look after them. The father was in prison for a very long period, and the mother was unable to cope, so it was her job to bring the children up for the foreseeable future.

Apart from the human costs involved, which were considerable, it set me thinking of the financial costs of the crime the father had committed. I have no idea what it was, but consider the following list of knock-on financial costs to the state that could feasibly be involved:

- hospital, and convalescence, costs for the victim, if it was a crime of violence
- income support costs for the victim, and their family, if they were unable to work as a result of the violence
- process of law costs – police, lawyers, court time, etc.
- prison costs – ten to twenty years of housing, feeding, guarding, the offender
- support costs for the offender's wife – counselling, income support, etc.
- payment of the mother we met to bring up the children
- ongoing costs, as a proportion of the children of criminals themselves take up crime

I am sure I have missed some, but the list does give some insight into the hidden financial costs of crime, over and above the human costs of the victim's suffering, the misery for the prisoner's family, and the waste of human potential for the prisoner himself.

Health services, too, were conceived in circumstances that were completely different from those existing today. The National Health Service in the United Kingdom was launched as a short-term expedient. At the time, shortly after the Second World War, most of the killer illnesses were *infectious* diseases. With the early diagnosis and eventual elimination of such diseases as tuberculosis through vaccination, it was envisaged that the nation's health would be improved to such an extent that health costs would *decrease*, and eventually very little funding would be required.

These diseases were reduced or eliminated, only for others to take their place, because, as it evolved, the major killer illnesses – cancer, cardiovascular – turned out to be diseases that could not be inoculated against. They were conditions that developed in the body through a combination of genetics, diet, stress and lifestyle. Cardiovascular diseases and cancers, of course, are primarily diseases of later life, so the more old people there are, the more cardiovascular diseases and cancers will be presented to doctors.

Not only do the major diseases affect the elderly in particular – of which there are more – they are generally very expensive diseases to treat. In addition, consider the attendant costs that the Health Service picks up for the elderly:

- more dentistry
- more opticians costs
- more prescriptions (more frequently unwell)
- more chiropody
- more ambulance costs (unable to get to hospital for check-ups)
- more district nursing (frequent home calls)
- home help costs
- home bathing costs
- meals on wheels

So the health service that was provided to sort out the nation's health – almost on a one-off basis – became a major devourer of tax revenues, for which there would appear to be an infinite, rather than a finite, demand.

The problem overall thus begins to become intractable. An ageing population means fewer suppliers of tax from incomes, and more demanders of expenditure on pensions and healthcare. Fragmented families, leading to more people needing housing and supporting, higher crime, higher unemployment and semi-employment, all add significant further weight to the social security budgets of developed nations. *It is clear that demographic and social trends are mostly uphill for the next twenty or thirty years.*

Extended family support emerges as a counter-trend?

The better-off will have to pay more in both taxation and hidden taxation (private healthcare, education, pension schemes, income insurance, etc.), but there will still be too little to go around. The cascade of wealth down the generations, envisaged by right-wing politicians, will not exist – apart from for the already well off – as savings and assets (such as houses) are taken by the state to fund care in old age.

There is, however, the possibility of a counter-trend to the fragmentation of the family emerging to lighten the burden on individuals going through periods of extended relative hardship. There is evidence from the United States of a marked increase in what is termed inter-generational giving. This mainly means grandparents helping out with the costs of bringing up grandchildren, but can also mean parents helping their own parents. The family transfers, that increase the spend of people on low incomes in this country, once more confirm the voluntary provision of support within families at times of need.

In my own experience, I see much more help between different family members, both our own and those of friends, than ever seemed to go on before. The somewhat sniffy attitude of, 'We can cope, we don't need your charity' seems to be a thing of the past. People are more open to admitting that they are hurting financially, and accept without demur any aid proffered. This aid goes in all directions – between brothers, sisters, parents, grandparents, aunts, uncles – and seems to be picking up pace. This could be interpreted as the first sightings of the return of the extended family.

As the welfare state retreats, the inter-family support systems it made redundant seem – I would put it no more strongly than that – to be reviving. The new form of the extended family does not, as yet, include the opening up of homes to relatives who have hit hard times. It does, though, involve financial and moral support, which is probably more appropriate to current lifestyles.

The new demographics

Most people, like myself, who have worked in marketing for a number of years, have seen the growing irrelevance of most demographic definitions of consumers. The term 'social class' now has an almost nostalgic flavour to it. Even 'age' has little relevance, as people's attitudes and behaviour patterns are now much less related to age and much more related to what has been called lifestage (single, married, divorced, young kids, second marriage, more young kids, etc.). This has spawned a whole sub-industry in defining consumers by attitude, life stages and behaviour (young professionals, empty nesters, DINKYs – Double Income No Kids Yet, etc.). The only element of the old-style demographics that still has resonance is geographic area, and even that is now only relevant on a micro level, as there can be significant differences in income, for instance, between streets, rather than between areas.

The most sensible definition that attempts to take account of the new realities I have seen recently is one that defines individuals, and geographic areas, by whether or not they have employment. As incomes continue to polarise, the economic element within demographic definition will intensify in importance. I therefore offer the following four groupings as being useful in recognising income as the most important driving force in grouping people into recognisable clusters. The reason for grouping people into clusters is not some fastidious tidiness on my part, but an attempt to gain some handle on how the developments of the next few years will affect different sections of the population.

I believe there will be four main groups that will develop over the next decade and beyond. These groups will have substantial overlap, and people will move between groups. The groups are:

1. The High-flyers
2. The Survivor-flourishers
3. The Strugglers
4. The Buggered

Let us have a look at their main attributes.

1. The High-flyers

As the term implies, this group contains people with large incomes, normally still from one job. These jobs will be in the provision of goods and, particularly, services, to the areas of commerce that are still making rapid productivity gains from the application of technology and the capitalisation on cost savings to be made from the skilful manipulation of the world's labour markets. For them the concept of the job is reassuring, despite their understanding of the volatility and vulnerability now inherent in the concept. They will be working long hours, usually under uncomfortable levels of pressure. Apart from the small minority that go on to run companies – for other people, or for themselves – they will begin to top out earlier and earlier.

This means the salaries that were just about comfortable in their thirties will be inadequate in their forties and fifties, as families grow up and consume more food, more clothing, and more money in all guises.

This will put significant pressure on family budgets and family relationships. It's easy to be generous when the money is flowing. Saying no to reasonable requests, when the month's money has gone, is a whole lot tougher.

A word to the High-flyers

High-flyers, almost by definition, can fall. If you are earning a lot of money, and you love your job – great. Relish every minute of it. But don't assume it will last for ever. Here are a few things that could nudge the applecart, either for the job itself, or the undiluted enjoyment of the income from it:

- health failure – natural, or stress-induced
- a close relative is in serious health or financial difficulties, and you are the only source of help
- your company is taken over, or the market changes, or the sector you work in is identified as an area for corporate withdrawal
- new technology replaces your specialised skill sets
- the company you have built in a specialist sector is drowned by the entrance of two major players
- you have a child with special needs, and the state withdraws all support for people with your level of income
- your parents, after exhausting their capital and liquidated assets, inconveniently live on after their bury-by date
- a child decides to become a vet, and needs deep funding for half a lifetime

You get the idea. Such challenges, for the High-flyers, will be particularly difficult, purely because they will be working such long hours, leaving them little time, physically or mentally, to devote to coping with them. On top of that, if loss of employment were to occur, it will be even more traumatic as their working life plunges from eighty hours a week to nil.

We have seen this at first hand. In our street alone, two High-flyers have lost their jobs in the recent past. Both found the difference in status very difficult to handle. They walked differently, avoided your eye, and tried to avoid taking the kids to school, even though they were available to do so. Both subsequently found new jobs, one full-time, and the other part-time, but though they were delighted to be wearing suits again, it took some time for their jaunty step to reappear. Much to our amusement, we later found out that one of the wives had always assumed that, because I seldom wore a suit, I too was unemployed!

2. The Survivor-flourishers

Probably most of the people reading this book will fall into this group. Some will still technically be High-flyers, but they will understand not only the fragility and vulnerability of the concept of the permanent job, they will come to perceive it as an anachronism, as the casualisation of employment continues apace. They will therefore be ready – both intellectually and emotionally – for their job to cease to exist. They will be preparing themselves for transition to the Survivor-flourishers group.

They, like those who are already members of the group, will understand the need for multiple income streams. They will understand the need for the quiverful of skills and mindsets that we will be exploring shortly. Importantly, they will understand that it is possible to be self-employed, self-marketing, and self-fulfilled; that it is possible to cope enjoyably with fluctuating and uncertain income, and even, with self-discipline, to flourish. Life will not be without its challenges, but their experience as Survivor-flourishers will have equipped them to deal better with them.

The interesting part will come in transmuting these challenges, so that they become life-enhancing, rather than life-threatening.

3. The Strugglers

This is the group that will have most ebb and flow between it and the groups above and below. Some Survivors-flourishers will find themselves sinking, hopefully temporarily, into this group, and some of the Buggered will find themselves rising, hopefully permanently, to reach this, and higher, groups.

The Survivors will be hurting financially, more or less permanently. They will have one, two, three, or even more jobs. These will be temporary, part-time, or both, and almost certainly poorly paid. Constantly short of money, and time, couples will see little of each other, but without the recompense of a swelling bank account that will dilute the angst of the time-poor High-flyers.

4. The Buggered

Excuse the language but, sadly, this sums up their situation all too appositely. Under-skilled, and under-educated, in a world needing fewer and fewer such people in its workforce, they will be, to all intents and purposes, buggered. Particularly so will be the younger men, themselves the sons of unemployed men, who will have been overtaken for what jobs are available by their female contemporaries. Some, who find employment, will escape. But most won't.

There are solutions, which will require new approaches (which may be the reworking of old approaches). Solutions must be found, in order to bring these people back into some sort of a dignified role in society. Failing such an initiative, this group, unwanted and ultimately resented by the better-off groups, will become an unemployable, alienated underclass.

They will have very little money, very little hope. They will feel deprived, rather than poor. Surveys show that the poor in developed societies do not regard themselves as poor. For them, the poor, and poverty, exist in Third World countries. Here in the West, they just can't afford things, and have precious few opportunities to change things (i.e. they're buggered).

The following summary of the findings of an investigation of poverty in the UK by the *Independent* newspaper gives some insight into what it is like to be a hapless member of the Buggered:

Poverty is humiliating. It's about living with other people's wallpaper. It's about having a social worker go through your cupboards to see if what you've bought meets their criteria of what you should be buying. It's about not having enough money to cover even the basics. It's about borrowing £50 from a loan shark, and having to pay back almost £200. It's about having to send your son to school in a yellow coat, because that was all you could find that fitted him for under £5 – all you can afford when you live off £73. It is about being refused a bank account, so that … you still have to go and collect your benefits from the post office knowing that you are an easy target for a mugger.

Poverty is about not being able to give your kids money for the cinema or the disco, so they associate with similarly disadvantaged kids, until they are finally drawn into crime. It's about the impossibility of encouraging children to read books, when there are none in the house, and they never see their parent, or parents, reading. It's about living in fear of something breaking down – if the iron packs up, you can't afford to get it fixed. It's about feeling inarticulate, unsupported, resented, worthless, and having little chance of changing things.

This rising tide will not raise all ships

Looking at these four groupings, it is pretty obvious that I'm not too optimistic about the lethal cocktail of global competition, technology replacing jobs, and uphill demographics producing widespread prosperity over the next decade or so. As a marketing person rather than an economist, I find most proper economists irritating from many points of view. Apart from their belief in their own intellectual superiority – which may be well founded – they seem to have two other shortcomings. One is that they never quote all the assumptions their projections are based on, and if you manage to find them out, their theories look somewhat less than robust. The other is that common sense does not seem to be their natural bedfellow.

Looking at the overall growth in economies, and particularly the rise in incomes of the more successful members of those economies, economists tend to assume that a rising tide raises all ships. They argue that the current restructuring of economies is no different from the Industrial Revolution, where there was widespread poverty, which was eventually rectified by growth in the overall wealth of the industrialised nations.

I have trouble with this fundamentally important assumption from two points of view. Both of them are based in common sense, rather than any understanding of economic theory.

The first is the denial of costs, prices and earnings vicious circle I talked about earlier. As global competition and technology both work their evil magic on jobs, and we move deeper into the Incomes Revolution, the continued reduction in the conventional forms of income will ultimately cause consumption to falter, and even decline.

Previous booms, from the Industrial Revolution onwards, were based on the efficiencies of mass production and mass marketing eventually leading to mass consumption. If technology means that goods can be produced cheaply in small quantities – which it does – and if it also means that fewer and fewer people have the jobs to provide the income for them to be mass consumers, it seems to me to be common sense that domestic markets for certain categories of goods that are not either essentials, at one end, or luxury at the other, will begin to lose their mass volumes. Markets, like consumers, will polarise into low price, or discounted goods and services, and high added-value, expensive goods and services. Manufacturers and service-providers caught in the middle ground could be in for a sticky time.

In the past, productivity gains usually fed through to higher pay, and more jobs. Now productivity gains flow through to higher pay for the few, and higher profits. *But fewer real jobs.* So in terms of potential consumers, there could be quite a large number of ships holed below the waterline, unable to take advantage of the rising tide. More importantly, and more worryingly, *it could already be high tide, and the lack of mass demand could cause the tide to begin to fall.*

The second reason I believe that we are now in a situation that is quite unlike the Industrial Revolution is *the lack of surplus people-absorbers available today.*

Twelve million people left Britain between 1850 and 1914. The United States and the colonies absorbed most of them. Many travelled in appalling conditions, taking the half-chance that conditions in the new worlds would be at least marginally better than those they were leaving. Most of those who stayed either had employment of their own, or had a relative who had employment.

Today, offloading surplus population to foreign lands is not an option, and hiding them is no easier. Young people cause particular problems. With hormones on the boil, they are prone to getting into bad ways if not fully occupied. Youth employment schemes are a not very successful attempt at hiding young people, and they fool nobody. With the loss of traditional youth-hiding methods, like conscription, or apprenticeship schemes, widespread youth unemployment becomes a serious, and public, challenge.

So the situation we face is new in two ways. In the current Income Revolution, jobs are being eliminated, leaving many unskilled workers with little chance of ever having conventional jobs again. They have nowhere to go, nowhere to be hidden, nowhere to be absorbed. The second difference is that, while the welfare state still exists, *they have to be paid for* by those lucky enough still to have taxable incomes.

The unemployed, and the partly employed (because the nearly-jobs – many of which, even if someone has more than one of them, still bring in insufficient money to prevent a household from having to claim income support from the welfare budget) are a significant on-cost for the state. This in turn precipitates more costs through deprivation leading to poorer mental and physical health, increased crime, and the necessity to house, as well as feed and clothe, those suffering from very low income levels. The responsibility of the state to look after its citizens in this way formed no part of the economic advances made by the Industrial Revolution.

If the Buggered category of citizens reaches a share of the population approaching 20 per cent, which is quite feasible, this would also have the effect of turning the tide from flood to ebb. They, in particular, could end up stranded on the muddy bottom, not only without a paddle, but with no way of reaching dry land.

To modify the metaphor to make it more apt, the tide will not relate to a sea, but to a series of locks. For the High-flyers, the level of water in the lock will indeed be rising, lifted by a flood of productivity gains from the expert manipulation of world labour markets and the exploitation of advances in technology. For the Survivor-flourishers the tide will rise and fall as lock gates open and close, in phase with their ability to organise their income streams in a world where no income is guaranteed. The Strugglers will be fighting a desperate battle to keep the level of water in their lock at least steady, rather than draining out, leaving them stranded, along with the Buggered.

So the conditions resulting from the Incomes Revolution are likely to be very different from those of the Industrial Revolution. There will be no raising of all ships by the extra wealth generated from the productivity gains from the new, and ever more ingenious, application of technology.

To make matters worse, the uphill demographics will cause the welfare state to shrink. This will make everyone except the High-flyers feel worse off. As welfare services – health, pensions, education, elderly care – are either rationed, or part-payment is demanded from those above certain income levels – the Strugglers and Survivor-flourishers will feel the loss particularly keenly. Had the welfare state never existed – as at the time of the Industrial Revolution – there would be no sense of loss. The dwindling of the welfare state – *care* from cradle to grave – will cause many of those deprived of its no-longer-affordable beneficence to feel extremely vulnerable.

Incomes from sources other than steady jobs tend to be staccato, and difficult to control. Sod's Law will apply to make matters worse. Services that historically would have been free, as part of welfare provision, will be needed by individuals or families just at the moment that their incomes hit a temporary low point.

Imagine you are a Struggler, or a Survivor-flourisher, and you find you have a minor health problem that is uncomfortable. It needs sorting out. You go to your doctor, who advises you to go for private treatment. You tell him that temporary financial difficulties have meant that you have let your private medical insurance lapse. He looks up the condition on the list to discover, because it is not life-threatening, treatment is no longer available free on the National Health Service. It will be at times like this, that if you stumbled across a passing economist, you would be tempted to drown him in his own rising tide.

FOUR

The First Step: Becoming an Independent Business Generator

IN OFFERING MY views on possible solutions from the challenges that lie ahead I rely largely on my own experience. I am lucky enough to have a traditional family, and I therefore talk from this viewpoint. I understand that many people reading this will be in a different situation, and some of my ideas and comments may seem less appropriate. For those people, please aim off, and see what can be applied to your own life.

My somewhat gloomy predictions for the financial abundance of most developed economies over the next decade or two may, of course, be quite wrong.

Imagine yourself back in 1950 forecasting the economy for the next two or three decades. The first fifty years of the century had seen a dismal economic performance, with wars, recessions and depressions. The five years between the end of the Second World War and 1950 had seen a time of severe hardship. Industries had been destroyed, we were heavily in debt to the Americans, and there didn't seem too much to be cheerful about. To make matters worse, goods were rationed. I am sure my lifelong love of sweets and chocolates originates in their being rationed when I was a child. The minimal quantities available per person left most people with a deep longing for more. At some deep psychological level this early deprivation left me with a permanent desire to eat as much chocolate as I can today – just in case it's rationed tomorrow.

From such a starting point in 1950, it would have been a brave forecaster who would have predicted the boom years of the 1960s, '70s and '80s, when the leaps in real incomes transformed the standards of living of all sections of society. So the next couple of decades may be a great deal jollier economically than I am predicting. This would not alter the two most intractable trends – the polarisation of incomes, and uphill demographics causing public expenditure to be reduced relentlessly and uncomfortably. Nor would it reverse the Incomes Revolution. The trends to de-massify labour, and put all but the core talent workers on a casual, just-in-time basis, are too well established. So if that is what is happening, what do we do about it?

We must create our own micro-economies

One can argue endlessly as to whether there will, or won't, be economic growth, which sectors will grow, which will decline – whether, indeed, economic growth is desirable anyway. The point is that we as individuals can do little to affect it, so we should be attempting to create our own booming micro-economies in the context of the new economic and social realities. This is not to say that we join the 'I'm all right Jack, pull up the ladder' school of thinking. Quite the reverse. Having had my cage rattled quite alarmingly myself, I came to understand that to survive as an individual in a world where income is becoming sickeningly fickle, you need a more broad-based approach than just efficient money generation. Life is fun, but you need to work hard on your mindset to make sure you enjoy its richness as you go along. That involves containing and transforming the worrying bits.

Remember: worry is paying interest on a debt not yet due. It is even sillier paying undue interest when you are ignoring the positive income from other areas of your life that financial focus alone won't let you acknowledge.

The agenda – quality of life *and* income

The important thing to understand is that the objective is to achieve an overall improvement in the balance between quality of life and the ability to survive well financially. This is not about downshifting. Downshifting – leaving high-pressure, highly paid jobs, to move to a normally rural, low-stress and low-cost environment – seems to me to run the dangers of utopianism.

It may work for some people, but for most of us I suspect that there would be two quite substantial challenges. The first would be that the reality of it would be closer to the poet Keats's 'Love in a hut, is – Love forgive us – cinders, ashes, dust.' The grubby realities of the simple life – arguments over whether purchases are luxuries or necessities, cars that break down, with no money to mend them (or if there's only one car, who gets it), children not understanding why they can't have the things they used to have – could create a new and even less pleasant form of stress.

The second would be that most bridges back to the original social context are burned. The day-to-day web of friends, colleagues, relations, etc. are left behind, just when such support is needed most. New friends may be made, but if conventional jobs are not part of the agenda of downshifting these can take time to make. Finally, if part of downshifting involves moving to lower cost accommodation, getting back to a similar house and location to the one you moved from, if you change your mind, could prove somewhat tricky.

If we assume that downshifting is not on the agenda, what is? *The agenda is to move consistently to a more holistic view of your own life, where you see yourself as a rounded human being.* Taking stock of where you are as a person is not easy, nor is it a one-off project. It takes effort, and constant reappraisal. It is wonderfully rewarding, but bloody hard work. Subsequent chapters, looking at the fundamentally important skills of personal development, attempt to illuminate the course I took, and the lessons I learned, in this challenging but rewarding area.

In basic terms, we are talking about rewards. Rewards, by definition, are what you earn for services rendered. These services are not merely for financial reward, but also for emotional and even spiritual reward. Work is required. There is no free meal ticket.

A simple example would be reward for services rendered as a father, mother, partner, husband, wife, son, daughter, nephew, niece, friend. What I am talking about is making a *career* out of these roles. Once you think through the implications of having a career as a father, or a partner, *you come to understand that career development is now involved.* This means turning up in time, doing what you are supposed to do, learning as you go, and undertaking regular appraisals of performance. Sounds a bit onerous, but it has two benefits.

The first is that it makes you rethink the importance of the role and the relationship in your life. High-flyers, in particular, because they have little time for anything outside their work, have a tendency to treat all relationships as an extension of work. Thus a husband, wife or partner tends to become the equivalent of another meeting to attend, or just another client or customer to satisfy. *Seeing that important other as a, possibly new, career, suddenly puts a new dimension on the importance of the relationship*. The relationship can't be rescheduled at will, or put off, as you would a meeting, or a customer, because something more urgent comes up. You can't treat a career like that.

The second benefit of seeing important relationships in terms of career development is that it keeps you up to the mark, by helping you to avoid sliding back into the old ways. Without the constant diligence supplied by a career development approach, it is all too easy, once the pressure comes on, as it inevitably will, to relegate significant others to being minor staff members, rather than senior partners, in the running of your life. A further benefit of looking at important relationships as a career is that setbacks can be put into some kind of context. You might lose your husband, just as you might lose your job, but that won't stop you having a successful long-term career as a wife, or whatever business or profession you specialise in. In essence, important relationships should be strategic, and treated as such, not tactical, and treated as expedients.

So we are talking about treating life in the round. (I would use the word holistically again, but I try to avoid it whenever possible, as I harbour slight doubts about what it means to people. It would be clearer if it were spelt 'wholistically', rather than implying it was concerned with the science of holes. On looking it up, I find that it comes from the Greek *holo*, meaning whole or total, as in holocaust, meaning all burned. Somehow it doesn't seem to help.)

Part of treating life in the round means having consistent standards of behaviour in all areas of one's life. This means integrity must underpin all activity, whether business or social. Several years ago I had dealings with a highly reputable company who recruited an aggressive new chief executive to sharpen up their performance. They got more than they bargained for. He was ruthless, and did things that took my breath away. His excesses eventually caught up with him and he suffered a humiliating, and very public, disgrace. I had dealings with a man who became one of his hatchet men, and the transformation of the man under the new leadership was disturbing to see.

Some years later, by sheer chance, I found myself sitting next to him at a dinner. I took the opportunity, and the courage offered by a few glasses of wine, to ask him how he could possibly have behaved as he did. His initial reply was the usual excuse 'merely obeying orders'. On being pressed for a more coherent response, he claimed that business morality and private morality had nothing in common. He maintained this view under close interrogation, and plainly believed that anything he did in a work context had nothing to do with any standards of honesty or morality he may have believed in outside work.

I found, and I find, this appalling and totally unacceptable. Something is either right or it is wrong, and the difference in context between work and family, or work and friends, has to be wholly incidental. Beyond that, if one of our most important goals is quality of life, that quality of life has as a starting point self-respect and self-belief. Self-respect and self-belief only come from integrity. Integrity, as Dr Stephen Covey has pointed out, comes directly from holding true to principles that are unchanging. It does not come from espousing values that change with time and context, and are thus a moving feast.

Being an Independent Business Generator helps create quality of income

If quality of life comes from achieving an inner dignity and satisfaction, through getting our life in better balance, money also helps. Lack of money makes it much harder to retain inner dignity. Money is an important element in life being both endurable and enjoyable, so let's not pretend otherwise. As Keats pointed out, romantic privation is a pretty thin concept, and normally ends up demeaning and reducing those involved in it.

Apart from any improvement in lifestyle we might wish for, there are some pretty basic funding requirements that will be required:

- general living expenses (including the exceptional, unbudgeted, costs that seem to crop up every month)
- savings (vital for funding income interruptions, thin patches, medical and dental fees, birthdays, weddings, holidays, etc.)
- pension (state provision will be risible, and any corporate schemes are likely to yield less than you expect)
- serious emergencies (serious incapacitating illness, aid for other family members, etc.)

I do not in any way underestimate the difficulty of achieving this financial programme. I am lucky enough to earn a considerable income from my various enterprises, but I frequently fail to achieve the desired combination of spending and savings. Like most people, whatever level of income I achieve, I always seem to need slightly more. Peter is often robbed to pay Paul, particularly when Peter is my tax savings account

(VAT is paid three-monthly and, being self-employed, I pay income tax six-monthly).

To underline the point, money is extremely important. We therefore need to hone to their most effective level our skills in generating income. We also need to develop coping stratagems for the thin periods, when the money isn't rolling in and the bills are. More of which later. In maximising the effectiveness of our ability to earn money, we must consider ourselves as Independent Business Generators.

All three words are important. *Independence* is crucial. Even if you have worked for a company for many years, and feel there is mutual loyalty involved, *start thinking independently now*. However much the firm may owe you, there is a dynamic in the air for replacing people with technology, supercharged by the forces of global competition, that even the employers most committed to their staff's continued welfare will find hard to resist. The bright-eyed new chief executive, brought in by the shareholders to increase shareholder returns, will not be looking at loyalty, or consistency of service. He will be looking at the business to identify who are the key talent workers who will form the core of the organisation, and whom he can let go, or keep on, working as temporary contractors to the company's core operations.

Step one, therefore, is to protect your income stream by making sure you are one of the core talent workers in your current job. This is probably the soundest strategy, but the important issue is *how* you accomplish this. It is unlikely that you will make yourself indispensable by just working hard. Working smart is the answer. How you reposition yourself to being a supplier to your company rather than an employee I will look at later in this chapter. What is important at this point is to recognise *that it is a major personal culture change*. Looking at yourself as an outsider, rather than an insider, is part of Comfort Zone Growth.

Comfort Zone Growth is about moving out of the areas of activity and thinking in which you are comfortable. If someone changes the song book, we must sing new songs. We won't necessarily forget the old songs, but we'll learn some great new tunes. We'll make mistakes in getting the tunes right, and we'll feel foolish doing it, but once learned, we'll have a much larger repertoire of songs.

Employment as a song book used to be a slim, simple, spirally bound volume. Now it is a large, rather messy, loose-leaf folder in which the pages are being changed constantly. Flexibility with a smile is what is required, and flexibility with a smile demands Comfort Zone Growth. Being an outside supplier is far less comfortable than having a contract of employment. But if your main client decides your services are no longer needed, at least you have a very clear idea of what services you can offer other clients.

In applying for employment, the difference between an Independent Business Generator, and a person looking for a job, is profound. An Independent Business Generator is not a permanent overhead (although in some circumstances may be offered a job, in the traditional sense). A IBG does not need costly induction and training. He or she does not need a car, or pension funding. If the relationship doesn't work out, it can be terminated painlessly. There is also a difference in mindset. The person looking for a job is automatically a supplicant. The IBG, on the other hand, is more of a commercial equal, in a mature buyer/seller relationship.

This description of the differences will not apply to every situation. Even if you believe that conventional employment is still relevant in the sector you work in, it's still worth getting out of your comfort zone, and rethinking yourself in these terms. The chances are that your sector will change sooner than you think, and repositioning yourself mentally will give you useful insights into what value you are adding in your current job.

Business is important as the second word because it is vital to recognise that whatever you do to earn money, it is a business transaction contracted between you and the person or company that employs your services. Even if you are a teacher or a nurse, you are still in a position of supplying services for financial reward. Rethinking yourself as a business will again give you more chance of ending up as one of the core talent workers, or at least being first in the queue when your organisation looks for key outside suppliers.

Generator, too, is an important word. The whole approach should be self-consciously proactive. *Creating income – both for yourself and the person, company, or organisation employing you – is the purpose of activity, and all energies should be concentrated on this goal.* Becoming an IBG is a *process*. Staying one is a process. It requires discipline to think yourself into the role, and to improve yourself in the role.

Even more important, Independent Business Generators exude a sense of integrity and strength. To onlookers, they feel no pain. This is not a journey for the fainthearted. Guts are required on the voyage. The good news is that, just as comfort zones can be extended, courage can be developed. It takes time to become a Mighty Lion, but all of us can make it in the end.

Becoming an Independent Business Generator is a process. To facilitate and steer this process it is helpful to complete certain steps. The first of these is to undertake a STOC Check, which in turn will lead to an IBG Action Plan. To get some idea of what is involved, let's look at the STOC Check of three fictitious people, Felicity Freshstart, Norman Newhope, and Simon Smartbutton. Felicity is a thirty-five-year-old, single, secretary/PA; Norman is a forty-six-year-old, married, accountant; and Nigel is a thirty-year-old High-flyer. They are in no way exceptional people. They, like all of us, have talents and strengths that can be developed. The process we will watch them go through will reveal how these talents and strengths can flourish, given the opportunity.

A STOC Check is a more holistic and insightful curriculum vitae. To give some insight into the differences between a conventional curriculum vitae and a STOC Check, let's look at Felicity's, Norman's and Simon's cvs and STOC Checks side by side. We'll begin with Felicity.

Curriculum Vitae: Felicity Freshstart

Background
A good secretary/PA, with experience of working with high intensity
   bosses
Energetic and effective in scheduling work programmes and sales meetings

Key Achievements at Boffins Technology
Re-organised, and runs, office and schedules of sales director, with great
   success
Helped establish better liaison between technical staff and sales people
Has organised several successful sales conferences

Additional Experience
Secretary to the Ringdon Amateur Drama Group
Captain of Boffins Hockey Club

Specialist Skills and Disciplines
As well as organising skills and enthusiasm, is fluent in all major word
   processing and conference technology systems

1996 to Present
PA to sales director, who is abroad more than 50 per cent of the time.
Responsibilities include keeping the department going in sales director's

absence, and creating continuous, seamless, communications between staff, clients, and sales director, whether in the country or not

__1992–6__
Secretary/PA to sales manager, Livewire Electronics

__Secretarial College to 1992__
Secretary to six senior purchasing executives, Plug and Switch Mail Order

__Education__
8 GCSEs; secretarial diploma

__Languages__
GCSE French and German

__Personal__
British, single, thirty-five years

From this you can get a reasonable handle on Felicity as an operator in a business context, if you are a prospective employer. But Felicity's STOC Check will look somewhat different.

STOC Check: Felicity Freshstart

__Strengths__
Ability to:
- work well under pressure
- work with difficult people
- prioritise, and deal with the important urgent first, rather than the merely urgent urgent
- problem solve with both clients and staff

Honesty
Reliability – always sees things through, and gets back to people
Kindness
Self-belief and self-respect
Good sense of humour
Healthy – good diet

Fit – regular exercise
Good at languages
Conquers loneliness with action
Strong and positive relationships with family and friends
Happy person, who makes others feel happy
Likes technology
Enjoys organising large sales meetings/conferences

Talents
Ability to:
  – create enthusiasm in others
  – make people feel relaxed
  – listen well
  – make others feel valued
  – make people laugh
  – build lasting relationships
  – spot wrong-'uns (men in particular)
  – cook well
Good athletic and sporting skills
Good actor and singer
Self-confident in meetings, speaks well

Opportunities
Opportunity to:
– become less vulnerable to situation at Boffins Technology (boss leaves,
  company restructured, taken over, etc.)
– gain more control over life

Challenges
Edging towards top of salary range (cheaper to replace with bright
  young thing)
Need to achieve Comfort Zone Growth – too comfortable in Secretary/
  PA role, amongst friends (major challenge)
Will need courage to reorientate life on own (no partner for daily
  support)
Will need all her skills to keep friendships and family relationships going
  through period in which she will be extremely time-poor
Challenge to keep motivation going, lacking external pressures of
  immediate family to support

As you can see, it tells us a lot more about Felicity than her curriculum vitae does. Now let's look at Norman.

Curriculum Vitae: Norman Newhope

Background
A excellent accountant running the accounts department of Delectable Foods, a privately owned chain of prepared food and meals super-markets
Efficient manager of a growing department

Key Achievements at Delectable Foods
Turned round Accounts Department by restructuring and retraining
Improved cash flow by restructuring supplier payments
Reduced shrinkage/staff theft by improved stock and cash controls

Additional Experience
Governor of Hottingbury School
Lecturer in basic accounting skills at Hottingbury College of Further Education
Treasurer of the Hottingbury Gardening Club

Specialist Skills and Disciplines
Highly skilled in the use of spreadsheets for business modelling
Special interest and expertise in waste and cost reduction

1995 to Present
Accounts Department Manager, Delectable Foods
Responsibilities include managing department, attending board meetings in role of Company Secretary, and setting of cost reduction targets

1990–95
Senior accountant, OK Foods

1980–90
Management Accountant, Sparks Electrical Retailers

1973–80
Trainee, then accountant, Lugs and Bait, Chartered Accountants

Education
7 GCSEs, 2 A Levels, HND Business Studies

Personal
British, forty-six years, married, two children

We've all come across a Norman in our lives. But let's have a look at his STOC Check.

STOC Check: Norman Newhope

Strengths
Ability to:
   – build and manage a team
   – take a proactive view (waste/cost control)
   – be a team player
Numeracy (and good with spreadsheets)
Integrity
Reliability (sticks at the task)
Strong sense of social responsibility
Sense of humour (particularly when things aren't going well)
Strong family relationships – good father and husband
Healthy – but tendency to over-imbibe
Popular with colleagues (possibly because not seen as a threat)

Talents
Ability to:
   – lead other people (gently)
   – develop Business Plans that people believe in
   – inspire trust
   – inspire love from family
   – see ways of improving things
   – see the funny side of difficult situations
Good teacher
Patience

Opportunities
Opportunity to:
- develop business opportunities, within current job, and outside
- get backing for business ideas (track record, accountant, inspires trust)
- become a more active Active Social Contributor

Challenges
Need to be more assertive – enough talent to be a board member, but
content to take minutes, and make contributions when called upon
Need to overcome tendency to doubt self, and question own abilities
To overcome tendency to talk self down (especially as he has always
delivered the goods so far)
To get fit – take regular exercise

Norman looks solid and content, even unambitious, but he has all the makings of a good IBG. We'll look at his IBG Action Plan later. Let's now have a look at Simon Smartbutton. Simon, as you will see, is a High-flyer.

Curriculum Vitae: Simon Smartbutton

Background
A very effective lawyer, specialising in commercial law
Excellent at absorbing work and getting it done to a high standard

Key Achievements at Charge, Charge & Charge
Youngest partner even at CC&C
Building reputation with clients for incisive analysis and outstanding service

Additional Experience
Member of Amnesty International – occasional adviser

Specialist Skills and Disciplines
Expert user of Information Technology to organise workflow, communi-
cate with clients, etc.
Specialises in commercial law within the IT industry

1992 to Present
Lawyer, now Partner with CC&C
Responsibilities include running his department, and advising
    on Knowledge development

Education
10 GCSEs; 3 A Levels; 1st Class Degree in Law; LLB.

Languages
French, German, Russian

Personal
British, thirty years, married, one child, aged four.

What the cv does not reveal is that Simon works about seventy hours a week and is close to crisis point. He is earning a huge salary and has no time to spend it. He sees little of his family and stress is building up at home, as well as at work. He is exhausted and knows he won't reach forty at this pace, let alone fifty. Let's look at his STOC Check.

Simon Smartbutton: STOC Check

Strengths
Ability to:
    – get rapidly to the heart of the issue
    – come up with imaginative solutions
    – work at pace, and under pressure
    – generate huge fee income
    – build a team of bright people
    – earn trust of clients
Ambitious
Single-minded
Great stamina
Technology pioneer
Good at languages
Reliability – whatever the pressure
Mover and shaker

Talents
Ability to:
- create enthusiasm in others
- speak well in public
- lead a meeting willingly to conclusion
- simplify the complicated
- combine speed with accuracy
Boundless self-confidence

Talents currently dormant
Good athletic and sporting skills
Sense of humour
Sympathy for the deprived/oppressed
Ability to develop caring relationships

Opportunities
Opportunity to:
- reorganise life, to avoid health breakdown, divorce, or both
- become a very worthwhile Active Social Contributor

Challenges
- Health – stress impacting negatively, eating too much, of wrong food, irregularly
- Fitness – non-existent – no cushion, in case of health challenge
- Family relationships not functioning properly – poor husband, non-existent father
- Impaired listening ability – too quick with the answer (especially in non-work situations)
- Seeming inability to get off work treadmill – intractable culture of long hours, highly competitive pressure, no half measures

Before we look at how to develop an IBG Action Plan, and what Felicity's, Norman's and Simon's might look like, a word about curriculum vitaes. Many will have excellent, up-to-date, cvs. For those, like myself, who find themselves without one, because one hasn't been required for a decade and a half, my experience may be helpful. I wrote mine out, after finding out the most up-to-date structure from a friend who had recently been through a similar experience.

I then gave it to another friend, who was also enormously supportive throughout, and gave significant practical support by getting letterheads and business cards designed and printed. The idea was that he would make it look beautiful on the word processor (he is an AppleMac enthusiast), and return it to me. He read it, and told me it was useless. He then rewrote it, and let me have it back. It was full of the most boastful puffery I had ever read. After a short discussion, I realised he was right. I was no longer chairman – I no longer even had a job – so low-key modesty was no longer appropriate. I toned down his worst excesses, and went ahead with his version.

If you are loath to ask a friend to render such a service, try to change your entire mindset when you sit down to compose your cv. Imagine you work for an advertising agency that has been given the brief of selling *you*. Look for the best, and dramatise it. If you find it embarrassingly fulsome, you're probably getting close to the target. It goes without saying that you avoid bullshit at all costs. It must be honest and accurate, but it must talk you up and dramatise all your abilities and achievements.

This is more difficult than it sounds, because effective operators do not go around claiming the praise for themselves, and are quick to give credit to others. Half the skill of getting projects agreed, or persuading people to do things, is to convince them that they thought of it themselves. It will therefore come as a bit of a shock to have to sit down and write yourself back into history. But it must be done. You are good. Communicate this clearly and believably.

An IBG Action Plan is not an advertising campaign – it's a rethink and relaunch of a complete brand portfolio

The development of the IBG Action Plan involves identifying and marketing the assets that you identify in the STOC Check. The STOC Check contains many of the soft, human issues, and is intended to gain a better insight into, and understanding of, your talents and abilities as a human being.

The IBG Action Plan is concerned with programming yourself to create income. It is unrepentantly commercial in approach. It concerns discipline, hard work and the understanding that most things coming out of it won't work at first. Some of them will never work. Enough things must be thrown against the wall for some to stick. No Business Plan on earth is guaranteed to succeed. Most fail, even those poured over by accountants and merchant bankers, and backed by millions of pounds of expert investors' money.

So don't worry about setbacks, and don't get upset when things fail. Success in business is about trying enough things, and never giving up. Just remember the story of Colonel Sanders. At the age of sixty-eight he was running his own fried chicken store in a small town in Kentucky. A bypass was built around the town, and he lost all his passing trade, which was what made the business profitable. He could so easily have drawn up the covers and said goodnight.

Instead, he set about thinking of other ways to make money. He hit upon the idea of selling the recipe for his method of frying chicken (which turned out to be finger-lickin' good). He tried a few fast food, and slow food outlets, but without success. No one was interested. He drove the length and breadth of Kentucky, and beyond, but without success. He was seen as a silly old man, who should have driven home and taken his recipe with him. After over 1,000 attempts to sell his recipe – yes, 1,000 – he made his first sale. And the rest is history.

Edison was said to have been looked at askance by friends and colleagues as he toiled away with experiment after experiment, attempting to invent the electric light. After 500 failed experiments, he was asked by a reporter if he would not be better advised to give up and admit defeat. His reply was that he now knew 500 ways *not* to invent it, so it would be much easier to find one that *would*. It took him more than 500 more experiments to crack it, but crack it he did, for which subsequent generations have been extremely grateful.

So discouragement is not on the agenda (more of which later). But strategic and intuitive thinking, imagination and ingenuity, all are. We are approaching on a broad front, because we don't know what will work.

The goal is *multiple income streams*, built around a core

You could be in one of several situations at this moment. You could have recently lost your job and be wondering what the hell to do next. You could be about to lose your job, or worried about losing it, or even be quite relieved if you did lose it. You could be reasonably secure in it, or you might even love it, but be interested in laying down some contingency plans, just in case. Whatever situation you are in, it is worth thinking about how you market your assets better, and how you either spread risk, or increase your income.

Multiple income streams (or diversity of income) are an intrinsic and important part of the Incomes Revolution. The aim at this stage is to identify a core business activity you are good at, that will be your main revenue earner – which may be your job – and build around it as many satellite opportunities as possible to bring in extra money. Many of these may not work, or will only work for a time. Some may grow into major earners, and change the whole balance of your income. In the oil industry there is a saying that the guy who wins is the guy who drills most wells. *We are all in the business of drilling as many wells as possible.*

If that sounds a tall order, don't be concerned. Basically it's about sitting down and looking at your STOC Check, and spinning out ideas of all sorts. But first apply the discipline of asking yourself a few structured questions.

1. What market are you in, and should you be in it?

Thinking of your STOC Check, and thinking in terms of your core revenue generator (probably your job) what are you good at, and what do you *like* doing? Are your strengths, skills and talents more applicable to markets other than the one you are in? If, for example, what you really like is the creative end of business, and you're in manufacturing, should you consider a shift to marketing? If you're in a service industry and you don't like people, should you look for opportunities in a business that values analytical, rather than people, skills? This sounds a bit like basic careers advice, which it is, but it's still worth thinking very seriously about whether your ladder is up against the right wall, before you continue to climb it.

2. Are you in the right sector of the market?

If you are sure that you are happy with the market you are in, which will provide your main source of income, are you sure you are in the right sector of that market? Are you better as a doer, or an adviser? Are your talents better suited – *or might there be a better market for them* – as a supplier, a retailer, or a service provider? What are the growth sectors? Are you already in one, and if not, how do you get into one?

3. Thinking of yourself as a brand, do you need a relaunch?

Are your current skills in demand in your market? Will they be more or less in demand as your chosen sector develops? Do you need to reformulate yourself, so **Brand Me** is the best on the market? What product development does Brand Me need to stay ahead, and be constantly in demand? How can you develop new skills that give you an initiative – a **Unique Selling Proposition** – for Brand Me? What subbrands can you develop to extend your appeal and give you a wider market? Is Brand Me's packaging (phone call, letter of introduction, curriculum vitae, etc.) better than the competition? *Do you talk, write and present yourself, like a brand leader?*

Thinking in these terms helps focus the mind on how we position ourselves in the market. You need to develop a **Brand Positioning Statement** that defines Brand Me, so that you feel like a brand leader, and others perceive you as such. What are your benefits to a prospective employer, client, or customer? What evidence do you have for the competitive advantage you claim for yourself?

A further important question is: *What investment in marketing support is necessary for Brand Me to be successful?* Preparation for your relaunch will be necessary. This will involve a range of activities, some of which will require investment. It is vital that you come across as someone serious, professional, committed, with a complete absence of flakiness.

You are now in the business of *perception management*. Perception management means what it says – managing the perception of Brand Me, from how *you* perceive yourself, through to how current employers (if you plan to relaunch yourself in your current place of work), or prospective employers or clients perceive you. How you perceive yourself has to be managed with clarity and precision. *It is a conscious act, in which you take responsibility for Brand Me.* Self-image and self-development are pivotal elements, both of which will be dealt with at some length later. Within this, there will be specific skill, or attitude, elements that need addressing urgently in order for Brand Me's relaunch to be credible to both yourself and others. These should be included within the **Planning and Evaluation Schedule** that accompanies the IBG Action Plan.

There is also the external perception of Brand Me to manage. This covers cards, letterheads, presentation folders, and other stationery to make sure Brand Me communicates to important clients. This will obviously not apply if you intend to relaunch with your current employer (although going through the motions may be no bad thing, as it will help clarify your positioning). This will need thinking about, as well as funding. All brands need investment to keep them viable. This ranges from product improvements, packaging updates, through to advertising and promotion. Brand Me is no different.

Probably the highest expenditure will be on product improvement. Training courses are not cheap, even the tape variety, but will be necessary to hone your skills and your ability to communicate them effectively. Short cuts are dangerous, particularly when something as important as your long-term earning ability is concerned. Your investment should, if possible, be an act of pride. I say this because you are now a brand – or business – *owner*. If you cavil about investment – or would rather someone else paid for you – you still have an *employee mentality*. It is important to break away from this thinking as soon as possible in order to rethink Brand Me as something you own, control, and are keen to develop.

But we get ahead of ourselves. Before we can relaunch ourselves as brands, we must develop our IBG Action Plans and Planning and Evaluation Schedules. Once these have been defined, reworked, and redefined, a Brand Positioning Statement can be evolved. These are sketched out below for our intrepid three: Felicity, Norman and Simon. It should be noted that only one Brand Positioning Statement has been worked out per person, and this in each case is for their most likely source of their core income. It will make sense for each of them to sit down and define their Brand Positioning Statements for their secondary lines of potential income. This requires work, but the *clarity* it will generate will make it easier to allocate resources. The likely winners and losers will begin to identify themselves, and the no-hopers can be weeded out. The apparent losers should be persevered with, as they may change in development, and metamorphose into winners.

Your own personal Brand Positioning Statement may be more complex, but it should not be *too* complex. It may sound contradictory, but simplicity and focus are still required, even if you are throwing a lot of things against the wall. You only have twenty-four hours in a day, and it's important to focus your efforts to make the best use of them.

Let's start with Felicity's IBG Action Plan. Felicity should focus on exploring the following possibilities:

Felicity Freshstart: IBG Action Plan

Core Income
either/or
– move from PA/Secretary to an executive within Boffins Technology
– become an executive with a supplier
– utilise conference-organising skills as freelance (major growth industry)

Alternative Core Strategy
– move to a service industry (e.g. recruitment) to utilise people skills

Secondary Income Sources
– develop home cooking business in spare evenings
– teach improved word processing/computer skills to fledgling IBGs
– explore other second income options

Personal Development Priority
– develop language skills – learn Spanish (second world language), or
  Chinese (will be the world's largest economy) – wider skills if has to
  remain a PA/secretary, useful for international opportunities if
  becomes executive, or goes freelance

Social
– become a worthwhile Active Social Contributor (see later)

From this, Felicity will be able to develop a Planning and Evaluation Schedule. This schedule is useful from two points of view, both of which are important. One is that it gives a timetable, with target times for action accomplished. Having specific goals is vital, because without a timetable they are merely dreams, and are unlikely ever to be achieved.

The second reason is that it focuses the mind on the Importance, as well as the Urgency, of each item on the action list. Without this focus, there is a tendency for everything to be seen as both Important and Urgent, with the result that very little ends up actually being done. The difference between Importance and Urgency has been defined in great depth, as well as great insight, by Stephen Covey in his outstanding books on effective leadership. In a separate talk, entitled 'First Things First' he tells a story about how he first came to see the distinction.

He was attending a class as a student, and the teacher had put an oblong fish tank on the desk at the front. From under the desk he brought out a bucket full of rocks and proceeded to fill the fish tank. When he could get no more in, he asked the students, 'Do you think I can get any more in?' 'No' they replied, because the tank was obviously full. The teacher then bent once more beneath the desk and pulled out a bucket of smaller rocks, which he placed in the gaps between the larger rocks.

'Is it full now?' There was less certainty this time, but the students thought it looked pretty full. He bent once more and brought out a bucket of gravel, which he poured into the pockets still remaining. 'Is it full now?' 'No!' they roared, suspecting there was more to come. They were right. He then brought out a bucket of sand, and repeated the process. 'Now?' 'No!' again, as he bent to retrieve a bucket of water, to fill the remaining gaps in the fish tank.

The teacher then addressed the class and asked them what they thought he was trying to demonstrate. There was general unanimity. He was trying to show that however full something appears to be, you can always get more in. And by extrapolation, however busy you are, you can always fit more in.

'Quite wrong,' said the teacher. 'What I was demonstrating was that if I hadn't put the large rocks in first, and had put the gravel or water in, I would never have been able to get the large rocks in at all.' And by extrapolation, if you fill your day busily knocking off the To Do list, the important things will never get done, because there will be no time left in which to do them. Covey goes on to make the point that some of our biggest rocks that we have to reorganise ourselves in order to find room for are our family – partners, children and parents.

Getting back to Felicity, and how she earns her rocks, we can begin to see how useful as a tool are the Importance/Urgency ratings in sorting out our priorities. The key for Felicity's Planning and Evaluation Schedule is I = Important, U = Urgent. Each of these dimensions is rating on a score of 1–5, with 1 being the highest score (most Important or Urgent) and 5 being the lowest. Here goes.

Planning and Evaluation Schedule: Felicity Freshstart

(We assume the date she is compiling it is 1 January.)

Project	By when	Importance rating
Move from secretary/PA to executive	June	I-1/U-1
Executive with supplier	Sept	I-1/U-3
Move to service industry	March following year	I-3 U-5
Dinner party business	March	I-3 U-2
Give wp lessons	Oct	I-5 U-5
Other options	June	I-2 U-2
Language skills	Sept	I-3 U-3
Become an ASC	Nov	I-1 U-3

Some of these scores can be debated, but some interesting points are thrown up by defining the goal in terms of Importance and Urgency, and putting some dates on. It shows that she ought to be putting out feelers quite soon with suppliers, in case Plan A (getting internal promotion) does not come to fruition. It also shows that she needn't do anything too active yet on moving to a service industry, although its mid-range Importance level indicates that a bit of background homework should be going on in the meantime.

It shows clearly that teaching word processing skills is probably a non-starter, because it is too labour intensive, and dependent on Felicity's presence. The home cooking/dinner parties business, on the other hand, could be delegated, when Felicity was away at conferences, with her leading a team of part-time cooks, all interested in diversifying their income streams, or just earning extra money.

Felicity now moves on to her Brand Positioning Statement. In fact she would write several, one for each of her different areas of strategic development. The one shown here is based on the assumption that her boss is too busy to listen to what she is saying, and is loath to lose such a good secretary/PA. He therefore hopes she isn't serious, or that it is some life-stage she is going through, and tries to fob her off with promises that they both know will never be realised.

She therefore starts executing the strategy of setting up her own freelance conference business, on the assumption that she can either actually start the business, or sell herself as a freelance organiser to a current operator along the way. The Brand Positioning Statement is the same for both outcomes:

Brand Positioning Statement: Felicity Freshstart

Brand Positioning
Conference Felicitations are business focused, effective, and memorable

Competitive Advantage
Felicity has complete understanding of your needs because she herself
ran conferences as a client

Specific Benefits
You can rest assured that a conference organised by Felicity will be
superbly organised, fun, and come in on budget

Support
Excellent track record in conference organisation (ratings very high in
post-conference research); Team Members confirm calm but firm
leadership, with style and fun. Superb people skills; problem
devourer; honest; life-enhancer.

Felicity will read and reread this Brand Positioning Statement, until she is living and breathing it. In all her meetings with prospective suppliers or clients she will live the role of Conference Felicitations. She is that brand, and its definition, in all its colours, will radiate from her.

We now come to Norman Newhope. For Norman, the IBG Action Plan has an element of risk, so it is important that he involves his family in these exciting new opportunities. His family, too, will have to undergo Comfort Zone Growth, as the familiar, safe, Norman of old begins to spread his wings and go for it.

Norman Newhope: IBG Action Plan

<u>Core Income</u>
either/or
– prepare proposition to board, to make him Finance and Operations
  Director, with operations manager reporting to him (benefit to the
  board, even better shrinkage/waste control)
– consider development of Business Plan to franchise Delectable Foods
  format, with self as first franchisee

<u>Alternative Core Strategy</u>
– develop Business Plan for concept that leapfrogs Delectable Food's
  offer (takes the best, and moves it on), and find investors for new
  enterprise (which he would run)

<u>Secondary Income Sources</u>
– explore opportunities in retailing gardening products (combines
  interests)
– earn extra income teaching private courses on spreadsheets, etc.
– explore other income options – possibly with wife

<u>Personal Development Priority</u>
– go on a good course that would transform his self-confidence

<u>Social</u>
– decide on more focused approach as an Active Social Contributor

---

Planning and Evaluation Schedule: Norman Newhope

Again, we assume we are starting from 1 January.

Project	By when	Importance rating
Finance and operations director	June	I-1 U-1
Delectable foods franchise	May	I-1 U-1

Better version of Delectable Foods	Dec	I-2 U-4
Retailing garden products	Oct	I-3 U-4
Private spreadsheet courses	Sept	I-5 U-5
Other income options	Oct	I-2 U-3
Course to produce Super-Norm	March	I-1 *U*-1
More serious ASC	Nov	I-3 U-3

Again, putting down target dates and importance and urgency ratings gives insights into Norman's priorities. He has to prepare his Business Plan for franchising the Delectable Foods format before he confronts the board with his plan to be a director. He then has the option of either using it (excising himself as the first franchisee) at his first board meeting, confirming their sound judgement in appointing this new ideas man to the board, or using it as a fully worked-out fallback if they don't buy Plan A.

What comes out as more important and urgent than anything is his programme of self-development, to ensure his propositions come from a serious businessman, rather than friendly old Norm. Again, spread-sheets, like word processor tuition for Felicity, goes down the priority list because it cannot be delegated, and is too time-consuming.

His garden products retail concept is still relatively important, both because it might work, and it would enable him to work with his wife. It is slightly less urgent than the new and improved version of Delectable Foods, as it is less likely (being new and unproved) to gain rapid backing from financial institutions.

Becoming an Active Social Contributor will be important to Norman, but must wait until the more pressing issues of his core income stream are sorted out.

Having absorbed the lessons of his personal development courses and study, the relaunch of New Norman will be possible. The following Brand Positioning Statement is focused on Norman's pitch to become a board director. He will adapt it for presentations to financial institutions, if Plan A fails, but the core will remain intact.

Brand Positioning Statement: Norman Newstart

Brand Positioning
A late flowerer, with business vision, initiative, and sound project
  leadership

Competitive Advantage
Rare combination of ideas, and gritty operation control (including cash
  flow forecasts that are actually delivered)

Specific Benefits
You know that Norman will be a good leader, totally trustworthy, and
  every penny will be spent effectively

Support
Norman's business forecasts have proved remarkably accurate, and he
  has run a tight ship with an accountant's eye for detail. Good with
  people; team player.

And now, Simon.

Simon Smartbutton: IBG Action Plan

For Simon, it will be far from easy. He has no time to think and feels,
rightly or not, that one serious error at work, or noticeable easing of his
work schedule, and he will be vulnerable to the predations of other, even
more competitive, partners. Simon will have to sit down with his wife
(assuming their relationship can be salvaged) and agree a joint plan of
action to resolve the situation. This will probably involve an extremely
aggressive savings plan. He is earning a considerable salary, so this
should be possible with both goodwill and a common purpose to work
towards. His wife, Fleur, is not currently working. A buffer of savings
will create options.

The most powerful option would be to take a sabbatical from Charge,
Charge and Charge, in order to get some distance from the pressures, to
sort his life out. Failing this, he should resign his partnership and leave,

to achieve the same objective. Simon and Fleur should agree their timetable, being aware *that everything will take at least six months longer than they think it will, to fall into place.* They can call their new venture Change, Change and Change.

Core Income

– acting as freelance consultant (to either CC&C, or one or two of his major ex-clients) as drafting expert (work relatively clean, and controllable, and less need of back-up departments)

Alternative Core Income
– consultancy in Knowledge Management, using latest IT applications (leading edge practitioner at CC&C)
– ad hoc work for local firm of solicitors (small practice with no commercial partner)

Secondary Income Sources
– Fleur returns to work (fall-back only)
– explore other income options with Fleur (when ready)

Personal Development Priority
– course on Active Listening

Social
– develop very useful role as Active Social Contributor with Amnesty International

---

Having talked through his IBG Action Plan with Fleur and convinced her that he is not just buying time, but serious about changing his lifestyle, they decide to give it a go. They are both perceptive and mature enough to know that it will not be easy. Their families and friends will be baffled and suspect the worst. As a couple they will go through challenges that would test a strong relationship, let alone one that is still in the rehabilitation ward.

Committing to the task, they develop their schedule.

Planning and Evaluation Schedule: Simon Smartbutton

Project	By when	Importance rating
Freelance consultant/drafting expert	Sept	I-3 U-3
Knowledge management	Sept	I-1 U-1
Ad hoc, local firm	Oct	I-4 U-4
Fleur back to full-time work	Never	N/A
Other income streams together	June	I-1 U-1
Active listening course	Feb	I-1 U-1
Role as ASC	Dec	I-1 U-4

Having decided to resign on the first day back at work after New Year's Day, they begin thinking through the projects. Discussing them, things begin to crystallise for Simon and Fleur. They realise that Simon will be almost certain to find the drafting work too intellectually undemanding. He will also miss the buzz of front-line client contact.

They therefore decide to go for Knowledge consultancy. Their discussions highlight the obvious snag, that consultancy, like the law, is personally very time-intensive. Simon will quickly be back into working long hours, and the income may well be lower than in the law.

Unwilling to let go of an idea that seems to have some legs, they continue to wrestle with alternatives, until Simon comes up with the solution. Like all good ideas, it is obvious once someone has had it. Within seconds, Fleur thinks it was her idea, and Simon is generous, and sensible, enough to confirm her in this view. Rather than consultancy services, Simon will offer software packages. He will develop specific packages for specific sectors (law, accountancy, etc.), which he will then subcontract to salespersons to sell on to selected client bases. His time investment will thus be more controllable, and the residual income from maintenance charges from his software packages will create continuous and, hopefully, increasing, revenues. At a later date, it might be possible to float the company on the stock exchange, or sell it.

Working together on the Planning and Evaluation Schedule was more enjoyable and stimulating than either would previously have thought possible. As a result, they brought the option of working together on a secondary source of income up the agenda, changing it from a gesture into a priority.

The active listening course also remained a priority (at Fleur's insistence), and her returning full-time to work dropped off the agenda. They both felt that they wanted to work as Active Social Contributors, probably with Simon doing work for Amnesty International, and Fleur helping out at the local hospice.

Simon's Brand Positioning Statement resulting from these deliberations was therefore drafted as a brand statement for his new company, Sapiens Knowledge. It is not a personal statement, but it comes directly out of his STOC Check, IBG Action Plan, and discussions with Fleur.

Brand Positioning Statement: Simon Smartbutton

Brand Positioning
Sapiens Knowledge Software packages give better access to more, and
    better-organised databases

Competitive Advantage
Market leaders in collation, organising and *editing* of information

Specific Benefits
Faster updating, and constant innovation, assures that your information
    requirements are satisfied faster, more easily, and more cost
    effectively

Support
Founder a recognised pioneer in the application of technology to
    acquire, organise and retrieve, relevant information

We have travelled the journey with Felicity, Norman and Simon through their STOC Checks, IBG Action Plans, Planning and Evaluation Schedules, and Brand Positioning Statements. We, along with them, are clearer on their first line of attack. Strategies and tactics may have to be modified later, but they are off to a flying start. All three of them are clear that they need either to develop, or protect, their core income stream, while they develop flexibility through other income sources.

They will have to visualise their Brand Positioning Statement, as they go to work, as they meet colleagues, clients, or customers, and particularly when they attend important meetings. Living and breathing it will help them to operate more effectively, whatever they end up doing.

And now, the snag. Yes, you've guessed it. I'm going to ask you to go through a similar process. If you accept the challenge and work out your STOC Check, your IBG Action Plan, your Planning and Evaluation Schedule, and your Brand Positioning Statement, it is very likely to involve an element of Comfort Zone Growth. As the fuzziness begins to be stripped away, and Brand Me begins to crystallise, you will start to feel the excitement rising.

At last you have the opportunity to be you and play to your strengths. The risks are high, but so are the rewards, not just financially, but in being able to move towards defining yourself as an individual, and in fulfilling more potential than you ever thought you had. If you're going to pull up the sheets, pull up the sheets of paper, and get a real buzz out of finding, and being, Brand Me.

Some Practicalities of Being an IBG

MOTIVATION, SELF-BELIEF, courage, excitement, positive enjoyment of life's rich variety. These are the most important practicalities of
being an IBG. But they form the heart of chapter seven, and this is
chapter five. This chapter is a far from exhaustive look at some of the
operational necessities of IBG-hood, and some of their implications. I will
also be asking you to think about things that tend to be thought of as
embarrassing and uncomfortable. Like selling yourself, and involving
your friends in the process. They turn out to be not the slightest bit
embarrassing – with practice – and eventually become great fun.

The Command Centre

Before getting into some of the grittier issues, let's step back and look at
how we control both the strategy and the operational details of
developing into an IBG. The most effective way I have found is to have a
Command Centre. The importance of the Command Centre goes beyond
its usefulness in managing yourself as an IBG, because it can encompass
the strategic and tactical management of your life as a whole.

If your home situation is difficult, or things are such that you don't
have a home, simply locate the Command Centre in your head. Even if
you are lucky enough to have a most sumptuous and well-appointed
office in your home, your true Command Centre should still be inside
your head.

Many of the great thinkers on personal development have identified
the **Quiet Room**, or the **Quiet Place** – located in the mind – as an
essential part of seeing issues with clarity, of isolating priorities, and

getting a perspective on events and conditions that otherwise can appear overwhelming. This time – twenty minutes to half an hour – and how it can help enhance your sense of control of your life, will be looked at more closely later.

Martin Luther King was said to have spent half an hour each morning in such contemplation. The busier his day, the more time he spent on thinking through his true priorities. He even foresaw his imminent death in such a session. But he also saw the bigger picture, which enabled him to press on, placing a lower priority on his own safety and life than on the success of the civil rights movement as a whole, and with it the benefits it would bring to millions of his fellow blacks.

The thoughts in your mental Quiet Place may not play such a momentous role in history, but may play an equally important part in your personal history, so they should be taken seriously and valued accordingly. The Quiet Place may be visited while you are still in bed, before getting up in the morning. Or it may be in a seat in the public library. Or as you travel to and from your job, or core income earner. Or in the office you create in your home. The important thing is that you see it as a Command Centre, and that *you are in control.*

I personally have a work environment that makes it vital that my Command Centre is inside my head. My wife and I share the dining-room table for our office and Command Centre. In fact, we could use a room at the top of the house as an office, but we both feel it is too far from where the action is – the kitchen, the children, the garden, and the front door (roller-blading in the street in the holidays). To be more accurate, I share the table, and she also takes most of the floor. Lizzie is immensely busy: doing community work, running our marketing business, and being a full-time mother. Consequently, she does not have a great deal of time for filing.

If someone comes round for a meeting, or friends come round for a drink, everything is bundled into plastic boxes and bags. As a result, she has become like a domestic bag lady, with her end of the table as the shopping trolley, filled with and surrounded by mounds and bags full of strange and often unvisited treasures. A friend who holds a very senior position in the corporate world recently came to see us. Seeing the table and its surroundings, he averted his eyes. With a slight shudder, he said: 'I can't bear to look at that.' In the light of his remark, we felt we couldn't tell him that it had, in fact, been specially tidied for his visit.

This regular quiet time – daily if you can achieve it – really does repay the effort of creating time for it in a busy day. The subconscious can get to work on the issues, both large and small. Solutions pop out, and knotty problems are resolved. This book is the direct result of such a session. Like most people, I have always secretly harboured a desire to write a book – a novel, rather than non-fiction, but no matter. I was thinking about my current income streams, and at the same time what I enjoyed doing most in my working life. The answer came that I not only enjoyed the conceptual work in writing the reports on the future of retailing, and consumer trends, for the management consultancy I worked with, but I also enjoyed the mental and physical act of writing itself. Beyond that, I relished the uncertainty, the serendipities, the adventures of being self-employed, with multiple income streams, some of which fluctuated wildly. The thought suddenly struck me that I could put all those things together, writing a book that plotted my odyssey, looking at how it fitted into developments now, and in the future, and seeing if there were any lessons to be drawn. It takes between fifteen minutes and fifteen months for the subconscious to come up with answers, but they always come.

The Command Centre's operational tool: the word processor

The main tool in my Command Centre is the word processor. This is *the* vital tool, and competence with it, if not mastery of its potential, must be high up the priority of skill sets required of anyone preparing themselves for effective existence in a world cut off from the support of corporate employment. The first time you are cut off from the corporate infrastructure can be traumatic. Suddenly all the things that seemed to happen automatically, don't. There's no typing resource, there's no photocopier, nobody to fax anything, nobody to dig out basic market figures and information, or go to the post, or arrange travel, or pay expenses. Everything now costs money. And takes time.

The word processor, however, is a wonderful tool. With it you can produce a professionally presented curriculum vitae, personalised for the recipient, documents, proposals, presentations, and – very important – invoices. Not only are they good looking pieces of work, they are adaptable and repeatable with minimum effort, and are *totally within your control.*

If you can't afford to purchase a new one, either get hold of a second-hand one (their resale value is very low), or get access to one belonging to a friend. Without this tool, you really will be struggling. A laptop computer is obviously even better, as it allows you to send and receive faxes and e-mail while you are travelling and, importantly, it is easier to remove from the dining-room table when guests are due.

A word of warning about computers. There is a *danger that they become part of your comfort zone, and an excuse for inaction.* It is all too easy to absorb time, ostensibly working on the computer, that would be better spent in more active areas of business generation.

Selling yourself as an IBG is merely the focusing of selling as a life-skill

Every day we sell things. We sell ideas to our parents, our spouses, our partners, our friends, and our colleagues. We even sell to our children: 'Do you think it would be a good idea to tidy your room?'

The more strongly we feel about something, the better salespeople we tend to be. 'I couldn't sell something unless I believed in it,' I agree. All you have to do now is *believe in Brand Me.* If it makes you feel better, imagine you are *helping someone to buy* Brand Me, rather than selling it. It's a good product, after all, and one worthy of being given a wider choice of potential consumers.

OK, how do we help someone to buy? We simply take the same commercial approach that we took in the last chapter, but extend it. We go back to your Brand Positioning Statement and focus it for specific targets. Whether you are looking for a relaunch at your current source of core income (your job) – to make your employers and colleagues see you in a new, improved, light – or looking for an alternative source of core income, or for secondary income, the method is the same. It hasn't changed since marketing began. It has been taught in all the classic textbooks.

Basically, it's about matching your product or service to customer needs and expectations. In terms of Brand Me, it's about finding people who need your product or service, and then dramatising your specific benefit and underlining your competitive advantage. And if you find the customer is looking for something slightly different, adapting your product as fast as possible, to beat competitors to the sale.

Remember, the customer is always right. At least in the short term. The customer is the buyer, so what he or she wants settles today's sale. In terms of being an alert IBG, however, it may be that you have spotted an opportunity that focuses on what the market will want in the near or medium future. In this case, some gentle education of the customer may be required, to demonstrate to them that what you are offering is what they will be needing tomorrow. Because you are the only one who has spotted this, and have the skill sets already in place, you are a very hot property and they should value you accordingly.

Brand updates: careers advice

Marketing is an iterative process. *That means you keep going till you get it right.* If what you are offering isn't what the customer wants today, or tomorrow, you have two choices. You either find a new customer, who is looking for the benefits Brand Me can deliver, or you reformulate Brand Me till you have a product that the market is looking for. The great advantage to being an IBG is that you are geared up to make product improvements, and see challenges and setbacks as exciting, rather than deflating.

The implications of this are clear. However much you enjoy working at the source of your core income, and however secure you feel, you must be constantly checking the market to see what demand exists for your skills, and how it is changing. So take soundings from your employers as to how their thinking is progressing. If this is not possible, or is inappropriate, talk to employment agencies that specialise in your field, or even competitors.

A word of warning. Your whole industry may be going down a blinkered path to perdition. If you were working in the mechanical till industry twenty years ago, however good you were, once electronic tills were available, you were in deep doo-doo. Your product couldn't compete. As an expert in fixing or selling mechanical tills, your skills were no longer wanted on the voyage. The choice facing you was to reskill, or get out.

Motorola, a world leader in consumer products, has both responded to and anticipated consumer trends throughout its recent history. It has done this by changing the industries it chose to be in. These have included radio, television, consumer and industrial electronics, cellular communication, and now satellite-based worldwide communications. To be a core worker at Motorola you would need talent, but you would also need flexibility, in order to survive the strategic adjustments necessary to stay in touch with where developments in technology and consumer needs came together.

When you look at what skills will be needed in your industry – indeed what might replace your industry – the key is to stay flexible, and constantly be readjusting and updating. Some of the new skills you may have to acquire in your own time, to ensure that Brand Me is up there with the brand leaders. Failure to update your brand constantly will mean it becomes a commodity, because its brand values are diminished. The most notable feature of a commodity is that it sells on price, not quality. Remembering that one of the significant aspects of the Incomes Revolution is the trend towards polarisation in incomes, it makes sense to make sure the market positioning of Brand Me is rich in added value, rather than down amongst the commodities, where the reward levels are plummeting because supply is larger than demand.

How Felicity, Norman and Simon sell themselves

After a brief excursion into forward planning for Brand Me, we are back to the less comfortable subject of actively selling ourselves. Not knowing the specifics of Brand Me, we return to our intrepid trio, launching themselves with gusto onto a changing world. In order to imbue the proceedings with a spicing of realism, I have thrown in a wobbly for poor Norman, to demonstrate the necessity of both pre-planning, and an ability to respond flexibly, and with courage, to changes in market conditions.

Felicity's marketing programme

Felicity decides to concentrate her marketing efforts for her core income on either setting up as a freelance, or getting an executive job with one of the top three or four companies in the field of conference organisation. She first of all re-examines her Brand Positioning Statement:

Brand Positioning Statement: Felicity Freshstart

Brand Positioning
Conference Felicitations are business focused, effective, and memorable

Competitive Advantage
Felicity has complete understanding of your needs because she herself
  ran conferences as a client

Specific Benefits
You can rest assured that a conference organised by Felicity will be
  superbly organised, fun and come in on budget

Support
Excellent track record in conference organisation (ratings very high in
  post-conference research); Team Members confirm calm but firm
  leadership, with style and fun. Superb people skills; problem
  devourer; honest; life enhancer.

Living and breathing her Brand Positioning Statement, she decides to take it a step nearer to realisation by having *business cards* printed. These will have the dual benefits of making her seem more professional to prospective clients, or employers and, even more importantly, to herself. The card is professionally designed and printed. It has her name and, at the bottom, the simple statement: 'For conferences that are effective and fun. And on budget.' At the top right-hand corner of the card there is a spotlight. Its beam illuminates the word 'fun'.

She then, by judicious questioning of her suppliers in the conference industry, finds the best four companies outside the ones Boffins Technology habitually uses. She finds the right person to target – the chief executive in one case, the operations directors in two others, and a conference manager in the fourth. She then finds the right person to talk to in a fifth company, that she does not want to work for. The last company will be her dry-run company, which she uses as a learning experience to get the bugs out of her selling techniques.

Felicity then sits down to compose a letter to the key man at this company. Before she sits down she undertakes a swift walk round the room to get her body and mind working well together, looks in the mirror, and tells herself – out loud – that she is the best conference organiser in the market, and she is about to write a great letter to demonstrate the point. This is her letter.

Gordon Twitcher Esq.,
Global Conferences.

Dear Mr Twitcher,
   Your company is recognised as one of the industry leaders.
   I have run several conferences that have been acknowledged by all who participated in them to have been both effective and fun (and they came in on budget!). I am now considering whether I become a freelance, or gain more experience with a company like yours, that specialises in the innovative use of technology in staging conferences.
   I will bring to your business not just a sense of fun and style, but the ability to increase profitability by controlling costs at all points in the development and staging of the conference.
   I have strong testimonials from companies I have worked for, should they be required.
   I will ring you later in the week to fix a meeting to see if it makes sense for us to work together.
   I look forward to speaking to you then.
      Yours sincerely, etc.

She constantly *reads the letter out loud* as she writes it, to ensure that it flows, and has the sound of good sense. It should really sound as if she is speaking, rather than writing, but she hasn't had enough practice to achieve that yet. She is concerned that it is a bit fulsome and over the top, but this is only a dry-run, so she would rather err on the side of oversell, than be too modest and demure.

She also includes a revised cv. She has developed this from a combination of her STOC Check, and her Brand Positioning Statement, so that it is slightly unconventional, but gives a much better idea to a prospective client or employer what Felicity has to offer. She had already done considerable *research* on Gordon's company, so she knows quite a bit about it. Like her introductory letter, she *adapts* her curriculum vitae to each prospect she writes to, *taking account of what her background research has thrown up*. This is on a special folder on her word processor, named Brand Felicity.

She is pleased that she has managed to include a *benefit for the recipient* (increased profitability) in her letter, even though she had to stretch a bit to get it in. She had also included the offer of a *testimonial*. And she *asked for the order* (an appointment).

Gordon Twitcher thought that the letter was a bit cheeky, but felt on balance it was worth investing time to see if Felicity lived up to her billing. Felicity was delighted to have got an interview at the first attempt, particularly as jobs in the conference business were so scarce they were never advertised.

Felicity now had to move on to *selling herself in person*. She applied herself to working out a long *list of questions*, for Gordon, to find out about the parts she didn't know about, and to *find out more* about the bits she did.

She knew she had to *dress for success*, so she put on her most business-like suit for the interview. All the day of the appointment, and especially just before going into Gordon's office, Felicity rehearsed her Brand Positioning Statement to herself. As she walked into the office, *she was Brand Felicity*.

Felicity also knew that selling in person is specifically about *helping the prospect to buy*. Once seated, *smiling*, in Gordon's office, Felicity concentrated on *active listening*, using several of the *questions* she had prepared beforehand. Her aim was to *build a rapport* as quickly as possible. She listened intently to the *answers*, and in so doing she *found Gordon's need* (no, he was happily married).

Gordon's need was for a financial controller, not a conference organiser. Gordon's hot button was cost control, because he was putting on some great conferences, but he wasn't making any money. *Without Felicity asking the right questions, this would not have emerged.* As a result she might have accepted the job that Gordon subsequently offered her, not realising the actual specification, whatever Gordon had said, was one of a position requiring skills in the area of accounting, not people management and creative flair.

Felicity went on to refine her approach and her brand marketing skills. *She began to like being Brand Felicity.* She turned down Gordon's job – gracefully – and managed to get interviews with three of the four companies she applied to. Some interviews went better than others, but Felicity *learned from the ones that didn't go well*.

One job offer came through, but before she had time to accept it, another offer materialised, from one of the conference companies that Boffins Technology used, who had got wind of the fact that she was on the market. They were very insistent, and the job offer had the added attraction that she would still be able to work with her friends and colleagues from Boffins Technology.

She now had a dilemma. Here was the perfect opportunity to become a freelance operator, offering to work independently for both companies. She was fairly certain that she could sell it to them on the basis that employing her as a freelance would reduce their fixed costs, and they would only have to pay her when they needed her.

As a freelance, if she were successful, she would be able to charge more, select the jobs she wanted to work on, and have more control over her life. As an employee of either company, she would gain from having a regular (though potentially lower) wage packet, with additional benefits (health insurance, etc.). In terms of security, there is little in it. As a freelance, if she were any good she could attract work from across the industry, whereas working for one company, if that ran into difficulties, she would be extremely vulnerable. There would, however, be no gaps in income stream while the job continued.

Both options were available, as she had not actually handed out her business card, stating publicly that she was a freelance operator. In each interview she had preferred the reassurance of having it in her handbag, to the very public statement of handing it out, and in so doing, risking a wry smile.

What to do? Both options had their attractions, so the decision was not an easy one. Fortunately, Felicity had recently taken up reading self-development books. Eager to put into practice some of the principles she had already learned, she decided to retire to her Quiet Place, an especially comfortable, and womb-like, armchair in her living-room. With her eyes firmly closed, Felicity reviewed the options. And then let her mind roam free and her subconscious get to work.

After twenty minutes, nothing. After thirty minutes, still nothing. Disappointed, but knowing she was already running late for work, she stood up, put her blank pad back on the table, and left for work. The following morning, she tried again. This time, after twenty-five minutes, the answer came, filling her brain like a full-blown rose. Deep down, Felicity had always wanted to run her own company. She had been held back by a lack of experience or training but, more importantly, by her scripting from her parents. Her parents, who were caring but very traditional, had always fussed over her two brothers, who were encouraged in everything they did and given plenty of advice on what subjects to study, and what qualifications to go for.

Her father, in particular, felt that Felicity, on the other hand, was just a girl, and shouldn't be worrying about such a thing as a career. She was attractive and personable, and these were adequate enough qualifications to get her very well set up in life with a suitable husband. This was very powerful scripting and, as a result, she had always felt a sense – entirely wrongly – of being a lightweight, who should have stayed a typist and concerned herself more with getting a man. Her subconscious came to her rescue, by telling her that here was a magnificent opportunity to rewrite the script once and for all. If she became a freelance organiser – an IBG in effect running her own mini-business – this would be an ideal launching pad from which to develop her own company, specialising in conference organisation.

As soon as she had the idea, she knew it was right. She smiled, took a deep breath, and decided to take the plunge. More of which later.

Norman's Marketing Programme

As an accountant, Norman understands more than anybody the importance of his core income stream. He realises that whatever income streams he develops in the future – and now he has been on a course to develop his self-image, and he is excitedly devouring personal development books, he intends to develop several – there is a fundamental need to have a *more-or-less reliable income stream that covers most of the basic overheads*. Delectable Foods was, and is, his chosen conduit for this income stream, so he has developed his marketing programme along the lines he outlined in the last chapter. Reading a passage a day from personal development books, he is growing increasingly confident of his Brand Positioning Statement, which was, you recall:

Brand Positioning Statement: Norman Newstart

Brand Positioning
A late flowerer, with business vision, initiative, and sound project leadership

Competitive Advantage
Rare combination of ideas, and gritty operation control (including cash flow
    forecasts that are actually delivered)

Specific Benefits
You know that Norman will be a good leader, totally trustworthy, and every penny will be spent effectively

Support
Norman's business forecasts have proved remarkably accurate, and he has run a tight ship with an accountant's eye for detail. Good with people; team player.

He works up the Business Plan for franchising the Delectable Foods format, and produces three copies on his word processor (he will run off more copies for the full board of directors if he is appointed and needs to present it at his first board meeting). One is for the chairman, one is for the managing director, and one is for himself. He is careful to call it a draft plan, to avoid any hint of arrogance on his part. He still hopes that they will agree to Plan A – Norman being elected to the board, with the operations manager reporting to him.

His plan is to put the proposal to the chairman and managing director the day before the next board meeting, so they have twenty-four hours to mull it over, before putting it to the board the following day. It is at this point that Norman's well-laid plans begin to unravel. The day before the board meeting, Norman goes down with a quick, but somewhat virulent, strain of influenza. He returns the day after the board meeting, weakened by the illness, but emboldened by two days of *visualising* himself fulfilling his Brand Positioning Statement, and *seeing and hearing the board of directors burst into spontaneous applause at the announcement of his election to the board*. He has also been working assiduously on his line of approach to the chairman and the managing director.

There are no minutes yet from the board meeting that Norman missed. Unconcerned, Norman requests to refix his meeting with the chairman and managing director that had had to be postponed through his illness. By chance, both are free that afternoon, so the meeting is confirmed for three o'clock. Rather than the fear that the old Norman would have felt, the new Norman – the Mighty Lion – is looking forward to it with eager anticipation.

At the appointed hour, Norman enters the chairman's office. The greeting is friendly. 'Good afternoon Newstart. Glad to see you're better.' The meeting begins. He has rehearsed his approach many times in his mind, and *visualised the setting*, and now he has to deliver it for real. He starts speaking, and is surprised at the strength and confidence of his voice.

'Gentlemen,' he begins, 'I have been working for Delectable Foods for some years now, and I think you have confidence in me as a safe pair of hands in all matters relating to the company's financial planning and controls. I have saved the company considerable sums of money through my cost control initiatives.

'As you know, cost savings within the stores was not originally in my area of responsibilities, but I took the initiative, and the successes are evident for all to see. I have also transformed the company's financial systems, which now deliver much greater control at far lower cost.

'My growing authority is not just internal. I am sure you appreciate that our bankers ring me directly with any questions on profit, or cash flow forecasts. And they seem to be satisfied with my answers.

'After thinking long and hard about it, I have come to the conclusion that at this stage of my career I need to make a move to ensure my talents and growing stature inside, and outside the company, are recognised. I may be a late flowerer, but I think you'll agree that I am bearing many fruits for the company.' (Norman wasn't sure this was grammatically logical, but he felt it sounded like the truth, and it tied in with his Brand Positioning Statement.)

Norman paused, but as he expected, his listeners were dumbstruck. He continued, warming to his theme:

'I enjoy leading my team, and I believe I do it well. I also lead projects well, and deliver them on time. At this time in my career, I find my business vision is widening, and I need greater challenges and responsibilities.

'My chief goal is to bring even greater benefits to Delectable Foods. I believe that Delectable Foods will derive more benefit from my talents – which I would be happy to quantify in terms of increased profitability – if I were to be appointed to the board of directors. I am confident that the resulting improvements in the bottom line will directly benefit shareholders, like yourselves. The role I see myself filling is that of operations and financial director. I recognise that I currently lack day-to-day experience of the stores, but with George Snakeoil reporting to me, as operations manager, this can be easily rectified.

'In conclusion, I would confirm that my first loyalties are to Delectable Foods. My aim is to continue to play a key role in building the company's success, but to be given the opportunity to be more effective in this role, by being given more responsibility.

'Gentlemen, I await your response.'

Norman sat silent. He experienced a mixture of elation and exhaustion. He felt he had performed well, although he was a bit concerned that he had put too many 'benefits' in towards the end. Too many, he felt, were better than too few. Knowing the importance of alert *posture and body language*, he resisted the urge either to slump in his chair while he recovered, or to leap to his feet and punch the air in joy. He'd done it! What a feeling!

Total silence ensued. Nobody moved. Eventually the chairman coughed. 'Newstart,' he said, 'Have you seen today's all-staff memo?' Norman hadn't. Catching up on work from two days away sick, he had not had time to attack his in-tray. 'No,' he replied. 'Why?'

'Well, in it we announced the election of George Snakeoil to the board of directors.'

Norman felt his insides melt. His brain went numb. He concentrated hard on keeping breathing. He had enough presence of mind to say nothing. Both directors shifted uneasily in their chairs, but Norman continued to say nothing. Slowly his brain began to work again.

This news was devastating for Norman. Not only were his plans completely overturned, but it was, in his view, very bad for the company. Everybody in the company knew that George Snakeoil was not a good operator. Everyone, that is, apart from the board of directors. Norman was acutely aware of his shortcomings, because he had witnessed the lack of control of some of the basic systems at first hand. As a good team player, and in his former incarnation as friendly Norm, he had never brought the deficiencies to the directors' attention, though he had been tempted to do so.

Friendly Norm, at this point, would have left the room. Overwhelmed and defeated, he would have gone off to lick his wounds. But now Norman knew he was a Mighty Lion. He didn't feel a lot like one at that particular moment, but he retained the presence of mind to hold his ground, until his composure began to seep back. Norman repeated one of his favourite *affirmations* to himself. 'I can handle it. *I can handle it.*' He then moved on to, 'I feel power and confidence in every activity I undertake. *I feel power and confidence in every activity I undertake.*'

Soon, sure enough, he felt the power and confidence returning. He then moved on to *visualizing* the board of directors bursting into spontaneous applause. This buoyed his spirits further, though not to the degree it had done earlier. He felt he should give them something to applaud.

It was now Norman's turn to clear his throat. 'Excuse me, gentlemen. I'm afraid I've embarrassed you.' Norman gave himself an *invisible pat on the back* for not saying, 'I've made a fool of myself.' 'No, no, not at all.'

They were quick to reassure him, and pleased to find something to say that was encouraging, but at the same time, neutral.

'Well, gentlemen, may I continue? I had anticipated that you might have had your own schedule for my advancement, which would be slower than mine, so I have an alternative proposal to put to you.' The chairman and managing director were mightly relieved to hear this, and encouraged him to continue.

Norman proceeds to outline his plan for franchising the Delectable Foods format. He briskly takes them through the benefits to the company – rapid expansion funded by the franchisees – as well as some of the challenges – control of independent operators, extra margin to fund. As he does this, he experiences conflicting emotions. On the one hand, he feels proud that he coped so well with a significant reverse, and he also feels good that he is conducting himself as a *businessman talking to other businessmen* – as equals – not as an accountant talking to his bosses.

On the other hand, he is aware that he is making a presentation, not having a conversation. In a sense, this is inevitable, because he has to outline his plans before they can have an informed discussion on his proposals. But he still gets the impression that the silence is more solid than it should be.

Norman outlines the Business Plan, hands them a copy, and concludes, 'So you see, gentleman, the major *benefit* is that we have the opportunity to increase our bottom line profit significantly at very low risk.' Again there was silence. Again there was an uneasy shifting in chairs. The chairman looked at the managing director, and the managing director looked at the chairman.

The managing director was the first to break the silence. Leafing through the Business Plan, he said, 'I have to say this looks very impressive, Newstart. And thank you for all the hard work that has gone into it. Unfortunately, when we talked to George Snakeoil a week or so ago, in preparation for his being brought onto the board, we asked him to give us his view of what direction Delectable Foods should go over the next few years. When he gave us his views, he expressly ruled out franchising as an option.'

'Oh, did he?' said Norman, trying hard to keep the scorn out of his voice. By now Norman was angry. He didn't have to visualise being a Mighty Lion, he *was* a Mighty Lion. 'And on what grounds did he rule it out as an idea?' The managing director replied, 'He said it was too difficult to control, and bad franchisees would give us a bad image.'

Norman almost snapped back, 'Too difficult for *George* to control,' but resisted the temptation. He thought for a bit, and began to realise that for the company's sake – and for the future employment prospects of all his colleagues who worked there – he ought to say something to bring to the directors' attention that everything in the garden was not lovely in the way store operations were handled at Delectable Foods. A few months ago this would have been inconceivable for Norman. He still had an *employee mentality*, so was more concerned with shielding colleagues from retribution, than in taking the *IBG's view*.

The IBG's view is one of an impartial businessman thinking about his core income stream as an external management consultant might. He or she is thus looking to protect it, for the benefit of him or herself, and others working in that environment. The lads-and-lasses-down-pub, all-mates-together attitude no longer holds water. Protecting weak or inefficient colleagues can pose a direct threat to core income, as the effects in the medium to long term are always serious.

This is not to encourage or condone in any way the telling tales on colleagues, or indulging in rumour or behind-the-hand chit-chat. That is negative, divisive, unethical and unproductive. What it does involve is not protecting, or supporting, actions or people that can damage the health of the enterprise. And, if appropriate, pointing out *objectively* to senior management the benefits of *improving specific operations and areas of action or responsibility*. As an IBG, you are *positive and action-orientated*. You will therefore include in your appraisal, verbal or written, *specific recommendations* to improve the situation.

Let's see how Norman deals with the situation. Norman considers the best approach. He is now *thinking and feeling like an IBG, as well as a Mighty Lion*. He decides on a course of action. He picks up the Business Plan and leafs through it until he finds the page he wants.

He takes a deep breath and says, 'One of the other chief benefits of franchising, which I rather glossed over in my verbal presentation, but which is worth serious consideration, is its positive effect on the standards of customer service. This is dealt with on page ten of this Business Plan. As you know, Delectable Foods is a concept that is able to charge more by adding considerable value in both the pre-preparation of the food, and also in the relationship between our staff and our customers.

'Franchising can take this a stage further, because each franchise owner depends for his or her livelihood on the success of that shop, so the standard of customer service will be extremely high.

'As you know [Norman is pretty sure they don't], our customer satisfaction research scores have been going down over the last twelve months [since George Snakeoil joined]. This is particularly worrying, as those of our competitors have been going up. One way of rectifying this would be to set standards in the franchised shops to establish a benchmark for the other shops to operate against. As I would be running the first franchised shop myself, I would be happy to accept the challenge of setting high benchmarks.'

The air seeping out of the managing director and the chairman was almost audible. There was another long silence. 'Have you seen those reports, Rod?' the chairman asked the managing director. The managing director looked uneasy. 'No. I was under the impression that the scores were good.' He looked meaningfully at the chairman.

At last the chairman spoke. 'Thank you, Norman. That was very helpful. We'll think further about your proposal, and get back to you.'

Norman left the office, with emotions even more mixed. He was delighted at his own performance, particularly his recovery from two body blows. Not to mention the fact that the chairman had called him by his first name for the first time since he had joined the company. But he was concerned about the position he was now in. He suspected the chairman and managing director were in a worse one, but that did not make him feel any better.

Norman pondered the situation as he went back to his office, to look at that all-staff memo.

Simon's Marketing Programme

Simon, if you recall, has decided to take up Fleur's idea of setting up Sapiens Knowledge Software, and now he is working out his notice with CC&C. In the words of Peter Drucker, the great management scientist, all great ideas eventually degenerate into hard work. And so it is with Sapiens. A company can be formed, legally, very quickly, but it then needs a strategy, funding, a structure and an action timetable. A Business Plan, in fact.

Simon knows the theory of Business Plans, and has read several, but has never had to write one. They throw up difficult questions like share structures, sales, margin, and profit targets on a three- to five-year projection, funding requirements and source of funds, as well as market analysis and competition analysis. Not to mention investor paybacks, and an analysis of risks and rewards for potential investors (including the bank, if an overdraft facility is required). This was not going to be as easy as Simon had thought.

The first question was, did he need investors, or was it something he could fund himself? Which, of course, threw up all sorts of further important questions. Like what speed would he have to move at, assuming his product genuinely was better, and would therefore be quickly copied by competitors. Simon was good at creating spreadsheets (which, by the way, are breathtakingly simple to operate, with the right Idiot's Guide – see back of book for a recommendation). He therefore created several different possible scenarios, including their cash flow implications, which didn't help him at all, because all it showed was that if he moved fast he would need to borrow money, and if he moved slowly, he wouldn't. Which is what his common sense had told him in the first place.

Simon then had a stroke of good fortune. On investigating the active listening course he had promised Fleur he would go on, he had come across personal development courses of all sorts. He had been dimly aware that such an industry existed, but had always thought it was for insecure Americans, or people with social problems. On dipping into some of the books, he found that they were not only quite challenging, and made sense, but that some of the ideas might even be worth a try.

The Quiet Place did not attract him, as he felt that he was someone who was excited and stimulated by doing, and by interaction with other people, rather than by communing with his own subconscious. In this, as he found out later, he was wrong, but at this time he was content to let his subconscious keep bubbling away below the surface, without ever asking it consistently for answers. It was still working of course, and still providing answers, but at a level a long way below its potential.

One concept that did excite him, however, was the **Mastermind group**. This is a timeless concept which was brought to general attention by Andrew Carnegie, using Napoleon Hill as his mouthpiece. Carnegie was a canny Scotsman who transformed the American steel industry. Napoleon Hill, one of the fathers of personal development books, was, in his early days, the scribe or amanuensis to Carnegie. Unlike Boswell taking down the pearls of wit and wisdom from the lips of Dr Johnson as he scattered them around the countryside, this was more or less straight dictation.

Carnegie gave to Hill the ideas and lessons he had compiled over a lifetime, as he took the US steel industry by the scruff of the neck and rewrote the rule book in the early years of the twentieth century. In so doing he had become an immensely wealthy man (see Carnegie Hall). Carnegie had hoped that his ideas would be incorporated into the US secondary education system, to give a better preparation to America's future business leaders. Then, as now, public educators resisted any tools that would help children acquire better life skills or learning efficiency (consider reading speed and effectiveness as a simple example).

One of Carnegie's ideas was the Mastermind group. Carnegie was many decades ahead of his time in terms of management techniques. His Mastermind group consisted of *fifty* key staff members, and to it Carnegie attributed all his accumulated wealth. A mixture of a **TEAM** group (Together Everyone Achieves More) and brainstorming sessions, this group of players examined the manufacturing, transportation and marketing of steel, to find ways of improving efficiency and effectiveness, and staying several jumps ahead of the competition.

Such groups and sessions are as worthwhile today as they were then. At Cobra Sports we invested substantial sums in staff training, believing customer service to be our most important benefit for customers. We had several of our own trainers, unusual for a company our size, but also brought in outside experts from time to time. We, the owners and senior managers, often sat in on these sessions to demonstrate how seriously we took this investment in training. In one such session, I remember the trainer handing us all a paper clip. He then asked us to write down as many uses for a paper clip we could think of. We all wrote down our list, some of which were dotty, but contained about two or three good ideas per person. The trainer then pooled the ideas and came up with a list of about twenty really good ideas. A powerful demonstration that Together Everyone Achieves More.

Back to Simon. He understood, as soon as he read it, the power and potential of a personal Mastermind group. He also understood that while a larger group was better, just one or two other people to knock ideas around with can be highly effective. The sum of two minds sparking together is always much larger than one can achieve on its own. Simon had already benefited from the Mastermind group that he and Fleur had formed which had thrown up the idea of Sapiens in the first place. He felt at this stage, however, that he would benefit from a wider base, and particularly from someone with up-to-date business experience.

He thought long and hard, but all the people he considered were either unsuitable or unavailable. But his subconscious was working. Thinking on and off during the day about possible candidates, he kept getting the odd image of Sydney bridge, in Australia, flashing through his mind. He thought nothing of it, but one day, as he was dropping off his son Jason at kindergarten (Fleur was at the doctor's undergoing tests for a hoped-for pregnancy) he bumped into another father who was performing the same task. He knew him only slightly, and had chatted to him at a recent parents' inspection of their children's works of art.

'When are you off?' asked Simon, dimly remembering that he was being moved by his firm to a new location. 'Four weeks,' was the reply. 'And where was it you are going?'

'Sydney', was the answer. Simon suddenly became interested. 'And what do you specialise in?' he asked. 'I'm a consultant in Information Technology.' Simon paused. He recalled that Peter (he even recalled his name now) worked for one of the global management consultants, and was a notable High-flyer.

'It's not often you have time to do this, is it?' Simon asked, indicating the milling children. 'Too right,' was the reply. 'I'm running down my workload, ready to leave, and I'm really getting a taste for it.' 'Have you got ten minutes?' asked Simon. 'Certainly,' replied Peter.

And so was born the Pacific Rim division of Sapiens Knowledge. Without Simon heeding his subconscious, and being open-minded enough to try the experiment of a Mastermind group, he would have taken the lower-risk route of a slow build-up of the company, with no external investment, with the attendant near-certainty that larger, better capitalised competitors would have copied his products, put more marketing clout behind them, and eventually sent him back into consultancy, or worse, the law.

Over the next four weeks, until Peter left for Australia, there were many Mastermind group meetings. Fleur attended some of them, and some took place just between Simon and Fleur. The net result was that a Business Plan emerged that was far more adventurous than anything that had been envisaged in the early stages of the project. Peter didn't operate in the Knowledge field (which was fortunate, as it meant there was no conflict of interest with his own core income stream), but understood how it worked, and how to find the relevant databases in different countries. Peter was interested in the concept for its own sake, but the real benefit for him was its potential to give him the opportunity to get off the High-flyer treadmill. He had enjoyed his short career as a father and husband, as his workload had wound down prior to relocation to Australia, and he wanted it on a more full-time basis.

The Mastermind group evolved a Business Plan that was bold and aggressive. It was agreed that the equity would be divided 45 per cent for Simon, 25 per cent for Peter, and the remaining 30 per cent would be sold to outside investors to fund the company. Simon would develop the products in broad terms, Peter would tighten up the technical specifications, and the software itself would be written in India, where the expertise base was high, but the costs were low. Simon would launch the products in Europe, followed by the United States, and Peter would do the same in Australia and the Pacific Rim.

They decided against banks and venture capitalists for funding, liking neither the rates of return on money invested that were demanded, nor the uncomfortable grasp that would be taken on very private parts of their anatomies. They decided instead to approach a select group of what are called high net worth individuals. This means they are rich. Simon knew several ex-partners of his law firm (and had a selective list of current partners as a fallback) who had accumulated wealth and were open-minded to ways of increasing it.

Simon, having written the Business Plan, with input from Peter, is now ready for action. He will first need to market it to potential shareholders, and then to potential customers of this software products. The principles are the same in both cases. First of all, Simon recalls his Brand Positioning Statement.

Brand Positioning Statement: Simon Smartbutton and Peter Pressenter (aka Sapiens Knowledge)

Brand Positioning
Sapiens Knowledge Software packages give better access to more, and better-organised databases

Competitive Advantage
Market leaders in collation, organising and *editing* of information

Specific Benefits
Faster updating, and constant innovation, assures that your information requirements are satisfied faster, more easily, and more cost effectively

Support
Founder a recognised pioneer in the application of technology to acquire, organise and retrieve, relevant information

---

From a personal development book on selling techniques (Simon is beginning to become a fan of the genre), he composes a letter to prospective shareholders:

Dennis Quillpen Esq.,
The Inkpot,
Sosslebury.

Dear Dennis,

Sapiens Knowledge: the Opportunity to Invest in a Business Start-up

We haven't spoken for some time, but when you were still active at CC&C I recall that you were open-minded to business ideas outside the narrow confines of the law.

I recently left CC&C to start a new business. As you may remember, I pioneered much of the structural organisation of our information base at CC&C, once the law reports and other source data had been transferred to computer discs. Since leaving, I have developed some of the principles of editing and rapid access much further. One of the main benefits of my systems is that the most untechnical of people can find what they are looking for very easily.

There is a huge need for the intelligent ordering of the massive amounts of information that are now available, and providing easy access to it. Sapiens Knowledge will do this with proprietary systems, for which there is worldwide demand. If you want confirmation either of the need for such systems, or my particular expertise in the area, please ring any of the current partners of CC&C. I'm sure they will reinforce my view of the size and potential of the opportunity – and my particular facility with Information Technology.

I have selected a small group of potential investors to fund what will rapidly become a multinational operation, as my partner will be building the business in the most dynamic markets in the Pacific Rim. Risks, of course, exist, but the potential reward could be huge.

Our Business Plan shows a possible placement of shares or flotation within five years. There would be no dividend for the first five years, but after that there is the likelihood of a substantial capital gain, or dividend income on any shares you leave invested. If this fits in with your investment programme, please let me know.

Shares are limited, so allocations may have to be made if demand outstrips supply. The timetable is a tight one, in order to get to market quickly. Our aim is to get the funding in place within four to six weeks, as the market is moving swiftly. If you are interested, please phone, or fax back the attached sheet, for a confidential copy of the Business Plan.

If we haven't heard from you within two weeks, we will assume that you do not wish to take it any further.

I look forward to the possibility of being in business with you again!

Yours etc.

Simon is aware that he should not really be using the word 'I' in a corporate context, as any corporate effort is by definition a team effort. He feels that the personal nature of the letter, and the fact that Sapiens Knowledge is still hardly a corporation, overrides this. He is comfortable, on the other hand, that he has incorporated other key criteria of writing sales letters, which he found in a personal development book he had bought for the purpose.

The *benefit to the recipient* is clear (financial gain), and the recipient has also been made to feel *especially chosen for this opportunity*. The offer of *testimonial* corroboration of his claims is clearly made, and an *incitement to action* is there as a first step towards *closing the sale*. Included too is a hurry-up to ensure that the recipient does not delay in his response, and the fax-back form makes it *easy for the reply to be completed* by hand and returned, with the minimum of fuss. He has also covered most of the points in his Brand Positioning Statement, using language more suitable to his target audience.

The result of his mailing is extremely positive, as the combination of a fashionable service category, and the chance to make a killing ahead of the market, is too strong to resist for most of the retired partners mailed. Without the need to mail the offer to existing partners, which could have had slightly embarrassing undertones, Sapiens Knowledge is launched, fully capitalised, and the adventure begins ...

So our three intrepid IBG's take another step down the trail to IBG-hood. As their understanding of the role grows, so their confidence grows with it. They have a great deal to learn, and many pratfalls await them. But they are on their way.

SIX

Alternative and Second Income Streams

A strong fish swims against the current. A dead one floats with it.

A *CORE INCOME* stream is of central importance to stay at least in the Survivor-flourisher group, if not to reach the High-flyers, in the Incomes Revolution. Two core income streams are even better. And half a dozen are better still. While having a banker income stream is vital, it is still important not to put all your eggs in one basket – just in case someone drops the basket.

This throws up one or two chewy issues. The largest of these is possibly the posture of some companies and institutions over exclusivity of employment. They recognise that employment has changed as a concept, and are quite happy to accept the benefits of the enormous flexibility the new situation gives them. *While they are happy to take, they are not happy to give.* They attempt to prevent workers having outside interests, even though they are unwilling contractually to underwrite any security of income as a quid pro quo.

The fact is that employers, like building societies and banks, want it all their own way. If anyone actually read a mortgage contract, or the terms and conditions of bank loans, they would never sign them. Most of them are totally one-sided, and as such, grossly unfair. This, sadly, is only discovered when the mortgage or loans are called in, and then the small print is leveraged up into the headlines, with draconian results for the defaulters.

It is becoming daily more unrealistic for employers to demand exclusivity of work from their employees. I am not for one moment suggesting that employees should be able to pursue other business interests in an employer's time. While working for an employer – for a core income, or an alternative or secondary income – the commitment to the job in hand during that employer's time should be total. What I am saying is that an employee's time, while not contracted to work for that employer, is his or her own. There should not, of course, be any conflict of interest. It is in no way reasonable for an employee to work for a competitor in his or her spare time, where information could be acquired or communicated that compromised either employer. But where there is no conflict of interest, employers should adopt the same *laissez-faire* approach as when they want to get rid of labour. '*I don't guarantee you job security, so I don't expect to control the time I don't pay you for*', would be a fairer position to adopt.

IBGs are easier, and better, to employ

Rather than fight a rearguard battle against their employees' need and desire to have diversified income, employers would be better advised to accept the paradigm shift and look on the positive side. For there is a positive side. *IBGs are much more effective operators than non-IBGs*. If you are lucky enough to employ an IBG, therefore, as either a core worker or as a contingent worker, you should be extremely grateful. Don't fret about divided loyalties. If you supply the core income for that IBG, they are going to be extremely careful not to mess it up, as what you pay them is vital to covering their monthly overheads.

Currently, companies recognise that, as the era of natural resource-based industries gives way to brainpower-based industries, *the skills and knowledge of the workforce are the only long-term competitive advantage*. Also, hierarchies within companies are weakening, and there are no very coherent structures to replace them. Loose confederacies of employees within an organisation are fine as a working principle when things are going well. When the pressure comes on, unless there is sense of coherent leadership, things can begin to fragment because a sense of common purpose was never established.

If hierarchies and paternalistic environments are slowly fading into history as ways of running commercial, and even non-commercial, enterprises, two things are starkly obvious. Firstly, employers are going to have to find new and better ways to manage confederacies of talent workers, who are self-sufficient and highly mobile. Secondly, *workers themselves will need to be more self-motivated*, as they will no longer be employees, playing a clearly defined role within a hierarchy, but will be more self-sufficient units within an association of workers with a common purpose.

IBGs will tend to be far better self-motivated, and more clear-eyed in general, than workers who are still looking for a comfortable framework in which to pretend nothing has changed. *Employees are used to being told what to do. IBGs are comfortable with the concept: 'If it is to be, it's up to me.'* IBGs get on with things. As such, they will need less supervision, allowing their managers to spend more time on the important, rather than the urgent, issues.

IBGs have the further advantage to employers that they are bringing a continually widening experience to the job. The *cross-fertilisation* with their other business activities brings new ideas, and fresh ways of looking at things, to their core income employment. IBGs *thus provide far more benefits than risks to employers.*

IBGs will manage their careers better, and training will be part of remuneration

IBGs will see their core income employment as somewhere to contribute as much as possible, in order to protect it as a core (non-fixed) asset. They will also be seeking to improve their ability to contribute and, with it, their *marketability*, inside and outside the company or institution they are working for.

Their marketability will be a combination of skills acquired and developed, and reputation and self-confidence gained through the successful achievement of tasks and objectives. *Training thus becomes an extremely important input into development of this combination of skills, reputation and self-confidence.*

Taking the generator in Independent Business Generator as a power generator, it can be considered, in this sense at least, as a machine. For the Independent Business Generator, therefore, as with any machine, *continual investment* is required not only to ensure it is performing optimally, and is at least as good as anything competitors have to offer, but also to provide the power to drive it. For an IBG – whether technical, professional, service, manager, sales, skilled or even unskilled, in orientation – *relevant training provides both the constant upgrading to optimise efficiency, and the fuel that will keep the machine going.*

As we have seen, IBGs as business owners understand that investment in their business is necessary and desirable. Training – relevant to future needs, not training for its own sake – will be expensive, *because IBGs need high-octane fuel and are extremely fuel-consumptive.* Training will thus come to be seen by both employers and employees as part of the overall remuneration package. Both sides benefit, and both sides should have input into what training is most relevant.

Training is relevant not just to the High-flyers and Survivor-flourishers. It is also highly relevant to the Strugglers and the Buggered. Relevant training can help anyone to improve their marketability. In the case of the last two categories, it is probable that the state will be the most likely provider of the training, making it more difficult, but just as important, to achieve a tight fit between what the individual needs and wants and what can be provided. Part of this training should be in *life skills* (see next chapter), as it is fundamentally important that everyone understands that he or she has talents which can be developed and eventually marketed.

Training can be liberating, and part of a Brand Me relaunch

As particular core income streams become cul-de-sacs, as will happen from time to time, the chance to relaunch Brand Me may present itself. This is an exciting opportunity to take a new direction and to develop new skills. It also provides the impetus for a **Brand Review**. A Brand Review will involve a comprehensive examination of the current and future market for your skills, how these need to be rethought or refocused, as well as an appraisal of your alternative and secondary income streams.

Indeed, alternative income streams may be promoted to core. Alternative income streams tend to be second, part-time jobs. Assuming that all income streams are addressed with the same high levels of talent and enthusiasm, it is highly likely the alternative income employer will be pleased to consider either an extension of hours, or a promotion to a more responsible role. Even apparently humble work, like part-time bar work, can be elevated to part-time, or even full-time, bar management.

If you are an insurance claims manager, changing to work as a bar manager, with less social hours and less pay, may not appear as the next logical step in a well-managed career. But if the majority of insurance claims managers' functions can now be more reliably performed by a computer programmed with a comprehensive list of criteria for paying or rejecting claims, *flexibility of response* is required. A reasonable income stream will have been secured, you will be operating actively in the economy as an IBG, *with all antennae tuned*, while you consider a Brand Me relaunch.

Taking a franchise may be a good idea, but it's a different strategy

One of the possibilities you may consider could be the taking of a franchise. Franchising is a powerful method of combining the energy and enthusiasm (and money) of individuals, with the opportunity to expand a business idea faster than the owners could otherwise achieve with the funds available. It is successful as a concept worldwide, because it allows entrepreneurs to build their own businesses, with the independence, wealth and freedom that can bring, while removing much of the risk through using a proven format as a vehicle.

While many franchises are very successful, there are risks involved and not all of them work. Even the most successful ones don't work in every location. Capital investment can be very high, so for most people it's all or nothing. *Taking a franchise is super-core.* There is no room for alternative, or secondary income streams. Taking a franchise can be a *very expensive way of buying yourself a low-paid job.* If you find after a few weeks you don't like selling hamburgers, or pizzas, or cleaning carpets, or giving driving instruction, twelve to sixteen hours a day, six or seven days a week, don't expect too sympathetic a hearing from your bank manager. You've got somewhere between three and seven years to make it pay out, so get on with it.

If you come through, the rewards can be great. Flexibility, however, even if you're successful, is noticeable by its absence. You can't adapt a franchise to your local market, or to your convenience. For obvious reasons the good ones are inflexible, and no variations are entertained. It is also worth considering that most of them cannot be willed on (the income from the sale forms part of your estate, but you can't will it on as a going business), so make sure you die at the right time.

If the total focus of a franchise appeals, and it does to many people, because it takes out much of the uncertainty – it has to work or you're in trouble – it is worth taking a very close look at what is involved before making a final commitment. Question, for example, *why the franchise is being offered.* If it is to take out risk for the franchisor – in an overcrowded market, like fast food for example, or because the economics don't work without the franchisee working seventy to a hundred hours a week at very low pay – be very careful. Talk to lots of franchisees – not the ones supplied by the franchisor as references – to see what really is involved. Remember that when the wheels start to come off a franchise format, things can get very tough.

I am possibly painting a somewhat negative picture of franchising. It is, after all, the classic route for the small entrepreneur with guts and energy to get a good reward on capital and time invested. I think my main reservation is the lack of flexibility and control in a world that demands both those qualities to an increasing degree. Most franchises are forced to be inflexible, to achieve consistency over a wide collection of idiosyncratic individualists, most of whom have their own theories on how to improve things. This tends to inhibit responsiveness to changes in market conditions.

This has the potential to make life very frustrating for a good entrepreneur, who can see market saturation approaching, or a shift in attitudes or behaviour that will damage his business, but has no power to adapt to survive because all control for his business resides elsewhere, with the franchisor.

From this, *I would argue that a franchisee is not an IBG.* On my definition he fails on one and a half counts. The main count he fails on is that he is not independent, because he is totally dependent on the franchisor for the direction, and to a degree, the development, of his or her business.

The half count he fails on is that he is a business person on one leg. While obviously franchising is a business, the essence of business is to have the ability to respond faster and better to changes in markets than anyone else. If the franchisor resides at a distance, possibly in a foreign country, and he controls all response to changes in the market, this essential skill is emasculated in the individual franchisee. If you take a franchise at the age of thirty-five or forty, there could be twenty to thirty years ahead of you in that business. While the franchise will evolve over time, it is worth considering what changes in the overall market could take place – let alone the entry of new, and different competition – before the time comes to sell up, and retire.

Multiple Income Streams means, by definition, more than one income

An alternative income stream is only really of relevance to those whose core income employment is less than all-consuming. High-Flyers, for example, will have no time for alternative employment, so secondary income schemes will probably be more interesting. The essential difference between an alternative income scheme and a second income scheme is *that alternative schemes tend to involve working for a second employer,* and therefore tend to be less flexible and less under control of the employee. *Second income schemes*, on the other hand, tend to be *independently controlled by the IBG, and thus more flexible in terms of time devoted to them*.

The central objective of diversified revenue, or multiple income streams is, of course, to give options. The larger the overall income, the more the financial dignity achieved and the less dependence on any one source of revenue. Dig the well before you need the water.

Leaving alternative incomes to one side as being, by and large, smaller versions of core incomes, let us have a closer look at their more flexible younger brothers. Second income schemes are a large, and very important, area of income diversification. They are not only flexible, they have the potential to generate more revenue than core incomes. And there can be other important reasons for building them, beyond the making of extra money.

The area of second income schemes is a very wide parish, and historically has contained some rogues within its boundaries: chain letters and pyramid selling schemes, to name but two. These are totally unacceptable because, as we have seen, principles and values must be aligned in all areas of our lives. This may sound obvious, but it is worth re-stating, because IBGs work in a highly flexible environment in which most of the old frameworks are missing. However tempting it might appear, there never has been, and there never will be, any such thing as a free lunch.

Much of Restoration comedy was built around the amusing spectacle of gullible people being gulled, or duped, by unscrupulous scoundrels. Ben Jonson's *The Alchemist* is a wonderful comedy in which many are duped into believing that a way has at last been found to turn base metal into gold. The three rogues – Subtle, the alchemist, and his friends Face and Doll Common – fleece various gullible fools such as Epicure Mammon by offering to produce the secret of their great discovery.

The interesting point to note is that in the morality of Elizabethan England, the gulled were as guilty as the gullers, and therefore not worthy of sympathy. The simple reason for this was that both sides of the deception were guilty of the same vice – greed. The transaction was driven by all parties wanting the same thing – something for nothing. Some second income ideas are based on a similar psychology, but it would take a comic dramatist of Ben Jonson's genius to make them appear remotely funny.

With that caveat in mind, second income businesses overall break into two main categories. Both are important. I am active in both, and enjoy the revenues, challenges and satisfactions of both. The first is the basic marketing ideas you can think up and run from your Command Centre. I know the Command Centre is located in your head, but we are talking here of ideas that originate in your head, and are run from the lowest cost premises you can find – probably, like me, from a room in your home. The second is to take a serious look at what network marketing has to offer as a method of building long-term income.

Second incomes form part of the Brand Me portfolio

All these activities will form part of your **corporate umbrella**. Just as a corporation such as Procter and Gamble has such diverse brands as Siegfried Sassoon hair products, Pringle's crisps, and Ariel washing powder, so you may find yourself with different brands within your portfolio. These are individual Brand Me products and services that may have no apparent relationship one with another, but each one has its own unique role to play.

As a simple example, your core income might be from journalism, or supply teaching, and your alternative income might be from part-time work at a leisure centre, or as a piano teacher, or coaching tennis. You might have second incomes from a variety of sources: growing specialist plants on your patio for resale at a local garden centre; trading in old coins; renovating old cars, or houses; spending a couple of evenings a week building your network marketing business. You are investing time in all these businesses. Not all of them will work – just as the majority of new product launches end in failure. But they are all different Brand Mes; they all have discernible benefits, and they all sit comfortably under the corporate umbrella of **My Corporation**. You should be serious about and proud of all of them.

Here we come back to the importance of the alignment of values. Whether it's Pringles, Head and Shoulders, or Pampers, it's still Procter and Gamble. The products are individually excellent, and brilliantly marketed. So it must be with My Corporation. You may be wearing different hats during your working week, but they are all *you*, and you must operate them to the same high standards. Just as, without thinking, you might play the equally different roles of mother/daughter, father/son, friend, helper, boss, beginner/expert, without feeling in the slightest bit uncomfortable – because they're all you – so the different Brand Me brands should sit equally comfortably within My Corporation.

This is obviously less relevant in the area of *investments as a second income* (although principles and values should still be aligned). It would still apply in something like the area of trading in old coins, because you are actively marketing goods, rather than inertly waiting for a return on an investment. Property, stocks and shares, and other financial instruments, all provide potential second income streams. The downside of these income streams is that, like franchising, they need capital to start with. They also need a close understanding of the market involved, or there is as high a chance of losing, as making, money.

Network marketing is as much about personal growth as financial growth

When my direct association with Cobra Sports came to an end, I found myself out in the cold world with a need to replace a reasonable size of income. I therefore sat down, applied all my marketing training, and came up with a long list of potential ways of generating income. For obvious reasons, I was extremely open-minded to ideas, from whatever source. One idea I would not have been open-minded to was that of network marketing. What I knew of it was distasteful. One heard stories of garages full of unsold stock, money lost, and hopes disappointed.

When I was approached about the business – I certainly didn't investigate it as a possibility – my receptivity was therefore pretty low. The approach was very low key – and almost didn't come off. An ex-employee spoke to me one day and told me that he had a friend who had a marketing business. He felt there might be some sense in our getting together, to see if there were any common interests to explore. Being open to suggestions, I agreed, and an appointment was subsequently made for a week or so later.

The meeting took place in the coffee bar of a well-known hotel, and the gentleman, about my age, bought me a Danish pastry and a cup of coffee. We sat down and began to talk. He was a good listener (although I didn't appreciate this at the time), and his most striking attribute was the sense of integrity that he imparted. On pressing him for what he felt might be the areas of common interest, he tabled the idea of network marketing.

I felt a flush of anger, and was on the point of leaving, when I noticed I had only eaten about a third of my Danish pastry. Being a lover of buns, I now had a dilemma. Did I storm off, disgusted, or did I finish my bun, and then make a more dignified exit? I decided on the latter course. And thank God I did, because the conversation led to a treasure chest full of gifts, of which I would otherwise have remained ignorant.

By the time I had finished the Danish pastry, the man's obvious integrity had started to raise doubts in my mind. How was it that this man could be involved in something shabby? Had I misjudged him, or had I misjudged the business of network marketing? As he spoke further the latter seemed increasingly the more likely. Eventually I decided to accept his offer to take a proper look at the business.

Having helped me over this hurdle, he then threw me another challenge. He explained that one of the benefits of the business was that couples could build it together. It was therefore important that Lizzie should see it, so at least she had a chance to make up her own mind. This put me in a real hole. I knew Lizzie's views on network marketing were even more vehement than mine, so I didn't fancy having to tell her that someone was coming to our home to show us how to fill our cellar with unwanted stock.

Knowing that business, and life, are about courage and risk, I agreed. I couldn't work out a clever way to tell Lizzie about the meeting, so I blurted it out that Michael and his wife were coming to show us a network marketing concept that looked interesting. A discussion followed. As is frequently the case in these matters, the persuasive logic that might be effective in business meetings seems to melt in the face of a partner's scorn.

Anyway, the meeting took place. Lizzie had everything crossed. Negativity radiated from every pore. She later admitted that her plan had been to listen apparently open-mindedly, and then at the end, politely, but firmly, to say no. My thoughts were along similar lines, but I couldn't admit as much to her at that point. After an hour of seeing the Business Plan unfold, and some products demonstrated, we were both in trouble. The thing looked like it might work. The products obviously worked well. There seemed to be no risks that were discernible, apart from the time invested in finding out whether it might work. And the company involved seemed to be financially sound, with strong business ethics.

We said goodbye to Michael and Mary, looked at each other, and in almost disbelief, said, 'Let's give it a go.' When Michael came back two or three days later, we signed up.

Network marketing has historically suffered a bad press, but is now emerging into a period in which it will be confirmed as a legitimate and effective method of distribution. It is highly efficient as a supply chain, because costs and processes are removed. Advertising and promotional costs are all but removed, and no retailers are involved, so goods are moved more directly to the end purchaser.

Network marketing, and the abuses it spawned, has a direct parallel in the franchising industry. In the United States, franchising was in its early growth years just after the Second World War. Abuses abounded, with the most common being the selling of a franchise for, say, a fast food business, to an operator for an entire state. The operator would then break the state into two or three smaller territories, and then sell the franchise to these territories to different operators, at a higher price. These operators, in turn, would break their territories into smaller regions, and sell the franchise at a still higher price. When an individual came to buy a franchise for an individual store, the thing collapsed, because so much had been taken out on the way through the chain, he could not possibly make any money. It was a classic pyramid-selling operation.

Things got so bad that in the early 1960s, *franchising came within six votes in Congress of being outlawed as illegal as a means of doing business.* It is worthy of note that historians of the McDonald's business attribute much of its early success not to its hamburgers, but to the integrity of the man who built the business, Ray Kroc. Ray Kroc would have none of these business practices. He would only sell a franchise one store at a time, and there was no mark-up at all on meat, buns, machinery, etc. Ray Kroc's profit was earned on a percentage of the overall turnover of a franchisee's business. His principle of success was therefore identical to those of a well-run network marketing business – *success only comes from helping other people to become successful.*

The rogues of franchising were mostly cleared out by legislation in the 1970s and '80s. The rogues of network marketing were mostly cleared out by legislation in the 1980s and early '90s. Rogues still pop up in both franchising and network marketing from time to time, but both industries are now run on ethical business principles, and both industries base their success on stimulating and releasing individuals' energy and enthusiasm to maximise the return for all parties concerned. If they are honestly and fairly constructed, they work. If they are not, they are short-lived.

Network marketing is like a personal version of franchising, but without the need to make binding commitments in either money or time. In some ways this can be a drawback. With nothing at stake, the exit route is wide open if success doesn't come in the first five minutes. Better that, however, than tying up capital, putting it at risk, and demanding a high price in terms of time, for a business method that may not be appropriate to the individual concerned.

It makes sense to investigate network marketing as a second income option, even if you end up rejecting it. One of its major benefits is that you don't need a strong curriculum vitae to do well at it. It is a career open to talents, and the most successful people cover the spectrum in terms of their original day jobs. The two most striking characteristics of the winners in network marketing are that they are people who like people, and that they already lead very busy lives.

Look at Amway as the benchmark against which to judge the others

Lizzie and I are Amway distributors. Anything I say should therefore be judged in the light of this bias. I have no knowledge of other network marketing organisations, so I can neither judge nor advise. As a marketing man, I should have examined the market before committing to become a distributor. Indeed, even within Amway, there are different distributor groups (the company does not deal directly with the public), which vary in the level of their professionalism. I undertook no such market research, but plunged in, and struck very lucky.

I will now attempt to define the total experience of what it is like for Lizzie and I to be network marketing distributors. As well as aiming off for my bias, use my analysis both to get a better understanding of what is involved, and as a benchmark for other second income ideas you might look at. Before I start, I would say two things. Firstly, we are not as successful financially in the business as we would like to be, or intend to be. This feeling is common to every distributor I have ever met, from multimillionaires downwards. Secondly, being a distributor is the most challenging, and at times infuriating, thing we have ever done. And we love it.

The simplest way to explain the business is to let me give you an insight into what there was about it that appealed to us. First, a few words about the company itself. Amway turns over more than $8 *billion* dollars annually and is growing at approximately $1 billion dollars a year. So it works. It operates in over seventy countries and territories around the world, so it is possible literally to grow rich while you sleep. It is debt-free, and one of the most creditworthy companies in the world, being regularly given the highest rating possible by Dun & Bradstreet. Its two owners are the fourth equal richest individuals in the United States. All eight of their children work in the business, indicating that it is likely to remain free from sale or takeover in the foreseeable future. Its products are environmentally friendly, and have been for forty years. They are concentrated, innovative, of the highest quality, and have a low cost per use. Most important of all, *they are products that everybody needs and uses regularly.* They are in the top half-dozen or so brands in the world in household cleaning products, cosmetics and skin care, and personal care products.

In Health and Fitness they are world brand leaders in diet supplements, turning over more than $1 billion dollars in this category. The plants and crops for these diet supplements are all organically grown on their own farms, and then compressed. This means they contain the trace elements and phytofactors that originally accompanied the mineral and vitamin intakes of Man when he was a hunter/gatherer.

Every product has a 100 per cent money back guarantee, used or unused. Even on cosmetics, if a colour is disliked after it has been used, a full refund is available. This means there is no risk in the system for either distributors or customers. The entrance fee to the business is under £100, which covers products and sales materials at cost, and is refundable for the first six months if there is a change of mind. What we particularly liked about the company, and the product range, was that we could make substantial *savings, through buying wholesale, on products we were buying anyway.* And they were delivered to the door.

We also liked the fact that you could have a business in several countries outside your home base. All you need for an international business is to know, or meet, people from another country who are interested in understanding the concept, and applying it in their own country. You don't even need to visit the country concerned: the system will look after it for you. There is, of course, less control doing it this way, but it can, in the long term, produce a significant percentage of the overall revenues of the business.

For Lizzie and me as distributors, there are several obvious benefits from such a company, and such a core product range. The longevity and success of the company is reassuring in itself. The high ethical standards can be confirmed by a telephone call to any government agency that deals with the company (e.g. DTI or Trading Standards). The *Times Educational Supplement* recently produced a pack for schools, containing fifty of the top companies children should look at for employment in all its forms in the new century. One of those companies was Amway. The innovative and cost-effective product range are a further reassurance.

What makes the difference on a day-to-day sales effectiveness level, however, is that nearly all the products are consumables. Most of them go down the drain every week. Even in recessions, people wash themselves and their clothes.

The companies who have copied Amway, and there have been many attempts over the years, mostly tended to provide high capital cost, non-repeat purchase products. The joy of the Amway core product range (and there are thousands of products outside it) is that all you need is a small customer base, who tend to become enthusiasts for the products, and their regular repeat purchase keeps the revenues flowing. Importantly, there are products in the range that can comfortably be sold by both men and women – men can sell car-care products, or mobile phones, whereas women might feel more at home selling make-up, or skin care products. This means it is much easier for couples to work effectively as a team in the business.

But don't run away with the idea that running an Amway, or any well-run network marketing, distributorship is about selling products. Sales of goods and services are important, *but the heart of the matter is helping other people to be successful*. Let's define how the business works. The business principle is that of *duplication*. Just as McDonald's, or any major retailer or service provider, gets one outlet right, then duplicates it – first nationally, and then internationally – so it is with network marketing.

How the business works

This means achieving a modest monthly turnover from fifteen to twenty regular customers who become loyal to the products talked about above. It becomes more like order-taking than selling, and is the cash generation part of the business. The source of these customers is straightforward and unembarrassing. As part of showing someone who is interested the Business Plan, you demonstrate some products. These are simple products, but stunningly effective to demonstrate. Of those who are not interested in looking further at the business, the majority are interested in buying some of the products demonstrated, or in taking a catalogue. This is where the retail customers come from.

The principle thereafter is simple. You then show the business concept to other people. Some of these are interested, like you, in earning a sizeable second income. Others decide they just want a small, regular income from retailing. Another group just want to save money on some great products by buying them at wholesale prices, and having them delivered to the door. Others still aren't in the slightest bit interested. Some even tell you it's pyramid selling, and illegal. Here you learn the first law of network marketing: *never argue with an idiot*. I was an idiot once, so I know. Michael didn't argue with me. He gently pointed out some facts, and left me to draw my own conclusions.

The two most important differences between network marketing and pyramid selling, by the way, are that, firstly, pyramid selling has an entrance fee over and above a minimal cost for sales literature. Bringing in new participants is therefore an immediate source of profit. The second difference is that distributors are encouraged to buy quantities of stock, to achieve higher discounts before selling it on, which is often non-returnable. In network marketing, the entrance fee is minimal, with most organisations incorporating no profit margin, and is refundable for twenty-eight days (six months with the better organisations). New distributors are strongly discouraged from buying any stock until firm orders have been taken from genuine retail customers. Unsold stock is refundable in full with most organisations, minus, in some cases, a small handling charge.

The reward system is simple. In most network marketing organisations, you are rewarded, for all the turnover in your group, on a commission basis. From this commission is deducted the commission earned by the individuals in your group, which is generally paid to them directly by the company. As a simple example, in the case of Amway, if you had six distributors in your group, each of whom had a group turnover that earned a commission of 6 per cent, the resulting group volume would give you a commission of 15 per cent. After taking away the 6 per cents earned by the front line distributors, this would leave you a monthly income of about £500. *£500 could make quite a difference in a thin month for an IBG.*

It is important to point out the source of this money. The money comes from the margin the network marketing company saves on your doing their work of advertising, promoting, distributing, and retailing. Of the price you pay for most products in conventional shops, approximately 50–70 per cent is for the advertising, promoting, distributing and retailing of the product. On some product categories it is higher. In network marketing these costs are taken out, so the prices can be reduced and the distributors given the margin instead. So it is a more efficient method of distribution.

The business sense of this is obvious. *You, therefore, are being rewarded for your role in the distribution chain from the savings you have made possible.*

Your reward is for finding, training, developing the people in your group, and in helping them to succeed. So you are not, as people who do not understand the supply chain and dynamics of network marketing sometimes claim, making money out of your friends. If anything, they are making money out of you. You have invested time and effort in helping them get into business, on a total risk basis, because they are entirely free to decide to leave at any moment they no longer wish to continue.

And this often happens. Circumstances change. Promotion at work, a new baby, friends who laugh because they don't understand. Many are the pitfalls that lead distributors – some temporarily, some permanently – to leave the business. Network marketing is not exploitative, and it is not easy. Rewards are earned. And large efforts earn large rewards. The total rewards for the very successful are interesting. The money goes without saying. What is unusual about network marketing is that the very successful *get their time back*. Most large incomes outside network marketing are tied to large inputs of hours to earn them.

In network marketing, it remains a spare-time income, so other income streams, core, or alternative, can be given up. Couples in their mid-twenties can give up their jobs, and become full-time parents. Similarly, a delightful couple we have met in the business have been able to clear their debts and retire from stressful jobs ten years early. They now play golf together several times a week. Interestingly, most people stay working in the business, even though they have incomes on which they could retire, wealthy, for the rest of their lives. The reasons they give are always the same. They get a real buzz out of helping people gain financial dignity and independence. And they enjoy the association with positive people in the business.

The other benefits can be just as important

I have learned more about business and life skills in general in the relatively short time we have been running our network marketing business than at any other time during my thirty-odd years in business. The reason for this is that *in a good network marketing operation, personal development and business development are much more closely aligned than in conventional business*. With no office, factory, or workplace to go to for daily support and guidance, the network marketer, *like the freelance IBG, is on his or her own*, in world that is neutral at best, and negative at worst.

For this reason, professional network marketing organisations, and the leading Amway groups in particular, have developed support infrastructures that are outstanding in their effectiveness. What they involve is a few basic tools – books, tapes, and seminars – and a system of *mentoring*. Your mentor is someone in the line of sponsorship above you (and is therefore more successful and experienced) to whom you particularly relate. This person, or persons, takes a particular interest in your welfare, and you meet with them regularly to review progress, to learn the business, and to set gaols. The role starts out as being that of counsellor, and develops into that of friend. You, in turn, then fulfil the same role for individuals and couples within your own group.

The books, within the basic tools, are personal development books, which contain a whole golden treasury of wisdom, of most of which I was totally unaware. Along with availability of books goes discipline. Part of the pattern for success in network marketing – totally voluntary, but worth following – is the discipline of reading fifteen to twenty minutes every day from a personal development book.

When I first heard this, I thought it sounded like some form of benign brainwashing. It is often equated to brain cleansing, which is nearer the truth. Negative events and influences are our constant companions in business, and life in general. A consistent diet of personal development and positive thinking books dilutes this negative, and allows it to be flushed away. Reading these books has a direct parallel in physical exercise. It takes application and training to get fit, and if training and application are relaxed, it is cruel how swiftly fitness can be lost. So it is with mental fitness.

The audio tapes, and the meetings, cover attitude and skills development. Since my early days as a fledgling IBG, before I entered network marketing, I had always invested in training courses and cassette programmes. These were often at significant expense. The cost of cassettes and seminars provided by the various distributor groups within Amway is infinitesimal in comparison, and the quality is often higher. There also tend to be more jokes. They are enjoyable, as well as instructive, which makes the whole thing more digestible.

People who do not succeed in network marketing – for whatever reason – complain that it has cost them money, because they bought tapes and books that are now sitting in a cupboard somewhere. I have two challenges with this as an accusation. The first is that any business, of necessity, requires investment, and network marketing is no different in this respect. The second is that had those tapes been listened to, and the books read, on a constant daily basis, with an open and receptive mind, it is likely that success would have been greater not only in Amway, but in work and life in general.

This is the point. *The training programme, and the discipline to stick to it, which are supplied by being plugged into a professional network marketing organisation, has far wider benefits to the individual than those confined merely to network marketing.* Personal growth – including goal setting, patience and delayed gratification, increased self-esteem and self-confidence, higher energy level, and positive thinking – is totally relevant to all areas of our lives (as we shall see in subsequent chapters).

It is no exaggeration to say that you will be a better wife/husband/partner/son/daughter as a result. If you have children, they will grow up into better adults if they see you overcoming challenges with courage and humour. Goal-setting, delayed gratification, and positive thinking are invaluable skills for children as they cope with growing up. And affirmations. Our younger daughter, when she was eight, was playing in a form rounders match at school. They were not doing well, so at the beginning of the second innings she had them all reciting, 'I'm going to get a rounder.' A rounder, for the uninitiated, is like a home-run in baseball (which was based on rounders). The result was extraordinary. Every child in the team got a rounder, *including one who had never scored one in her life.*

The benefits of association are also significant. We are all aware of the danger of association with dubious people. We advise children to stay away from certain types, because we believe they will be a bad influence. The same is true of association with positive and uplifting people. It is, of course, even more relevant to IBGs – and freelance IBGs in particular – as positive association gives a framework, a reference, and a plugging-in point. Positive people look for the good, and praise it, and this attitude can be invaluable as a support when things look temporarily dark. Meeting with sane, professional, positive people can be an effective and heartening supercharge to the feeling of optimism and achievement that is the stock-in-trade of the IBG.

The other aspect of the seminars that is worth mentioning is recognitions. The first experience of watching distributors being invited up on stage to have their hand shaken for what, to an outsider, would appear to be somewhat insubstantial achievements, is a slight culture shock. But then you realise four things. The first is that on any motivation-rating matrix for the most important factors in measuring job satisfaction, recognition is always at, or near, the top. Remuneration is far lower down the scale. The second is that in most employment situations, recognition is almost totally absent. Stories abound of big hitters in the business and professional world being moist-eyed when at last receiving recognition for very humble achievements in the world of network marketing.

The third thing you realise is that when you in turn get recognised for your first, faltering steps in the business, it is unexpectedly enjoyable. And fourthly, when you at last have your own distributors to welcome up on stage for their achievements, the feeling is quite heady. Such recognitions make for the ultimate win/win situation. The recognised, the recognisers, and the audience, all partake in the experience, which is both edifying and uplifting.

A small but significant example of the power of recognition is demonstrated by the actions of the brother of a colleague. He had worked his way up the system to become the general manager of a chain of garages. It was a stressful job, particularly because the improvements he would like to have made in the delivery of customer service were not achievable, as a result of the owners, not him, controlling the budgets. His working day was therefore a continuous succession of customer complaints and staff problems.

He planned his escape, and organised his finances, so that a complete change was possible. He is now a breakdown mechanic with the Royal Automobile Club. The hours are unsociable. He works in all weather conditions. And everyone is pleased to see him. The appreciation he receives from broken-down motorists is warm and heartfelt. The *recognition* he receives for his work, makes it, for him, a dream job.

Amway, as the brand leader, is the network marketing business to check out, so others can be compared to it, as a benchmark. Investigate particularly if they are likely to be around for the long term. A network marketing businesses that is well run, and well structured, is the most forgiving business in the world. You can't go broke. You can't get fired. No overdraft is required. And you can make any number of mistakes, and still get it right in the end.

It does take some guts, because many people are comfortable floating with the stream, and say 'No,' as a matter of course. 'No' is the comfortable thing to say. It saves thinking, and it avoids action. It also avoids the possibility of failure. But both the financial and human rewards for persevering can be huge, and not just within the business. One of the most important skills, rather than attitudes, you learn, is that of enjoying talking to people.

I used to speak when spoken to. I was a friendly enough cove, and liked talking to anyone, but I didn't go out of my way to speak to people. Because in network marketing you are looking for lookers, you talk to anyone. It's part of Comfort Zone Growth. If it's appropriate, you take the initiative. You walk up to them and say, 'Hello. I'm Tim Drake.' Or, in your case, something more appropriate.

From this, delightful conversations can ensue. On the majority of occasions, network marketing is of no relevance. When it is, it's great, because you have found someone who might be able to benefit from the business. When it's not, it's great, because you will either learn something you didn't know before or, as has happened to me on several occasions, you will meet someone with whom, as an IBG, you can do business in other areas of your activities. Without the stimulus of my network marketing business *giving me a reason to engage*, I would never have met these people, and the income from subsequent activity would never have been created.

Four core reasons for an IBG to engage in network marketing

The first core reason, of course, is its ability to provide income to cover overheads, and its potential beyond that to give you financial freedom. Financial freedom is different from financial independence. Financial independence means you have paid off the mortgage, have a pension fund going, and can survive if the shutters have to be pulled down for any reason. This contrasts with most people in employment who, if they lost their jobs and were unable to find another, would be struggling to keep their car and their house after twelve months. Financial freedom means the ability to take off, on a whim, to exotic places in the world, knowing that when you return, you will still have more money in your bank account than when you left.

The second core reason is that in network marketing the luxury of being depressed is inexcusable. It is a reason to be proactive (and active) at times when nothing else in your portfolio of multiple income streams seems to be remotely active. The positive charge you will get from associating with positive people will permeate your entire business activity, and reactivate other income streams that appeared dormant.

The third core reason is close to the second. It keeps you plugged in to human networks at times when you could start retreating or withdrawing. Its potential for cross-fertilisation is enormous. You will find that over time you create numerous friends and business colleagues – all of whom you have yet to meet, and whom otherwise you would never meet

– if you engage in a network marketing business that is well-structured, is viable, and has a good support system.

The fourth core reason is that it gives you something to hope for. It is said that the three key elements needed to achieve happiness are extremely basic. They are: something to do; someone to love; and something to hope for. Network marketing can give you all three. Particularly something to hope for. There is always the possibility that distributors in your group – whom possibly you have still to meet – may develop into the most successful distributors in the history of the business. Your eye may be on a slightly different ball at the time, but your group, supercharged by the energy of these pioneering spirits, will bring you wealth beyond your wildest dreams.

As you may have deduced, I am quite positive about the benefits of professionally organised network marketing. Even people who have left the business and do great things elsewhere often attribute their later success to what they learned while they were on a regular diet of the books, tapes and meetings. In a wider sense, network marketing is the embodiment of modern management thinking.

It is a collection of *empowered business men and women – all independent, yet interdependent* – who react to their empowerment with a release of energy. This manifests itself in initiative-taking and business creation. They form part of a **Learning Organisation**, which is constantly finding out more about itself and its markets. This enables it to adapt and improve its products, services and methods of distribution, which, in turn, ensures that it can better satisfy its customers. The win/win process that evolves is customer inclusive, because it creates unmatchable value – products and services that have more benefits at lower prices. The goal of all marketers is thus achieved – customer *commitment*, rather than just customer satisfaction.

Time management becomes a crucial issue

Time has to be created for all this activity. Whether you are an IBG with a job as your core income stream, with the need to build second income streams to provide either financial security or financial freedom, or you are a freelance IBG, with core, and alternative income streams, plus secondary incomes for the same reasons, you will need time to do it all.

You must also remember that if your principles and values are properly aligned, you will also be finding time for the important things in your life – which include family and friends. There are two sources of time. One is the more effective use of your working day. The other is the more effective use of your private time.

A later chapter will touch on some of the principles of time management. Suffice it to say at this point that all of us could organise our time more effectively, and many of us have considerable slack to make up in this respect. Take two small, specific, examples in the area of time management at work (even if work is in your home).

The first example is the handling of paperwork – letters, memos, invoices, etc. Start by freeing up an hour early in the day, when you are not available for meetings and, ideally, take no phone calls. Take all the morning's mail – and the current contents of your in- and pending-trays, if they exist – and sort them into three piles. The first is things to action now. The second is things you're not sure about, and would normally go into the pending tray. The third is for immediate filing, possibly time-dated for future action.

Then take the second pile and allocate it between piles one and two. Having done that, take action on pile one, and file pile two. On the second, and subsequent days, only ever have two piles, which are always cleared. This is stage one of saving buckets of time that would otherwise be used picking up pieces of paper, reading them, putting them down, and performing exactly the same actions, on the same pieces of paper, until either something is done, or it is too late to do anything.

Stage two, when you have mastered stage one, *is only ever to touch a piece of paper once*. Pick it up, and take action on it. Reply to the letter or memo, pay the invoice (and lodge it in your books), accept the invitation, make a personal key-point summary of the document (read it actively with this in mind). Deal with that other massive time-waster – e-mail – in the same way. Read it, take action, clear it. Don't leave it hanging around, causing electronic clutter and a sense of guilt. If you find you need it later, you can always ask for another copy.

The second example of time-saving through effective time management is the control of meetings. Meetings swallow time like a storm-drain swallows water. Even if you are not the most senior person in your circle of work colleagues, most managers are open-minded enough to listen to constructive suggestions on how time might be saved. It is, of course, better if the principles of meeting management are adopted across the company, or institution, you work for. The rules are thus universal, and all meetings have a far better chance of being effectively run.

Meeting disciplines demonstrate the difference between efficient management and effective management. A meeting can be efficiently run, but if there is disagreement, or misunderstanding, on what it aims to achieve, and if the wrong people are at it and are coming and going as other pressing duties demand, it can be totally ineffective. A basic formula for running an effective meeting would be as follows.

Decide on the specific objectives and outcomes desired. Think through who should, and who should not, attend the meeting, *and why*. Itemise the agenda, including attendees, and define the length of time each subject should last. Leave space for action agreed, to be taken by whom, and by when. Circulate a summary of the above points, with a brief justification for each one.

Fix a time for the meeting and ask for feedback a minimum of forty-eight hours before the meeting is scheduled to take place. Adjust the objectives and personnel in the light of the feedback. Keep the meeting to the agreed time schedule. At the end of the meeting, the chairman summarises the decisions reached, and the action required, by whom, and by when. He or she then fills in the agenda form, and this constitutes the minutes of the meeting. This is later circulated to all those affected by the outcomes of the meeting.

This sounds mechanistic and lacking in the soft, human values, important in any organisation. And so it is, but the enormous waste of time, effort and frustration it avoids makes it eminently worthwhile.

The issue of family time versus business-building time

The effective use of your time that is not contracted to your core, or alternative income streams, is more challenging. On the one hand you have to create more time for your family and friends. Neither family nor friends can be organised like a business meeting. Here the soft issues really are important. Time itself is as important as what is said or done. *In this situation, the only quality time is quantity time.* Intelligent listening and time efficiency are not happy bedfellows. It takes time for someone to talk through a problem, particularly if the problem being talked through is only a smoke-screen for something more serious. Rushing the problem would never get to the real issue.

On the other hand, you need to create time for secondary income businesses. The morality of investing time in building time in secondary income businesses is clear. Children and families should of course be cared for, and loved. Assuming that babysitting and support can be provided, the absence of one or both of the spouses or partners, for one, two, or even three evenings a week, while the income or incomes are being built, can be justified on several grounds.

The most important reason for building secondary income streams is, by definition, to increase the size and security of the family's total income. This is of fundamental importance. A child's self-respect and learning capacity is enhanced if it can have the right books, diet, shoes and clothes, school trips, specialist classes in music, art, etc. that are appropriate. Tertiary education, gap years to gain a wider experience of the world, all need funding. Insufficient money to fund any of these things can cause anguish both for the parents and the children. This can be heightened if parents live in an area where public education is poor, and the only way to achieve a reasonable standard is to invest in private education.

If a consistent framework of love and support is available to children, the temporary absence two or three nights a week of one or both of the parents will be relatively small in its potential negative impact, compared to the potential benefits of the extra income generated *to provide the children with a more effective education.* Furthermore, there are benefits beyond merely the extra income which could make the difference between an adequate, and a good, education. Of these, one of the most important is the release from the stress and family tension caused by insufficient money to cover what children perceive to be the basics.

Another is the example set by the parents to their children of the crucial virtues of discipline and courage. It is good for children to see their parents taking on challenges willingly, persisting at them, and refusing to give in when success is not instant. The struggle for success is what gives it value. For children to see this fundamental life principle at first hand can be enormously helpful. If a personal development programme for the parents is involved as part of the process, the personal growth of the parents will not only enhance their abilities as parents, but will imbue them, and the children, with a positive attitude that makes each day more enjoyable, regardless of situations and events.

So where does the time come from? Overall time, and life, management is the long-term solution, but in the short term *the most likely answer is from television time.* Most people watch television for getting on for thirty hours a week. Just giving up ten of these hours could provide the time to transform the income of most people. The majority of our friends claim they don't watch much television. They do, but they tend not to include things like news programmes, which they consider worthy, and therefore not to be counted as indulging in watching TV.

Lizzie and I used to be great news watchers. Sometimes twice a night.

Watching the news is a curious phenomenon. Consider, for a moment, young people. Their distinguishing characteristic is generally that they are busy enjoying, and participating in, life. What they seldom do is watch the news. Consider, also, what you do on holiday, when you're busy, having a good time. How much news do you watch? Very little in my experience. Consider, finally, what elderly people do. They watch a great deal of news. Elderly people are probably better informed on what is going on than anyone else in the country. Is there a pattern here?

I would submit that there is. I would further submit that the pattern is clear: the more you have to do, *the more full your life, the less news you watch*. If you have little that is constructive to do, without realising it, you are bored, which is all the stimulus you need to turn on the news. Or if you are looking to reduce your own problems by watching others who have bigger ones, again you plug in, like a drug addict, to a regular fix of the news. Busy, successful people tend to invest TV time elsewhere, and catch up on the important news in a newspaper.

If this sounds a bit smug, it is not intended to be because we, too, used to be news junkies, so we know it is not easy to go cold turkey. We still do watch selected programmes – including, occasionally, the news. But more frequently we will either be out building our second income business, or we will play games, or do something – anything – together as a family. Sitting separately in the same room staring at a television only qualifies marginally as doing something as a family. It's better than sitting doing it in different rooms, but only just. Having said that, watching some programmes – especially comedy programmes – can enhance family relationships. Laughing together can unite generations. In the words of Francis Bacon, 'a sorrow shared is a sorrow halved – a joy shared is a joy doubled'.

For us, what at first was a discipline, but is now effortless, has had the additional benefit of making our children more selective. If we come into the kitchen (our television room) and they are watching something on TV, we tend to ask, 'that sounds a bit average. Is it any good?' Sometimes we word it slightly more strongly, but the point is they are mature enough in their judgement now to say 'no', and turn it off.

So, for most people, giving up some TV watching is an important source of new time.

Another source of time is sleep. Most people who sleep long hours do so because they are bored. They think they are busy, and tired, but there are energy sources they are not tapping. I now sleep about two hours less a night than I did during my conventional business career. I worked hard, and thought I was exhausted. I now work hard, and find I have more energy on less sleep.

There is nothing particularly clever in this, it is just a combination of motivation, positive thinking, and regular exercise. Regular exercise is Important, rather than Urgent, and whatever the pressures (and sometimes it is *very* difficult) must be fitted in somewhere. You feel healthier, sleep better, and you have more energy.

Positive thinking is also important. Anyone can do it. Imagine two scenarios. In the first you come home from work exhausted. All you want to do is to slump in a chair, have supper, watch television, and go to bed early. A friend rings up and asks you to play tennis, and then have a drink with some great mutual friends that you haven't seen for years. Suddenly, you're energised, out of your chair, and onto the court.

Imagine then that you are at a trade show, or a conference, in a foreign country. You see some wonderful exhibits, or hear some thought-provoking papers, and meet some exciting new colleagues, or suppliers, and have a great time socially. The entertaining is terrific. You are up till all hours, and back working again early in the morning. You are full of energy, despite very little sleep, and loving every minute of it. After two days you come home, and that night you feel exhausted. You find it difficult to stay awake, and give a sketchy outline of the event to your partner, and retire to bed early. The point is that if that conference or trade show had gone on for another night, *you would still have been living it up till all hours.*

So tiredness is a state of mind. The good news is that it is possible to find new energy that can *extend the quality and the quantity of your working day, and your playing day. Time management – and more importantly, life management – is both possible and necessary for an IBG.*

Developing as an IBG is potentially a much larger and more significant process than just getting yourself better organised to cope with the Incomes Revolution. *Fundamentally, it is about taking steps to take back control of your life.* It is about developing improved life skills, and achieving a better balance in the work that creates our multiple income streams. Our goal in these income streams is to find, or create, work that is more satisfying, that we actively enjoy, and which gives us reward, recognition, hope and, ultimately, freedom.

Most of us are – or have been – dead fish floating with the current. Our fins may have been working hard – very hard – but our brains have been dead, because they have been transfixed with the rigor-mortis of the old paradigms of jobs and careers, with preferment in someone else's gift. The new situation of the *Independent* Business Generator *gives us back our sovereignty. It liberates us within the system, to create our own lives and revenues.* The personal growth which is ours to achieve in this new environment gives us the opportunity to grow strong mentally as well as physically, and to swim against the tide.

SEVEN

Personal Development and Mind Leadership: Getting Control of Your Thoughts Before You Get Control of Your Life

HOMER SIMPSON, THE father in the US cartoon series *The Simpsons*, is a wonderful comic amalgam of the characteristics that most fathers would recognise in themselves, although they might not be too ready to admit to it. He is very funny because he is a painfully honest mixture of very human emotions and reactions. In one episode he is disturbed by his son, Bart, who wants something urgently. Homer, lying on the sofa, wet towel on head, snaps irritably at Bart, 'Leave me alone. Can't you see I'm lying here trying to worry?'

Shakespeare, as always, got there first, and when Hamlet, reflecting on the death of his father, says, 'There is nothing either good or bad, but thinking makes it so' he encapsulates the message of most personal development and positive thinking books. Homer Simpson, in turn, encapsulates the futility of worry by dramatising its non-productive, and often counter-productive, effects.

We are talking, in essence, of *leading* our mind, rather than being led by it. Further, we are talking about leadership, and not just management, of the mind. Leadership is about having a vision, about creating new possibilities, about inspiring all the elements involved to contribute to the achievement of that vision. Management is more about control, about using resources well, about operating efficiently within accepted paradigms.

To oversimplify to make the point, leadership is about effectiveness in life, and management is about efficiency in life. The best definition of the difference between effectiveness and efficiency that I have come across is that of Stephen Covey, who is probably the leading-edge thinker in this area. Covey defines efficiency as cruising along the highway in a car that is superbly tuned, economical on fuel, reliable, comfortable, and easy to drive. *He then points out that if the car is travelling due south, and your destination is due north, then the car is efficient, but totally ineffective.*

All of us have the potential to be great – in business, in the community, in the family. None of us will achieve the total realisation of our greatness, because that realisation is a journey, not a destination. One thing is sure, however, and that is that unless we can set a goal for greatness, and follow it passionately, we will remain rooted in our current perceptions of ourselves and our abilities. Leaders break patterns, and move the whole game onto a new level.

The underlying precept of this book is, in a sense, that the interruption in traditional employment patterns, and changes in society as a whole, contain within them the possibility of releasing new personal energy and potential. *Wearing the Coat of Change with enthusiasm allows us to develop as individuals in new and exciting ways. We have music within us, and change will be the catalyst that enables us to find instruments on which to play it.*

Mind Leadership looks for New Dimensions and New Ways to Add Value

Managing our minds, so that we can control the tendencies to doubt our abilities, and to want to return to our comfort zones, is important. But it is not as important as *leading our mind to conceive new possibilities* that transcend the dead-hand limitations of the facts as they are currently perceived.

The whole knowledge and wisdom base of personal development, and positive thinking, are the vital underpinnings we need for proactively coming to terms with life and for radically increasing the satisfaction and enjoyment we get from it. Most personal development thinking has two different goals, which frequently become confused. The first is the more limited, but immensely worthwhile, goal of giving us coping strategies. The second is that of putting us on the road to fulfilling more of our potential.

When we get blown off-track, as continually happens as life lobs its grenades at us, positive thinking can help enormously, but more to help us cope with, than to transcend, the situation. Cheerful coping is sometimes a triumph in itself, but **Leadership Thinking** would attempt to go a step beyond and take an initiative. Great men, like Abraham Lincoln during the Civil War, when things were going badly for the Yankees, or Churchill, when total victory for the Nazis looked inevitable in the early years of the Second World War, have the ability to transcend their situation. Gandhi, Martin Luther King, and Nelson Mandela, similarly, could see beyond their personal situations to a bigger picture.

Our personal actions may not change the world in this way, but they may change our personal worlds, and the worlds of those around us. To create a mindset of **Mind Leadership**, therefore, rather than mind management, it is worth having two questions that we constantly put to ourselves, especially when things get challenging. To be proactive rather than reactive, we should ask ourselves:

– *What do I see as the bigger dimension?*
– *How can I add new value?*

The first question demands that we step back, review, and rethink the situation in a larger context. What other elements could be relevant, that we hadn't considered before? What else in our, and other's experience, could have a bearing? If I were the future chronicler of this event or situation, how would I put it in a wider historical perspective? What is the bigger picture, and how does this fit in?

On the second question, there is an imperative to contribute some new thinking. There is also an imperative to *take some responsibility* for the situation. If it is to be, it's up to me. What can I contribute that is new, different, and no one else could contribute? I know that I am unique, and that there is no one else quite like me. So how do I apply *my* unique talents to enhance the situation, and use a fresh approach to address what seems to be an intractable situation?

The basics of personal development and positive thinking

We are getting ahead of ourselves. Let's step back, and have a look at some of the elements of the life skills that are provided by personal and positive thinking development programmes. As an exercise in *perception management*, which is what it is, let's first examine two different ways of looking at our current situation.

A Homer Simpson, lying there trying to worry, might come up with a view as follows:

– no job security
– polarisation of incomes

- polarisation of regions
- emergence of a deprived underclass
- deterioration in law and order
- spreading drugs culture
- growth in dependency culture
- hospitals and schools deteriorating
- old age frightening (little care, or income)
- growth in age-related illness (cancer, heart)
- structural unemployment

And so on. Now let's look at a different perspective on our achievements over the past several decades:

- numbers doing dangerous jobs reduced (coal mining)
- not tied to job for life
- employment more diverse, and interesting
- more labour saving devices (dishwashers, washing machines)
- average living standards higher
- high rewards for talented people
- tertiary education much wider
- wide access to arts and sport (TV)
- medical advances improving quality of life
- low costs transforming travel opportunities
- birth control reducing unwanted pregnancies
- mental health better understood
- better fed, better understanding of diet
- living longer
- better informed (wider access to information)
- only one – democratic, and well intentioned – superpower
- working from home avoids waste of time commuting
- cleaner water, cleaner air
- reduced telephone charges and mobile phones transform personal communications
- fax and e-mail transform business communications
- personal computers transform ability to access and process knowledge
- personal computers transform data transfer (e-mail, EDI, etc.)
- wider variety of leisure opportunities (Disneyland, safaris, adventure holidays)

And so on. As many teachers of positive thinking have pointed out, we are living in the Golden Age. We are privileged to live in a time of so much accessibility, and choice, in knowledge, travel and communications in general. We are generally better educated, better fed, better off, and in better health than our parents' generation, have more interesting and more varied employment, and have a greater variety of leisure opportunities.

We therefore have the framework in place to enjoy fuller, more satisfying lives. The only thing that stops us is the Homer Simpson in us, looking for something to worry about. Estimates vary between 75 per cent and 90 per cent as to the amount of things worried about that never actually become reality. Remember the saying quoted at the beginning of the book about worry being the interest on a debt not yet due? The avoidance of paying this interest, and with it the creation of stress and anxiety, is what much of this chapter is about.

What I intend this and the following two chapters to achieve is to give some insight *why, as potential IBGs, we need to get out of the straitjacket of conventional thinking, and to get the strength – and supercharge – of personal development built into our very cores*. I will also look into the origins, development, and concepts of positive thinking in particular and self-development in general. This is not intended to replace the need to study the subject thoroughly, and regularly (indeed daily), in order to achieve what I term Mind Leadership. Three chapters can in no way replace the collective wisdom of great teachers across time.

Because the subject is huge, and the groundwork therefore extensive, Felicity Freshstart, Norman Newhope and Simon Smartbutton will not get a chance to put some of the ideas into action until a later chapter. They will bring into clearer focus some of the key concepts outlined in this, and the subsequent, chapter.

Untether your mind – jump out of the jar

The more stories you read in self-development books about people transforming their performance, and the more your personal experience confirms that you are capable of much more than you ever thought you were, the more you come to understand and believe Edison's statement: 'If we all did what we are capable of doing, we would literally astound ourselves.'

The challenge we have to overcome, as many writers and teachers have pointed out, is to remove the false ceilings we impose upon what we perceive to be our capabilities. The two analogies that are normally presented are the fleas, and the elephant. If you put fleas in a jar with a lid on, the fleas jump, and continually hit the lid. Eventually they learn that jumping so high is fruitless exercise, and they jump low enough to avoid giving themselves a headache. If you then remove the lid, the fleas continue to jump to a level just below the top of the jar. They are free to escape, but they are conditioned to believe there is nothing beyond the small space in which they are confined.

Elephants, similarly, go through a similar process of *horizon limitation*. As baby elephants, they are tethered by a sizeable stake and try as they may, there is no escape from it. Being elephants, they never forget this lesson. As they grow older, they can be tethered by the lightest of stakes, which, if they were to try, they could remove effortlessly. Again, they are free to escape, *but their minds are tethered to a smaller reality*.

Houdini, the great escapologist, unwittingly supplied an example of **Tethered Thinking** when, on a visit to Britain, he accepted a challenge by a gaol in the Midlands to escape from a special cell, fitted with a double lock. Houdini realised that two locks would take longer than one, so he demanded a full hour to perform the escape. As usual, he smuggled tools into the cell to aid his escape, and set to work. He managed to unlock the first lock, but couldn't budge the second one. He tried and he tried, but couldn't shift it. Finally, after two hours of abortive effort, he became totally frustrated, and flung himself against the door. It swung open. There was only one lock on the door. The other lock was on Houdini's mind.

We, like Houdini, have locks on our minds. We are tethered to limiting paradigms of what we believe to be possible and, in particular, what we believe ourselves to be capable of. *Leadership thinking therefore looks not only for a larger dimension on a problem or an opportunity, but it also looks to create a larger dimension for our personal talents and capabilities. It stimulates us to achieve personal growth by visualising the possibility of that growth*. This is why a defining characteristic of leadership is the ability to think outside the box.

The box contains logic. Logic and greatness are antipathetic. All the world's great inventors, explorers, warriors, political, religious, and business leaders, have been men and women who have carried on to achieve greatness when logic would have given ample rationalisation to stop. People whose minds are tethered by logic do stop. Leadership thinkers ignore logic, and carry on. They visualise themselves growing as individuals to achieve great goals, and great outcomes. And, thriving on the risk involved in achieving greatness, they are content that if they do not achieve a glorious victory, they will at least have the satisfaction of failing magnificently, and achieving far more in doing so than if they had taken the comfortable route of setting lower goals in the first place.

The lower our sense of self-worth, the shorter the rope that tethers our minds

In order to be capable of bursting free from the tethered logic and the limiting paradigms of conventional thinking, it is necessary to have strong self-belief, and a high sense of self-worth. If we believe ourselves to be weak and unworthy, we will not be able to resist even light pressure, let alone to keep fighting long after the world has concluded that we are mad.

Dr Maxwell Malz was a plastic surgeon who, many decades ago, wrote an excellent book called *Psycho Cybernetics*. The book is more readable than the title and concerns Malz's journey of discovery of the power that self-image has to make or mar people's lives. He found that after operating on some of his patients to remove unsightly moles or birthmarks, they still believed themselves to be ugly. Despite the evidence to the contrary in their mirrors, their perception of themselves was that nothing had changed. Malz therefore set about altering their self-perception, by helping them to release the mental tethers that were constraining them.

In terms of our individual potential, we are all prone to suffer from a below-optimum sense of self-worth. For those of us whose sense of self-worth is beneath our actual worth, rather than our potential worth, the implications can be serious. It is the worst kind of poverty, because it can reduce individuals to walking shadows, ruining their relationships, their lives, and their futures.

Self-worth is probably the single most important attribute for the IBG. If your self-worth depends on your position and your income, you are likely to find life as an IBG extremely challenging. Imagine that you lose your core income. If your self-worth was predicated upon it, and the position it gave you, developing alternative and second income streams until the core was replaced will be much more difficult. A person's sense of self-worth is communicated in body language as well as attitude.

At various times during my business career, I have been involved in recruitment. If someone sat in front of me who had a magnificent curriculum vitae, but was communicating a low sense of self-worth, the first question was, 'It's not clear on this cv. Are you currently working with the last company on this form?' The answer was invariably no. The person concerned was probably no worse an executive than he or she had been two or three months previously, but you could *smell* the lack of self-esteem that had resulted from being, however temporarily, out of work.

The challenge then was to evaluate not only whether the person could do the job, but whether their self-esteem could be rapidly rebuilt to enable him or her to do it effectively. Frequently, if I took the risk, it turned out that it could be, and the person was successful. But if the sense of self-worth had been retained in the first place, the individual concerned would have avoided carrying around the ticking time-bomb of self-doubt from interview to interview, and would positively have enjoyed the process of finding a better job.

However far along the never-ending path of self-development someone is, he or she will still suffer from fluctuating self-esteem. *The key point is that this fluctuation will be between high and very high.* It is important to understand that *there are no short cuts to a robust and resilient sense of sense of self-worth.* It is based on two things. The first is mastery over self. Genuinely to like yourself, you have to be *worthy* of being liked. Principles and values need to be aligned, and a worthwhile vision should be in place. This vision may start as something quite humble, as we shall see in the next chapters, but may develop into something larger and more inspiring.

Once you know yourself, and have worked diligently on mastering yourself, you will like yourself, because, on a very simple level, you will know that you are honest, unmanipulative, constructive, that you enjoy giving to others, and are exhilarated by their success.

This leads directly on to the second point. A sense of self-worth needs constant consolidation and reinforcement. This is achieved by daily affirmations and visualisations. The crucial point is that these affirmations and visualisations are far more effective if they confirm reality. You can, as they say, fake it till you make it, but you've got to be intent on making the reality match the image in the shortest time possible if you are interested in success on a long-term basis. In Stephen Covey's phrase, the law of the farm operates. What you plant is what you get. If you plant weeds, weeds is what will grow. If you're looking to get rich quick, and plant corn in late summer, hoping for a quick autumn harvest, all you'll get is rotting corn seeds.

Courage – one of the IBG's chief ingredients – comes directly from self-worth

The wonderful thing about a strong and well-founded sense of self-worth, is that it can carry you through whatever life throws at you. You'll be able to fight the shite, because you'll know that whatever comes up, you *can* handle it. As an IBG, this is especially important *because the only security you have lies in your capacity to perform confidently and effectively in a number of different roles*, each of which forms a separate income stream. This ability to interact *confidently* with different people is fundamental to success in these different enterprises.

Because the paternalistic framework of the job only exists – if it exists at all – in the more limited sense of the core income stream, flexible response to opportunities as they present themselves – and creating them if they don't – is the defining characteristic of the successful IBG. Leaving aside network marketing – which may or may not be appropriate to an individual IBG – it is quite likely that there will be little opportunity to associate with other colleagues on a consistent basis.

There will thus be times when discouragement nibbles at your entrails. Discouragement is an interesting word. It literally means having your courage removed. This implies that having courage is the natural state of affairs, and losing it, by definition, is unnatural. Hang onto this thought. Courage is the daily companion of the IBG, so it is good that it is a natural state. Comfort Zone Growth is about having the courage to push the boundaries back a little further each day. Fluctuating and uncertain income streams are about having the courage to carry on, with confidence and enjoyment, when there is no guarantee that bills will be paid when they are due.

The need for courage simply means your qualities as an individual are being tested. If you have achieved a state of integrity and well-founded self-worth, you will pass the tests as they present themselves. Once your self-esteem enables you to be a consistently positive, cheerful and confident person, two benefits flow from this achievement. The first is that your clients and colleagues will always be pleased to see you, and any challenges you are facing will not impact negatively on your relationship with them. The second benefit *is that your cheerfulness will be genuine*, because it is based in a well-founded belief in your inner qualities, and thus your ability to handle whatever life throws at you.

The origins of personal development and positive thinking

Many of the concepts of positive thinking have their origins in the Greek philosophers, the Bible, and great works of literature. One of Shakespeare's preoccupations is the difference between image and truth, perception and reality, which touches centrally on this area. Indeed Hamlet again features in the annals of positive thinking when his ultimate killer, the noble but misguided Laertes, is being given worldly advice by his father, Polonius: 'Assume a virtue, and you have it.' Coming from Polonius, this is shallow advice, but like much of the speech, contains many verities ('But above all else, To thine own self be true') which in the mouth of a more worthy man would have carried considerably more weight.

Positive thinking really began to become recognised as a genre of education, life skills and literature, between the two world wars. America was its birthplace and cradle, with writers such as Dale Carnegie, Dr Maxwell Maltz and Napoleon Hill, who, as we saw, started out as the mouthpiece for the other Carnegie (Andrew). Dale Carnegie's *How to Win Friends and Influence People* sounds hokey as a title, but is a book of profundity in its understanding of the basic mechanics of human relationships, and rewards close reading. The lineage then passes through Norman Vincent Peel and Earl Nightingale to the more contemporary writers and communicators.

Amongst these, Stephen Covey has moved the whole conversation on by giving it an intellectual depth, and rooting personal development in the character, rather than the personality. Anthony Robbins has added further dimensions in his application of Neuro Linguistic Programming, and there have been other great teachers and communicators along the way, such as Zig Ziglar, Dennis Waitley, Brian Tracy and Susan Jeffers.

All writers in personal development borrow freely from each other, and from the timeless wisdom of the great writers and philosophers of the past. Most of the ideas are shared, with each author adding a slightly different twist, and adding his, or her, own fresh insights. There are also dozens of other writers, some good, some OK. The books vary dramatically in length. Some are long, and densely packed with stimulating thinking and stories to illustrate the ideas. These are the parables, if you like, to dramatise the lessons and truths the writers wish to communicate.

Some of the books are very short, and have illustrations that seem to have come out of kids' comics. They are, none the less, all worth reading, because in almost every one there is a nugget or two of distilled wisdom that strikes you in a fresh way. However culturally bizarre one or two of the books, and particularly their covers, may look, the time they take to read (quite short, in the case of the slimmer ones) is always time well invested. It requires a similar sense of humility to that of Emerson's Sage of Concord: 'In every man there is something wherein I may learn of him, and in that I am his pupil.'

Daily personal development can change your life, and contain the negatives

What is interesting about personal development books and tapes is that they strike different chords in different people. Books I think are brilliant, Lizzie may not find as stimulating and helpful, and vice versa. They also mean different things to you at different times. I find that I reread books, and because I am at a different stage of personal development, I find important ideas and helpful insights that had entirely eluded me on first reading.

A recent example of this was an idea that Lizzie found illuminating in a book she was reading. It is an illustration of what I am talking about now – how you can be blind to something under your nose, because your focus is elsewhere. Try the idea now. You have to be honest doing this, otherwise it loses half its effectiveness. Look around the room and focus intently on everything you can see that is *blue* in colour. Look again at them, and get them securely into your mind. Close your eyes and try to remember all those blue objects, and where they sit in the room. Now keeping your eyes closed, mentally look around the room, and identify all the objects that are another colour, chosen at random – say green. You will find that your memory can recall the blue objects, but the green objects are few in number, and mainly guessed at. It's an excellent dramatisation of selective vision – and it had passed me by the first time I had read the book.

Recommending books for other people to read is therefore difficult, as the chord they struck with me doesn't always resonate with somebody else. Or it might be the right book, at the wrong time. If you haven't read these sort of books before, I would therefore suggest that you read four or five before making a judgement. And whatever your judgement, go back and reread the first book. You'll find, for the most part, that it's like reading the book for the very first time.

It is important (and urgent) that you find fifteen to twenty minutes *every day* to read the books. If it isn't regular, their effect is enormously diminished. Like physical exercise, their power for good begins to decline after forty-eight hours of neglect. The reason for this is simple. *We are faced all day, every day, with a continuous stream of negative information – much of it from within ourselves – that needs distancing and controlling.* Regular doses of positive programming from personal development reading and listening *give us the opportunity, and more importantly, the power, to control it, and replace it with a consistently positive and life-enhancing approach to our lives.*

The simple message is: we can't control other people, and we can't control the happenings in our lives, *but we can control how we react, and how we feel.* This is news for many people. It certainly was for me. But this awareness has been around for many centuries. Samuel Johnson articulates it clearly: 'The fountain of content must spring up in the mind, and he who has so little knowledge of human nature as to seek happiness by changing anything but his own disposition, will waste his life in fruitless efforts and multiply the grief he proposes to remove.'

We are not talking about quick-fix, temporary, solutions

Continuous personal development, if it is approached maturely, is satisfying and extremely challenging. This is because we are working on developing our core character traits, how we perceive ourselves, and how we interact with the world. This does not mean that we will not be talking about techniques that can extract you from a sticky corner, but it does mean that we have to get our basic principles and values aligned before we can hope to take on the world on a consistently effective basis.

In the terms of Stephen Covey, who is outstandingly good on the elements and dynamics of character, integrity and personal effectiveness, we must achieve private greatness before we can achieve public greatness. He further defines it as a necessity to achieve private victories before we can achieve public victories. This means we become honest internally – keeping promises to ourselves – before we can hope to keep promises to others. When we can trust ourselves, particularly when the pressure comes on, and the cracks threaten to appear, then others will in turn trust us in the profound sense of knowing we are more than fair weather friends.

Talking the talk is useless, and dangerous, unless we walk the walk. Or, as Socrates put it with a little more dignity: 'The greatest way to live with honour in this world is to be what we pretend to be.' The deep truth of this is obvious. The public victories – possessions, status, qualifications, titles, financial success, the people with whom we associate – *all give us borrowed strength, and are thus temporary.* These attributes are very attractive, and enjoyable, but their function beyond that, in most circumstances, is *to prop up our inner insecurities.*

True security comes from being at peace with ourselves. *That means liking ourselves.* Not in some sticking plaster way that gives a quick fix of self-regard in between bouts of self-doubt, or even self-loathing. It is useless telling ourselves that we are wonderful, and visualising ourselves triumphing in the areas the world holds important – wealth, sporting prowess, business success, personal attractiveness – if inside we feel ourselves to be shams, hoping desperately not be found out.

The source of this self-belief that gives us inner peace is a profound sense of our own integrity, and maturity. This is far bigger, more complex, and hard to achieve, than it sounds. Integrity, as a word, comes from the Latin word 'integer', meaning whole number, not broken into fractions. It has thus come to mean honesty in a whole sense, rather than in any partial sense. Consistency over time is a further element involved in the concept. For an IBG, or for anyone living a full and challenging life, this has implications in many dimensions. Not only are we talking aligned principles and values between what goes on inside us, and what goes on outside, but also across all the areas of activity in our lives.

Integrity can thus be distinctly uncomfortable. Wholeness means no bits missing. The elements, too, have to be total. Loyalty is 100 per cent, or it is nothing. If you are loyal 99 per cent of the time you may feel you qualify as being above average, but the 1 per cent totally undoes the value of the 99 per cent. If you are faithful to your partner 99 per cent of the time, but you sleep with someone else on the hundredth occasion, your fidelity is worthless. And you know it. So it is with other aspects of personal integrity. It's a very tough standard to aspire to, but the standards are absolute, not relative. If, however, you can attain and maintain it, the sense of self-respect and self-belief it can deliver is awesome.

The need for maturity alongside integrity is what prevents it from becoming smug and self-congratulatory. Maturity is gained from two main sources. One is the sense of humility which comes from knowing how much *courage* it has required, and still requires, to achieve integrity, and how many shortfalls there were along the way. Secondly it comes from the ability to exercise *patience*, and to understand the challenges others may be going through in trying to achieve it.

I was extremely fortunate in the timing of my own discovery of the teachings and concepts of personal development. It came directly from my becoming involved in network marketing, and occurred at a time that could not have been more felicitous. Perhaps it was a case of when the student is ready, the teacher will appear.

The six months of consultancy with Cobra Sports were in a strange way soothing, and helped to heal the inevitable wound incurred by the personal loss of the business. I was given the comfort – you might even say security blanket – of an office, secretarial support etc., and I was still surrounded by old friends – now ex-colleagues – who kept me involved in the developments within the business. When, at the end of the six-month period, I cut the umbilical cord and left, I began the very different experience of working from home.

I loved the feeling of being with my family, but I also missed the positive association with colleagues who shared a common purpose. *This is the dangerous time for anyone making the jump to become a freelance IBG.* For a period you are neither fish nor fowl. You are no longer employed in the conventional sense, yet you have still to graduate to becoming a fully fledged, wholly self-sufficient, Independent Business Generator, and it is not uncommon to suffer from moments of disorientation and doubts.

It was during this period that I was exposed to the thinking of some of the great teachers in personal development, through the programme of books and tapes I plugged into – somewhat unwittingly, and full of reservations – in the network marketing organisation I had joined. *Without the support of this programme there must exist some doubt as to whether I would have survived in the long term outside the system of conventional employment.* This – in addition to the obvious potential for difference-making second income – is the reason I stressed the importance of the option of examining a professional network marketing organisation in the last chapter.

Without the constantly reinforced self-belief that comes from personal growth within a programme of personal development, very few individuals will have the consistent intestinal fortitude to survive – smiling – the inevitable reverses and disappointments that can be the constant companions of the IBG. Suddenly without the support of the culture provided by a position in conventional employment – however inimical that employment might have been – the individual is cruelly vulnerable to these body blows, particularly in early life as an IBG.

Personal development, using some of the concepts and techniques I will outline in the next chapter, is far more than a sticking-plaster solution to periods of difficulty or self-doubt. It gives the opportunity to grow as an individual, and genuinely to relish the challenges, to learn from them, and to emerge stronger, with senses of perspective and humour intact.

For me, it was the catalyst that enabled me to grow into the role of the Independent Business Generator. It has allowed me to be able to revel in being home-based, independent, and excited by what life had to offer. Whatever your personal starting point, a programme of personal development will help you to grow as an individual, get more out of life, and even more importantly, put more back into life.

EIGHT

Some of the Key Concepts of Personal Development

If you think you can, or you think you can't, you're right
Henry Ford

LIFE ISN'T EASY. Nor is personal development. What personal growth and personal development can achieve, which is of fundamental importance, is to change the mindset from one *of being a passenger to one of being the driver*. Having control of the vehicle is far more enjoyable and satisfying, however bumpy the terrain, than to be thrown around in the back of the vehicle, a victim to both to the terrain and the limitations of an unknown driver.

Taking back responsibility for our lives, and controlling our responses to what life throws at us, enables us to become winners rather than losers. We are on the front foot, accepting setbacks as necessary preliminaries to a more fulfilling victory. We are no longer on the back foot, waiting for the next body blow, half expecting it to despatch us to the canvas.

These sporting metaphors may seem simplistic, and indeed some personal development literature verges on both the simplistic and the patronising, but the reason is that the step from defence to attack is a very simple one. Not easy, but simple. Once you have made it, you realise how profound is the difference in outlook. *You begin to enjoy the fight.* A glint comes into your eye, and you become filled with the certainty that you will win the war, even if individual battles are lost.

I believed I was a strong and positive person. To a degree, I was. But most of my life had been associated with relative success, and I had never been asked to dig deep, without the reassuring infrastructure of a work, or academic, environment around me. If I am right in the belief that I am one of many scouts on a new trail that will be followed by future armies, the fact that I have found the tools of personal development of pivotal importance, should cause even the most self-confident of doubters to open their minds an inch or two to examine some of the concepts involved.

It is possible to survive and flourish as an Independent Business Generator without consciously and actively becoming involved in a personal development programme. I would argue, however, that such a programme will not only significantly increase the chances of success, it will make the journey considerably more enjoyable. Not only will it be more fun, it will be more educational. I learned a great deal about myself, as well as others, during my journey.

I am strong, and I am worthy – the subconscious runs the show

This chapter deals with some of the basics of personal development: the power of the subconscious – to help us, or to hinder us; also the necessity to create and control our own thinking, which in turn leads to an understanding of the transformational nature of positive response.

Someone coming new to personal development and positive thinking – as I did – has a great deal of ground to cover to get to grips with the basic framework of the subject. The largest and most challenging part of the framework is the power and influence – for good or for bad – of our subconscious minds. Before coming to understand its importance, I tended to dismiss the subconscious as so much psycho-babble. One simple demonstration of its power was the first step in changing my mind. If you are similarly sceptical, you too should *try this simple exercise*, to untether your mind, and open it to the potential of the subconscious.

The demonstration works best in a group, but works effectively with just one other person. I first came across it in a book by Susan Jeffers, an exceptionally gifted teacher and educator, who in turn learned it from another teacher. The demonstration consists of asking someone to stand up, holding his or her arm parallel with their shoulder, and to repeat the words 'I am strong, and I am worthy' ten times, and with feeling. Most people feel pretty silly doing this, but they enter into the spirit, and then wait attentively. You then attempt to force their arm down towards the ground, which is extremely difficult, because the arm is rigid to the shoulder.

Next you ask the same person to repeat the phrase 'I am weak and unworthy' ten times, and with feeling. You then repeat the operation of pushing the arm down, and find it goes down with little resistance. The extraordinary thing about this demonstration is that not only does it always work, but it doesn't matter what order you do it in, or even if the person pushing the arm down is kept out of the room, to keep them in ignorance of which set of instructions were given.

I had personal confirmation of this when we demonstrated it to Lizzie's four brothers. One of them is of a somewhat sceptical frame of mind, and had expressed the view on more than one occasion that positive thinking was for the birds. We went around the table, varying the instructions, and it worked every time, until we got to doubting Thomas. I was more concerned than he was, because for him to have proved it to be fraudulent would have caused us public – and private – embarrassment.

I asked him to be strong and worthy first, and after correcting his tendency to mutter, heard all ten positive statements. He is an ex-professional diver, and is very strong, so I was in no way surprised that his arm was immovable. Then came the test. I could see the glint in his eye, and knew that whatever the words he spoke, they would be fighting a strong desire to keep his arm firmly in place. 'I am weak, and unworthy', he said, just audibly, ten times. I stepped up, looked him in the eyes, and to my enormous relief, forced his arm straight down. He was not amused.

Look at the positive – it's the best chance of survival

The best way to keep your head, when those around you are losing theirs, is to look at what is positive. The injunction 'stay calm' might work. 'Don't panic' won't, because it programmes into the mind the negative aspect – panic – leaving a very high likelihood that the mind will freeze, and panic will ensue.

A dramatic example of positive thinking saving the day occurred during the Apollo 13 space mission in 1970, since made into a film. Deep in space, an oxygen tank exploded, cutting off the electrical circuit to the command module. Mission Control in Houston and the three-man crew watched in horror as one system after another started to fail. Meltdown was approaching, not only for the spacecraft, but for the crew and Mission Control, whose brains began to melt down at the horror of what seemed to be happening. Like rabbits caught in the headlights, brains, too, were beginning to malfunction.

The situation was saved by the intervention of Gene Krantz, the flight director, who changed the whole orientation of thinking, by asking one simple question: '*What have we got on the spacecraft that's good?*' Thinking now about what was working, rather than what was not, changed the mindset of all concerned from, 'This is a disaster', to 'Let's get on and solve this.'

Anthony Robbins illustrates the same point, when he describes taking lessons in how to drive fast cars at great speed. At one point on the test drive there is a brick wall on a very tight corner. He is told by the instructor that if he looks at the wall, he will hit it. The only way to get round the corner without hitting the wall at speed is to look at, and concentrate on, the exit point of the bend. Robbins goes into the bend at speed, and can feel an almost irresistible magnetic pull from the wall – both for his eyes, and for his car. He manages to force his eyes onto the exit from the bend, and makes it. But he knows that if he had kept looking at the wall, he would have hit it.

Fighting the *intense magnetic pull of the negative* is another manifestation of the need to untether the mind from inhibiting forces. Unless the mind is untethered, the combination of a serious problem, together with a brain working at quarter speed – if at all – can potentially be overwhelming.

Thomas Edison, throughout his life, was not a man to be overwhelmed by negative events or influences. When he was sixty-seven, an age when many men would retire from the challenges of life, he faced yet another situation that had the potential to overwhelm him. His factory burned down. Not only did he lose all his workings and prototypes, he discovered that the factory was insured for under $250,000, and the damage was estimated at $2 million.

On the morning following the fire, he was on the site of the still-smouldering ruins of the factory. Many had arrived to offer condolences. They gathered round to hear how Edison would respond to the disaster. 'Friends,' he said, 'there is great value in disaster.' Pointing to the gutted factory, he continued, 'Look, all of our mistakes have burned up. Thank God we can start anew.' Three weeks later, Edison unveiled to the world the first phonograph.

The subconscious takes orders from the conscious mind – so control the negative Chatterbox

Two important points emerge from these demonstrations. The first is the enormous *power* we have over our subconscious minds, and how that power is handed over in turn to our bodily functions. The second point is that the subconscious *is neutral, and cannot differentiate between good and bad, or between positive and negative.* It is non-judgemental. It listens, and believes everything we say – however true, or untrue, it may be.

Whole books have been written on this subject (*What to say when you talk to yourself* and *You can't afford the luxury of a negative thought*, to name but two). It is of fundamental importance because it deals with the scripting we give ourselves. This scripting will determine whether we take positive control of our lives or we remain victims; whether we respond positively to challenges, or we look for a way out; *whether, ultimately, we decide to be winners or losers.*

The negative **Chatterbox** thus forms an important element in the victim culture. Victims enjoy telling themselves they are victims, and it forms part of the reinforcement of the comfort zone of misery. The Chatterbox welcomes worry, and negative thoughts of all kinds, and proceeds to articulate them for internal consumption.

Talking to yourself is a universal phenomenon. Psychological tests indicate that between 70 and 90 per cent of this self-talk is negative. That means we are confirming to ourselves that we can't do things, or the world is against us, or that it's bound to rain next week when we want to play tennis. The original purpose of this negative chatter is probably to provide an insurance against disappointment. *What it becomes is a monstrous and continuous self-fulfilling prophecy.* We talk negative to ourselves, and we get negative as a result. We tell ourselves that we can't do something, or that we'll fail if we attempt it and, as Henry Ford pointed out, we are right – we can't do it, and we fail if we try. Just as we told ourselves we were weak and unworthy, and couldn't hold our arm up.

The subconscious is a great friend, but it cannot take a joke

The subconscious – our willing servant, as the eastern philosophers call it – can be our strongest friend, and staunchest ally. *Unlike friends, however, it does not have a shared value system. It is a computer.* We programme it, and it produces answers. If we supply the right programming, we get the right answers, and if we programme it incorrectly, we get the wrong answers. If we supply positive inputs, we get positive outcomes; if we supply negative inputs, we get negative outcomes.

Because the subconscious is a computer, it has no sense of humour. Once you have understood this, your own repertoire of humour becomes more circumscribed. Any joke at someone else's expense, however kindly meant, can, and does, hurt. The recipient of the humour may laugh, but his subconscious feels the pain, because it can make no allowances for the value-overlay of humour.

This is particularly true for children, who have a more direct link between their subconscious' view of their self-worth and the cutting edge of the joke's humour. Drole little putdowns become unfunny large putdowns to the subconscious, and directly affect the self-worth of the butt of the joke. A friend of ours tells a story from her childhood, when she ran all the way home from school with the wonderful news that she had earned a mark of 98 per cent in her physics exam. She gasped out the news to her parents. Her father's only comment, without looking up from his paper, was, 'What happened to the other 2 per cent?' Very drole, but our friend is still hurt by the remark, thirty years later.

The subconscious is one of the most widely validated concepts of psychology, philosophy and religion. It has two important positive functions. The first is to be the *repository for our self-worth*, and to be the catalyst that enables us to envision and pre-live success, in order to prepare us for its arrival and to make sure all the elements are in place for its achievement. The second is to come up with solutions – that are *invariably right for us, and often new to us* – to difficult questions on what line of action we should take in a given situation.

The first function of the subconscious, as the repository of our self-worth, plays a pivotal role in self-development thinking and teaching. The programming tools are visualisation and affirmations, which I will come to shortly. The challenge lies in gaining control of these programming tools for the good, rather than allowing them to be continually hijacked by the bad.

Most people programme themselves for failure. They constantly give themselves failure instructions. They set themselves negative goals ('I'll never get that promotion', 'I can never lose weight'), and when they fail, they blame their upbringing, their education, their marital situation, or their impossible boss. They nestle so deeply into their Comfort Zone of misery that any encouragement to set positive goals, or to take responsibility for, and control of, their lives, is resisted with the stubbornness of a teenager trying to avoid getting up on a Sunday morning.

Your subconscious has the answer

The second role for the subconscious – to come up with solutions – is equally important, but for most people, grossly under-utilised. The subconscious is to be found in the Quiet Place – the private time you reserve in your mind to restore balance and perspective through quiet contemplation – and needs to be communicated with regularly (half an hour per day) to be properly effective. Most of the great religious and political leaders (Jesus, Moses, Confucius, Mohammed, Buddha, Gandhi, Lincoln, Churchill, Mao Tse-tung and Martin Luther King, to name but a few) spent considerable amounts of time alone, meditating and communicating with their subconscious minds. Some of this solitude was enforced, behind prison bars, but the individuals concerned got the taste for quiet reflection to gain perspective, and discover a new dimension, on the problems and challenges that faced them.

There are countless stories told of extraordinary, serendipitous events that followed from people listening to the promptings of their subconscious minds. One of these is told by Susan Jeffers about an experience that happened to her. While thinking through the implications of what was happening in her own life, and the work she was doing as a psychologist, she was communing one day with her subconscious when she received a clear message to go to New School. She was puzzled, because it was a college in New York with which she was unfamiliar, having done her graduate and doctoral work at other universities in the city.

None the less, she jumped into a taxi, to see where her subconscious would lead her. Having arrived, she found her way into the building, to attend, she assumed, a workshop. She met a woman in the corridor, who asked why she was there. Without thinking, she replied, 'To teach a class on overcoming Fear.' She was astounded at her reply, as the thought had not come from her conscious mind. She was even more astonished at the woman's response. 'Great,' she said, 'I'm the principal of the college, and I've been looking for someone for six months to teach a course on overcoming Fear. The deadline for outlines of course material is midday. You've got twelve minutes to write your course outline.' This happening changed Jeffers' life. She became a teacher and educator, wrote *Feel the Fear and Do it Anyway*, and changed the lives of many other people as well.

The Jeffers case history is a good one because it not only demonstrates the subconscious at work, but also the crucial aspect that the best

exponents stress – *take action immediately*. The instructions and suggestions issuing from the subconscious should be written down on a pad
held ready for the purpose and, if possible, acted upon instantly. *The
instructions are time dated, and are relevant for now*, not next week or for
next year.

Briefing your subconscious – affirmations

Affirmations are the secular versions of prayers. They are framed to
communicate with the subconscious, just as prayers are framed to
communicate with the soul (with God as an additional interlocutor).
They are repeated frequently and consistently, because spaced repetition
helps to confirm and consolidate the message.

The Christian believer saying, 'Lead us not into temptation, and
deliver us from evil' imparts a briefing to the soul in the same way as my
saying, 'I feel power and confidence in every activity I undertake'
imparts a briefing to my subconscious. Both messages are communicated
because we both know we are likely to come under pressure during the
course of the day, which will put both sets of statements to the test, and
us along with them.

Affirmations, like prayers I assume, are extremely valuable in arming
yourself for life's challenges. To be effective (although nobody is quite
sure why) they must be in the *present tense*, and they should obviously be
positive. 'I am strong and I am worthy' works, whereas 'I will be strong,
and I will be worthy' doesn't.

Making up your own affirmations for reading, preferably aloud, each
morning, on getting up, and each evening before going to bed, can be
fun. It's also very helpful in adding strength to parts of the IBG armoury,
and indeed, personal armoury, that need working on. Affirmations can
usefully include your Brand Positioning Statement, and your personal
Mission Statement (see next chapter). This clarifies to the subconscious
who you are, and the principles and values with which you approach
life.

Affirmations tend to be private – shared between you and your
subconscious, and possibly your mirror – but I will share one or two of
mine to give some insight into how yours might be articulated. I have a
card on which I have written my affirmations. It is important that they
are written down. It is important also that they are semi-public. This is

you *going on record to yourself and your subconscious.* So if a family member finds the card, this should only add further to your resolve to accomplish the things you have written down to achieve.

Don't worry if on some of them you are only taking the first steps – we are talking about a journey, not a destination. You will, in any case, gain respect for identifying what you want to become, and taking positive action to achieve that state. Note that all the affirmations are in the present tense, and all are positive ('I am calm,' works, but 'I will not be angry,' doesn't).

My first affirmation is, 'I have a fantastic positive mental attitude.' I affirm this because I know that it is vital that I make it true 100 per cent of the time, not 90 or 95 per cent of the time. My next affirmation is, 'I am a person who feels power and confidence in every activity I undertake'. This is to confirm that whatever situation I find myself in, I know that I can not only cope, but cope well. It prods me into looking for the bigger dimension, and the new added value, when the strong temptation is just to cope until things settle down a bit.

'I always show grace under pressure' is an affirmation that, on some days, needs repeating with some frequency. It helps me to be on my best behaviour, whatever has hit the fan. I sometimes, when in a situation demanding the reiteration of the affirmation, find myself asking myself, 'What does Grace look like?' which brings a shaft of humour into the situation, as well as taking it halfway towards being a visualisation (see below).

Another affirmation is, 'I feel joy and good humour all day'. This is an interesting and important one. If our objective in life is to be happy, let's try to fulfil it as frequently as possible. No waiting till we've got more money, are slimmer, a relation who invited herself to stay has left, or that promotion at work comes through. Let's be happy now. There are many happenings in the course of a day that can be the source of joy, and can contribute towards happiness. *This affirmation helps us to avoid waking up one day to find that life is over, and we've forgotten to be happy.*

There are two helpful variations on this, which I thought sounded totally daft when I first heard them. The first is to smile at yourself when you first look at yourself in the mirror each morning. Sometimes this takes real effort, but is always worthwhile. This is a genuine smile, not a sickly grin. This gets easier and easier with practice, and the reason it works is that it is impossible to smile broadly without actually *feeling* better inside. The second variation is to stand in front of the mirror and say ten times, with feeling, the word 'enthusiasm'. By the end you really will be smiling – partly because what you are doing is so manifestly silly, and partly because it works.

A further small affirmation that I don't make every day, but sometimes wish I did, is, 'I am good at receiving advice when driving.' Lizzie is not a back-seat driver. She sits in the front seat, but on the passenger side. To be fair, my concentration is not always total, and family lives are important. Also, my sense of location is not perfect (I am dyslexic in topography – I can be in a ski resort for a fortnight, and still not know how the lifts and runs connect up). The persistence of the advice does, however, at times demand constant reaffirmations during relatively short journeys.

One of the roles of affirmations is to enable the garden of the mind to be cleared of the weeds, briars and brambles that sprout there with such profusion. Once uprooted, as any gardener knows, something productive or beneficial has to be planted quickly, and tended carefully, to prevent re-encroachment by the undergrowth. Affirmations are the seedcrops that will ultimately flower and provide the fruits which enable you to be productive and effective as an individual.

Affirmations can also be used in a more tactical way to address specific challenges. As we will see later, in Susan Jeffers' Pain to Power vocabulary, (pages 169–70), the specific programming of the mind to handle difficult situations positively can transform the chances of success and, indeed, survival. On a more trivial level, affirmations can be used to contain those frustrations that we know are coming, but are still difficult to cope with. One such challenge for me is negotiating the Péripherique – the motorway system around Paris.

We have to negotiate a sizeable portion of this complex road system two or three times a year. The challenge is that the cars move very fast on it, but the French take a perverse delight in confusing travellers with signage that keeps changing the names of the towns you are aiming for, on a seemingly random basis. This is not my topographical dyslexia – Lizzie is totally concentrated on it as well. At least 10 per cent of the traffic on the Péripherique could be removed, if the people using it were given the information to get off it at the correct exit. On the last couple of occasions I have made affirmations that I would not succumb to a loss of temper at the signage system. I have managed to last about five minutes longer each time, but I have yet to survive the course.

What this small example demonstrates is that affirmations do work, but they are not easy. Undoing a lifetime's scripting cannot be achieved overnight. Dramatic and almost instantaneous effects can be achieved with some of the applications of Neurolinguistic Programming, as we shall see later, but even here, considerable effort often has to be applied to establish, or maintain, the states that enable, or paralyse, our ability to act effectively. The point is that the hard work is rewarded. Behaviour – and lives – can be changed for the better by the application of these simple techniques that man has been aware of, in the form of prayer, for centuries. The key elements to their success are *repetition and conviction*. Unless affirmations are made regularly, and with *belief*, their effect will be noticeable, but a long way below their true potential.

A small additional affirmation for the Independent Business Generator might be the use of the IBG initials in a further context. At times of challenge (like being turned down for a project, or going into a tough meeting), the following affirmation may be helpful: *'I'm an Independent Business Generator. I'm an IBG, and I'm Bloody Good!'*

Briefing the subconscious – visualisations

Visualisation is the three-dimensional, multicoloured, singing-and-dancing version of affirmations that enables the subconscious to prefigure future achievement or success. It is a basic and fundamental human attribute, and one that can literally be the difference between surviving and not surviving.

When Victor Frankl, the Freudian psychologist, was examining the discriminating factors that enabled him, and many like him to survive in the hell of the Nazi concentration camps, the key factor was the ability to visualise another reality. There was no pattern in terms of education, health, strength, or upbringing. The one thing all the survivors shared – and the future survivors of similar harsh treatment in Korea and Vietnam – was the ability to visualise. Each survivor had a vision of something beyond their current suffering, something more worthwhile, something worth hanging on for.

This underlines the importance of each individual having a vision of something, outside and larger than themselves, that gives their life some meaning. The very existence of a mission lifts the eyes to something more meaningful and enduring – and in so doing provides something to live for – at times when quiet surrender could be an attractive option. Such a vision gives a further *raison d'être* for integrity, *by providing a purpose that binds together the core values that make up self-worth.*

One of the most powerful – and difficult to achieve – applications of visualisation is to focus your mind daily on *the person you intend to become*. Create a clear mental picture of that person – and see it in full colour, and add sounds and smells, if they are appropriate. The emotional values you add to the visualisation are vital in making the full connection to your subconscious, which acts only on thoughts that are mixed with emotions. These techniques are, of course, widely validated in fields like sport and business, where the peak performers are nearly all visualisers. They all see, feel, and fully experience their success before they achieve it.

One or two of my own visualisations may help to throw further light on this crucial area of personal development. As well as visualising before getting out of bed in the morning the person I intend to become, I also, throughout the day, have certain visualisations that are specific to my own business targets. These take the form of visualisation of the rewards I have committed to giving myself for the achievement of these targets. One of these is a sit-on lawnmower for our house in France. We have an area of grass to mow that would be considerably facilitated by a sit-on, rather than a hand, mower.

I have taken longer than I would have hoped to achieve the target in question, so I am still using the hand mower, though I could easily purchase the sit-on mower I want. Herein lies the important principle of *delayed gratification*. The principle of delayed gratification says that your rewards are not taken until they are earned.

Ray Kroc, who built the McDonald's business, was the embodiment of delayed gratification. Although by no means a wealthy man, and fifty-six when he took over the operation, he still did not pay himself anything for the first six years he was building the business. Taking premature rewards devalues all goal-setting and always ends in tears.

I have pictures of the mower I want (it's a red one), and I visualise myself sitting on it. The sun is hot, I can smell the new-mown grass, and the machine is so efficient it will be no time at all before I can sink into the pool, or open an ice-cold beer. The reward for another goal is to take the family to Disneyland. Again I visualise the plane door opening and the Florida heat hitting me as I emerge, blinking, into the dazzling sunshine. I can hear us shrieking as we go down watershoots and roller-coasters. I can feel my affirmations about liking hamburgers working, as I find every bite delicious.

A visualisation for a less specific target – abundant financial wealth – is arriving at our French home by helicopter, cutting out the rather tortuous journey, whether by train, car or plane. I can hear the noise of the helicopter, and I can see the trees blown by its down-draught. The grass is flattened as we run, crouching, for the house. A final, small visualisation is the more familiar one of driving straight at golf. Intensely visualising long, straight drives, can be surprisingly effective. Unfortunately my concentration is not yet good enough for it to work on every hole. But it will be.

Negative visualisations work in a similar way. Take another example in golf. If you are approaching a green surrounded by bunkers, with a pond between you and the green, your only chance of hitting the green is to concentrate on it, to the exclusion of all else. Once the mind dwells on water or sand, you are visualising failure. The *negative magnet effect* comes into force, drawing your ball into perdition.

The new dimension of NLP

Neurolinguistic Programming utilises visualisation in many of its techniques. Anthony Robbins, one of its most effective exponents, even had attendees at his early seminars walking across red-hot coals to demonstrate to them that if they achieved an empowered state, and visualised fire-walking with no pain or harmful effects, they could achieve this feat with no other training or support. Robbins is a powerful writer and communicator, and repays close study. One of his underlying precepts is that we all have enabling states, and paralysing states.

Enabling states are states in which we feel joy, confidence, love, inner strength, ecstasy, belief. Paralysing states are states in which we feel anxiety, confusion, depression, fear, low self-worth, sadness, frustration. Our behaviour tends to be a direct result of the state we are in. If we are in an enabled state we are Mighty Lions. We operate at optimum effectiveness, and feel empowered to take on the world. In a paralysed state we feel feeble and find it difficult to initiate or lead. We tend to coast, until we begin to feel enabled and resourceful again. It is Robbins' goal to teach us to control our states, so that we can be in a resourceful, enabled state either most of the time, or, failing that, be able to summon up such a state at will.

Changing moods and creating moods incorporates action we can take to control not only ourselves, but to a more limited degree other people as well. Robbins demonstrates that it is important to *interrupt the pattern* of a mood to achieve success. This usually involves changing the physical posture, which induces an immediate opportunity for change in emotional mood. These interruptions of moods can be particularly helpful with children. If a child is crying, the first thing to do is to attempt to get the child to look up, and keep looking up. It is very difficult to cry when you're looking upwards, and this can often do the trick on its own.

Failing that, get the child involved in some positive action, like walking, running or jumping, to interrupt the mood pattern. I put this teaching into practice soon after reading it. My three-year-old niece came to stay with us, a child of outstanding power and vehemence in the performance of temper-tantrums. I did not have long to wait. She soon produced a magnificent display, throwing herself onto a small sofa near the doors leading out to the garden. I walked over, opened a door, grabbed the child, who was operating at full throttle, carried her into the garden, and pretended to throw her into the goldfish pond. The effect was instantaneous. She stopped crying, and roared with laughter. I then had a problem. For the next quarter of an hour she insisted that I kept pretending to throw her into the pond.

The experience left me exhausted, but determined to try other pattern interrupts, and mood control techniques. One of these techniques Robbins calls anchoring. An anchor is a sensory stimulus linked to specific state. Pavlov's dogs were anchored by the bell to produce a state of salivation, ready for food.

In the extrapolation made by Robbins you pre-construct a whole battery of positive feelings, and anchor them in a simple physical gesture – say, making a fist. So if you were an athlete, for example, you would visualise yourself at a point when you were at peak condition, winning a specific race. You would then relive – physically and emotionally – what it felt like on that occasion. This reconfiguration of the event should be done with great intensity. You should re-experience the sight, the sounds, the smell – all the sensory experiences – of what it felt like to be at peak performance.

The next step is to stack several of these experiences, and anchor them all into the same stimulus – say, the clenched fist. I tried this, and had dramatic results. I anchored four experiences from my own life. The first was running out onto the turf for a game of rugby I had played in at Twickenham. I could see the intensely green grass, I could smell its wet odour in the rain, and I could hear the almost overwhelming roar of 65,000 people. I felt as if I could run through a brick wall. The next experience I anchored was the first London marathon, which I ran with my brother and two close friends. It was our first marathon, so for all of us it was uncharted territory. The point I relived intensely was running past Buckingham Palace at the end of the race. We all held hands as we ran, grinning stupidly in the drizzle, and crying our eyes out.

The third experience I relived was the end of a meeting I chaired – the first of a think-tank of chief executives I brought together as one of my early initiatives as an IBG. As I drew the meeting to a close, one of the members kindly asked for a round of applause for the chairman, which was unexpected, and delightful to receive. The fourth experience was similar, as it involved a speech I made at a charity dinner, which fortunately was well received. I intensely relived standing there, with the audience receptive, and the applause coming where I had hoped it would.

I was not comfortable with Robbins' rather American example of a fist in the air, or a high five, as it might have caused some embarrassment at the delicate point of a meeting or presentation that wasn't going too well – the sort of time I might need some supercharge of confidence that the anchor was intended to provide. I therefore used a pressure by my thumb onto my forefinger in a closed fist as my trigger point for the anchor. I tried it out once or twice in dry-run situations, and it seemed to work.

A couple of days later I went for my usual three-mile run and, as is the case from time to time, I started to struggle to sustain the already slow pace some way before the end. Without thinking, my fist closed, and my thumb bit into my forefinger. I found myself surging – running much faster than I intended to. It was uncomfortable, to say the least. This kept happening, and it was some time before I realised what was going on. I had triggered my anchor. I was a Mighty Lion athlete, but I was running in the body of a clapped-out lion. By the time I arrived home I felt like I had run thirteen, rather than three, miles. I have since relocated my trigger, to avoid such painful mistakes happening again.

Living out visualisations: <u>act as if</u> – the three most powerful words in personal development

Visualisation, like affirmations, require effort but, as my personal experience demonstrates, can produce dramatic results. Doug Hooper tells the story, which took place during his time teaching prisoners, of an inmate named Carl, who was disablingly shy and introverted. He even had trouble saying his name. Hooper was teaching a class on visualisation and telling the prisoners that anything was possible, if only they would believe it. The prisoners decided to put Hooper on the spot. Carl was out of the room at the time, so one of the prisoners suggested that when he came back, Hooper should make him into a great public speaker. The class roared with delight. Hooper, with trepidation, accepted the challenge.

When Carl came back into the room, Hooper took him to a corner, and spoke quietly to him. He told Carl he wanted him to try an experiment. He reassured him that he wasn't going to ask him to say anything, but he did ask him to go back to his seat and try to visualise what it would be like to be a great public speaker. He then suggested that he should visualise walking to the front of the class, *acting as if he were a great speaker*. Still acting out the role, he would make a short speech, which would produce a standing ovation of five minutes. Hooper then suggested that when he had visualised this for twenty minutes or so, he should walk to the front anyway, turn, look at the class. He could then either continue to act as a great speaker, or, if he didn't feel like saying anything, go and sit down again.

Carl reluctantly agreed and returned to his seat. Hooper watched him out of the corner of his eye for the next twenty minutes or so. Carl sat there with his eyes closed, with a grin occasionally flitting across his face. After almost half an hour, Carl opened his eyes, stood up, and strode purposefully to the front of the class. Brushing Hooper aside, who was standing there open-mouthed, he turned, and started to speak. He gave a fifteen-minute speech, which was brilliant, and received, just as he had visualised, a five-minute standing ovation. Hooper was obviously delighted, but said that he lived to regret his action. Thereafter Carl couldn't stop talking, wanted to offer his opinion on everything, and developed into a consistent pain in the neck!

This is exactly what Polonius was talking about when he said to Laertes, 'Assume a habit, and you have it.' *Acting as if* is one of the most intense forms of visualisation, because all the physical, mental, and emotional aspects come together as *you literally act out your visualisation in a real-life situation*.

Doug Hooper had a similar challenge to Carl, when he was phoned by a lady with what seemed like an insoluble problem. Her son was on the high school basketball team, which had not won a match all season. That Saturday they were playing the league champions, who had not lost a match all season. Morale, understandably, was at rock bottom, and some of the boys didn't even want to play in the match, not wanting to experience the humiliation at first hand. The mother pleaded with Hooper to come and work some magic on the boys. Hooper hadn't a clue how he would turn the situation round, but he accepted anyway.

The reason he accepted was interesting: he had made a promise to himself that to ensure his own personal growth would be as fast as it possibly could be, *he would accept any project that could result in him learning something*. This was a fundamental attempt to achieve rapid Comfort Zone Growth. He was in his late fifties at the time, and it ultimately resulted in his becoming, in his early sixties, both nationally recognised as a great motivational teacher, and financially comfortable for the first time in his life.

Back to the story. Hooper went to meet the boys at the mother's home on the Friday evening. He by now had a strategy. He would apply the same thinking as he had in the case of Carl. The boys arrived. Their heads were down and they couldn't meet his eye. They were all dreading what the next day would bring. Hooper sat them down, and said to them, 'OK, boys, forget the real situation. I want you all to close your eyes, and *act as if you are the team that are league leaders*, and haven't lost a game all season. Imagine yourself running onto the court, bouncing with confidence, because you *know* you are going to thrash the other side. Imagine yourself shooting from far out, and all the shots going in. And most of all, imagine the end of the game. The crowd will rise, and both teams of supporters will give you a five-minute ovation.'

Hooper stayed with them for an hour or so, helping them to visualise the situation intensely, and advising them to continue the visualisation when they went to bed that night. He then returned home. Late the following evening, he received a telephone call from the mother, who was totally hoarse, but ecstatic. All he could understand from her was that her son's team had won 71–70. A week later he received a cutting from the local newspaper in the mail.

The report of the match detailed the extraordinary happenings of the day. The reporter marvelled at the fact that when the bottom-of-the-league team came on, they bounced around the court, high fiving, so that 'anyone would have thought it was they who were the league champions'. He went on to describe the boys shooting from enormous distances, with the majority of shots miraculously go in. He finished the report by saying that at the end of the match both sets of supporters were so excited, and so admiring, that they gave the team a five-minute standing ovation.

An Abundance Mentality can transform the situation

An **Abundance Mentality** (Covey again) was a new concept to me, and took some growing accustomed to. It is one of the character traits that needs to be developed to achieve primary greatness. My personal scripting of the genuine scarcity of the postwar years – make do, and mend, was the slogan – has made this challenging to achieve.

My father was an extremely generous man, who had to live with financial challenges that would have made a smaller man bitter with what life had handed him. He had very few options, if any, to escape from the situation in which he found himself. His father had died suddenly when he was still at school. He had to leave school at sixteen to support his mother. Having no chance of going to university, or to qualify as an architect, as he wanted to do, he took what in those days was a good job – he joined a bank. As he started to climb the career ladder, war was declared. He had already volunteered as a reservist, and was taken straight off to join the army. For six years when he might have been building a career, he was a serving officer in the Royal Artillery.

The point of this history is that when he was demobilised in 1945, he had a wife that was no longer working (mothers didn't in those days), and two young children. His salary as a major was £1,000 per annum. When he returned to the bank, his salary was £400. He attempted to emigrate to Canada with his wife and young children, but was prevented by his mother, who interceded with some heavy moral blackmail. So, at the age of thirty-six he set about taking more exams, and working his way up the ladder again. The labour market was oversupplied, so it was many years before his approached £1,000 again.

As a result of the shortage of money for anything but the essentials in those years up till the mid-1950s, he developed a habit of turning off electric lights and appliances if they were not being used. He took it to such an extent that we offered to climb into the refrigerator to check that the light went off when the door was closed.

I vowed I would never do the same when I had a family. Despite my best intentions, I continually find myself a slave to my early scripting, and cannot resist the urge to turn off any light or appliance that is not in use. Fortunately, I can now justify it to a degree on environmental grounds (avoiding waste of the earth's natural resources), but the real reason is that it stems from a **Scarcity Mentality** with which I was imbued in my formative years.

The Scarcity Mentality as a concept is much larger than trying to save money on electricity bills. Essentially, it is about seeing life as a pie, with only so many slices. If someone has a slice, it means there is less to go around. This applies to all resources, not just possessions or money, but success, praise, gratitude – even love. Most people, whether they are aware of it or not, are scripted in a Scarcity Mentality.

The implications can be profound. They feel, knowing it to be irrational, that if a friend, or even a member of their family, meets with success, that they themselves are in some way reduced. They resent success in others, because it means there is less success left for them. They have trouble sharing power, because shared power, rather than potentially enhancing the overall effectiveness of an operation, is merely a direct dilution of their own power, and thus effectiveness.

The other side of the coin is equally true. Their own successes are enhanced if others suffer setback, or even failure, as a result. They fight on a win/lose strategy, and find the concept of win/win negotiation woolly-minded, soft and unrealistic. *For an IBG such a mentality can be enormously inhibiting.* An IBG's strategy is to build a wide range of core, alternative and second income streams, so that when some wither and die, either others deliver more copiously, or new ones spring up to take their place. A Scarcity mindset at times of employment loss, or an arid spell when two or three streams dry up at once, could cause the mind to freeze, and a sense of impending endless drought to take over.

For this reason, if for no other, it is important to develop an Abundance Mentality. An Abundance Mentality sees richness of resource everywhere. With more than enough to go around, no one needs to go short, and everyone can rejoice at the success of others. Francis Bacon's approach of 'a joy shared is a joy doubled, and a sorrow shared is a sorrow halved', was coined for those with an Abundance Mentality. Power, responsibility, and decisions can be shared without danger. Any situation can be improved, made bigger and richer, because there is plenty of goodwill, talent and generosity to go round.

Win/win is the natural mindset for those people who can achieve the Abundance Mentality. It requires courage, consideration, generosity, but above all the fundamental *belief that the cake can be made bigger for the benefit of all.* Small thinking, begrudging others praise or recognition, adversarial relationships – none of these has any place in the thoughts – or feelings – of someone with an Abundance Mentality. It does, of course, require both a strong sense of self-worth, and courage, to think and act consistently in this way.

One extrapolation of Abundance thinking that I have found extremely helpful was suggested by a practising psychologist who is also a very successful distributor in the network marketing group to which Lizzie and I belong. He suggested carrying a minimum of £100 pounds in your pocket, or handbag, at all times. Creating a float of £100 could be quite challenging in itself for some people, but it could repay the effort. As an IBG, however much income you are generating, the flow of income can be extremely uneven. A core income stream is likely to be regular, but for people, like myself, living on a combination of consultancy, business projects, and network marketing, much of the income is spasmodic, as clients pay at different speeds.

The monthly pay day doesn't happen, but the rest of the world is still sending you invoices on a monthly basis. To make matters worse, however much you are earning, you tend to spend at a slightly higher rate, as hitherto suppressed needs reveal themselves and require satisfying. The money comes in more slowly than expected, leaving a gap in the cash flow forecast. At such times, you feel strapped for cash, and can easily start to worry. Every reasonable request for cash from the family is greeted with an inner groan, before the money is handed over, slightly grudgingly, making all concerned feel reduced, and even guilty for asking.

Carrying a £100 in cash does not, as I expected, cause you to spend more, because it is there, but it does enable you to hand over *cash you would have spent anyway* with a much more open heart. It is a win/win situation. The recipients don't feel guilty, and you don't feel that unattractive and negative mixture of emotions – resentment at an unexpected reduction of sparse funds, and guilt that you're not providing well enough for your family, and not doing it with enough grace and generosity.

No one can hurt you without your consent

The £100 float in the pocket or handbag is an interesting example of our need for all the help we can get along the way to significant personal development. If our attitudes were right in terms of an Abundance Mentality we would not need physical cash to help us feel abundant. The reality is that, as we travel along the road to developing ourselves as fuller, more positive, contributing, and happy individuals, we need a few props along the way. All the time we are striving – and succeeding – in getting onto the front foot in controlling our lives and our responses, we keep being forced onto the back foot – fighting the shite, and trying to contain its ability to unsettle us.

While we fight the daily battles with the light weaponry, it is fundamentally important to develop the heavy artillery that will win the war. As we develop greatness inside, the attitudes that will enable us to fight life's daily skirmishes will fall into place naturally. *The heaviest weapon we have – which is nuclear in its potential power – is the understanding and belief that we control our own responses and feelings.*

In the words of Ghandi, 'They cannot take away our self-respect, if we do not give it to them.' While great leaders and thinkers have instinctively felt this down the ages, much early twentieth century psychological thinking followed the determinist philosophy of Sigmund Freud. Freud believed that early upbringing and experiences conditioned our responses, which gave us a predetermined response pattern to a given situation. Thus conscience, or the super-ego, was a social product, and the scripting of behaviour was so powerful as to be incapable of being influenced by individual will.

Victor Frankl was a Freudian psychologist who, as a Jew, was put into various concentration and death camps during the Second World War. His parents, wife and brother died in the gas ovens. He was tortured, humiliated, and given the job of body removal from the ovens. Alone and despairing, he came to find what he later called 'the last of the human freedoms'. The Nazis controlled everything about his situation and condition. Everything, that is, *apart from how it was going to affect him.* This was the antithesis of determinism.

Frankl visualised himself lecturing to students, after the war, expounding on the lessons he learned under torture. He did this even while he was being tortured. He eventually developed an inner freedom, which used elements of memory, combined with elements of imagination. He became an inspiration to other prisoners, helping them to find meaning and dignity in a situation that appeared desperate, and without hope.

This fundamental freedom to choose our response to a situation is at the heart of the development of integrity and a proactive attitude. Our behaviour and our feelings are a function of our *decisions*, that in turn flow from our sense of self-worth. Our conditions and situation provide the framework, but not the response itself. *We* decide our response, so there are no excuses. Reactive people fail to do this, and become *victims* to their situation. *Proactive people take responsibility for their feelings.* They are driven by their own set of values, that transcend those of the conditions around them.

Proactive people carry their own weather with them

This striking phrase of Stephen Covey sums up the ability all of us have to direct and control our own responses. There are no exceptions. Doug Hooper provides a good example of this. Hooper was a volunteer prison visitor in one of the toughest prisons in America, who taught proactive response to some of the most intractable situations imaginable. He taught there once a month, applying the lessons he had learned himself in studying the subject in his spare time.

His insight into carrying your own weather around came before such a visit, when, one day, he was walking along a street with a friend. The friend stopped at a kiosk to get a newspaper and some matches. The newsvendor was gratuitously rude, but Hooper's friend was charming back. On querying the newsvendor's ill-humour, his friend told him that he was always like that. Puzzled, Hooper asked him why he treated him with such friendly courtesy in return. The friend replied, 'You don't think I'm going to let someone like that control how I feel, do you?'

Later, Hooper was talking on the subject to the inmates of the jail, many of whom were serving long sentences for serious crimes of violence. One of them, with the unlikely name of Pearl, stopped him, and challenged him for personal advice. His situation seemed hopeless. As a prisoner who had no privileges because he was constantly being provoked into attacking staff, he was being woken at four o'clock each morning to be marched off to perform some demeaning punishment. His particular problem was that the guard who woke him each morning was vicious in his behaviour to him, and he was worried that one morning soon he would crack, doing the guard some serious physical damage.

Hooper saw that the situation looked impossible for Pearl, because he believed he had no power to influence his situation. Hooper's response could have been diagnosed by Frankl. He took the course of explaining to Pearl that the guard obviously had problems himself, because no happy person, with a sense of self-worth, would behave in that way. He suggested that Pearl's response to the volley of abuse at four in the morning, should be to say, 'Good morning, guard.'

A month later, Hooper returned for his next visit in some trepidation as to what might have happened. He need not have worried. Pearl immediately asked for permission to address the rest of the class. He told the class how he had carried out Hooper's instructions, and that the effect had been stunning. It had stopped the guard in his tracks. Within days they were chatting together, and after four weeks, Pearl was now being woken very gently. They were getting along like old friends.

It's not what happens, but how we respond to it – Positive Response is transformational

Taking positive action to change our thinking about a situation that seems impossible goes a long way to transforming the situation itself. **Positive Response** – rather than mere positive thinking – acknowledges the realities of the situation, and *acts* upon them positively. Feeling follows action, so we feel better about the situation, having taken the positive action.

We are not talking about smiling-as-we-sink, pretending things are great, when they are obviously not. We are talking about *looking for the good*, and responding to serious challenges with courage and maturity. It is about making choices to be brave, when everything is conspiring to excuse a quiet drawing up of the covers. It is about resorting to mind leadership, so that the larger dimension is looked for.

Prisoners of war who underwent torture or brainwashing in Korea and Vietnam were extensively screened on returning home, to discover why some had coped with what they had experienced, while the majority had not. The findings confirmed Frankl's experiences. The ones who, like Frankl, survived well, all had one thing in common. They had a vision of life that was larger than the experience they were going through. For many, this was religious belief. For others it was a belief in the important benefits of freedom and democracy. The harder their captors tried to dissuade them, the firmer their beliefs became.

The positive and courageous response to a challenging situation can transform that situation not only for the person caught in the heart of it, but also for other people involved. My father was an example of such a response. Having stuck for forty years to a job he did not enjoy, he had for a long time yearned for retirement, to spend time with my mother pursuing their interests together. The bank tried very hard to entice him to stay on, but he was adamant. Within very few years, he contracted lung cancer, and was given a year to live.

At this point it would have been very easy for him to become resentful with the cards fate had dealt him. Having seen his brother die of lung cancer two years previously, he knew the physical challenge would be considerable. Rather than putting his head down, and sinking, he lifted his head up, and *resolved to make his last year the happiest year of his life*. The effect was extraordinary. I visited him most weekends, and I got to know him better than I would have done otherwise. He made each weekend a time of humour, and at times, joy. I always left on Sunday evening in a happier mood than I had arrived on Friday evening. He transformed his situation in a way that made it a happy year for all of us, despite our knowing its inevitable finale would be his death.

A Positive Response to a situation means, by definition, you cannot be its victim

By unwittingly applying the rules of Mind Leadership, my father transformed his situation, and removed himself from being its victim. He looked for a larger dimension (the goal of it being the happiest year of his life), and he added new value (by being genuinely amusing and cheerful, when he could have been lying down recovering from coughing fits). He remained in control of the situation, and did not allow himself to become its victim.

Susan Jeffers is especially good on defining the importance of a positive response to maintain control in situations that could easily overwhelm. Her memorable injunction, *'If life gives you lemons, make lemonade'* gets to the heart of the belief that underlies the work of most personal development thinkers and writers, that action-orientated positive response is geared to helping you create meaning and purpose out of whatever life hands you. Saying 'yes' to a situation, and getting on with it, demonstrates both courage and realism. Pain is acknowledged – for denial is potentially lethal – and rebuilding starts from an honest and solid base.

Jeffers relates the moving story of Charles, a young gang leader from the ghetto, who is shot through the spine in a gang fight and left paralysed from the waist down. His life is shattered and has no meaning. The hospital is about to give up on him and put him back without support into his tenement block, because he shows no inclination to cooperate with any rehabilitation. He realises his last chance is about to be blown, and sets to with a will. Once he took the decision to stop being a victim of his situation, and to start building from the new base, Charles grew daily as a person.

As well as mastering the skills of a wheelchair, he mastered the skills of social interaction. For the first time in his life, respect was not earned by demonstrating physical toughness, but by entering the give and take of everyday life with something to give as well as to take. He became an inspirational youth leader, fighting the culture of drugs and crime in his own ghetto. The last image we have of Charles is at a party organised for some elderly people by the youth workers. Dancing is announced, and there is some understandable reluctance to start the dancing. Charles drives his wheelchair onto the dance floor, starts spinning in time to the music, shouting, 'Come on!! If I can do it, you can!' He had come a long way – through his own ultimately positive response – from being the self-pitying victim of a gangland shooting.

The Victim Mentality creates its own vocabulary

Settling comfortably into the **Victim mentality** in any situation that demands courage is understandable, because it is the natural thing to do. We are conditioned to respond in such a way because telling stories to each other about the things that went wrong are part of the stock-in-trade of everyday conversation. The car that broke down, the illness or the injury we have sustained, the awful boss, the difficult children, the disastrous holiday, all form part of a pattern of our daily sufferings. Nothing ever goes right for us. We revel in the humour of the mishaps that befall us. Indeed, comedians make whole careers out of telling bad luck stories.

The danger is that what is intended as self-deprecating humour – 'Listen, this is drole, you'll never guess the latest disaster that happened to me' – becomes over time crystallised into a consistent mindset. We become the hapless victim of a world that conspires to frustrate and afflict us at every turn. We control neither the situation, nor our response to it. Instead, we derive a certain comfort from being a victim, because it gives us an emotional bond and kinship with the rest of humanity, who are also suffering from fortune's slings and arrows.

From the mindset of the victim flows the vocabulary of the victim. All responsibility is abnegated. 'Things happen to me – I can't control them' is the unspoken precept on which the victim mentality is based. *'It's not my fault' is the implication of all victim thinking.* What develops from this thinking is a *comfort zone of misery*. Humour can confirm this comfort zone as a good place to be, as there are plenty of people ready to identify with it, and establish a warm sense of fellow-suffering.

The reversal of the vocabulary is the first step in reversing the mentality, and with it the pernicious attractiveness of its comfort zone. This is step one in Comfort Zone Growth. It is the most difficult step, because it means breaking old, and comfortable habits. It is like a plane taking off – all the effort is at the front end, getting it airborne. Language is the key, because it has the power to lead the reorientation in thinking.

'I choose' replaces 'I have to'. 'Let's look for a bigger dimension on this – what are the alternatives and consequences?' takes over from, 'There's nothing I can do'.

Eventually, as the shift in vocabulary takes place, away from victim, towards control and responsibility, the ability develops to achieve a proactive, positive response. At this point fundamental shifts can take place. 'I get tense every time my boss comes near me', or 'the way she treats me tears me apart', can become 'I control my feelings', or 'I'm responsible, and in control'. There is a long distance between the two approaches, but the ground can be covered in a relatively short period, if there is a commitment and determination to do so.

This progress from victim to controller via the development of non-victim vocabulary is recognised by many of the personal development teachers and writers, and is well defined by Susan Jeffers as the movement from Pain to Power vocabulary. The most important shift in thinking via language she covers is that from, 'What will I do?' to *'I know I can handle it'*. The confidence of knowing you can handle anything life can throw at you is immensely reassuring. Repeating the phrase frequently to yourself keeps this reassurance topped up.

Enjoy working for Team me

The message of this chapter is that there are some excellent and effective personal development tools available to help you enjoy operating as an IBG. The Independent part of being an Independent Business Generator means that you have to learn to enjoy the sometimes *radical change in outlook required in the shift from being a player in one team, to being a player on several teams*. Apart from your core income stream, which may be more traditional in team orientation, your other activities will all feature you as a part-time actor. In some of the roles you will be a star. In others, you will be a bit-player.

The only consistent element through all your performances is **Team Me**. While you, and only you, are the team leader, you have a superb coach in all the personal and business development literature and cassette tapes that are available to enrich your mind and develop your life skills. Teams have great games and merely good games. Teams have great seasons, and merely good seasons. As team leader, it is your job to ensure you are up there consistently with the high flyers.

One of your jobs as team leader of Team Me will be to fulfil the role of a leader. This includes consistently taking the initiative in Comfort Zone Growth. To discover new continents you have to lose sight of the shore. This demands both courage, and a vision as to what lies in store on the new continent. To be a leader, you also need to be able to cope well with a crisis. A crisis will test your growth, and show – to yourself, and to others – what you are worth. Further crises will show how much you've learned, and how much you've grown in the meantime.

Leadership, too, is about persistence. As Winston Churchill so memorably put it, in his shortest speech ever, at a Commencement address in the United States, 'Never give up'. Keep failing until you succeed. The mark of a true leader is someone who keeps going when everyone has stopped. Persistence is one of the most dramatic demonstrations of your belief in yourself and your abilities. There is truth in the saying that success and failure are on the same road – success is just farther on down the road.

Another fundamental element of leadership is the ability to inspire people to want to follow you (I'm not talking about the Hitlers, who lead through fear). Leaders, above all, are confident people. They generate positive energy, they sidestep negative energy, and you feel you can trust them. They have integrity. With some leaders these aspects could be true as far as any follower is allowed to see. On the inside there may be cracks in the façade, but the leader is skilful enough for them never to show.

If you are leader of Team Me, you can look underneath the curtain. As leader, and led, you know the truth of your qualities. This makes it even more imperative than ever that you walk the talk. Despite Groucho Marx's brilliant line, 'All great men have integrity; if you can fake that, you've got it made', integrity can't be faked on a consistent basis. As Covey says, if you want a happy marriage, *be* a good husband, if you want a good relationship with your children *be* a good father, if you want to be trusted *be* trustworthy.

The gut issue is that you can't share something you haven't got. You can't make your family happy unless you're happy yourself. And if you can't achieve happiness, you can't count yourself successful as a human being. It all comes back to peace of mind through aligned values, integrity, and a well-founded sense of self-worth. And achieving sufficient insight and support from self-development programmes to grow internally as well as externally into the role of leader.

The good news is that it is achievable. Mind leadership, which is at the core of the process, builds, step by step, the robust inner worth, which in turn, manifests itself on the outside by a resilient and attractive confidence. By looking for a larger dimension, and to add new value,

Team Me becomes accustomed to *looking for ways that any situation can be improved, and not giving up until some answers have been found.* Whatever part of the IBG's range of incomes is concerned, the colleagues and clients he or she is working with will find this approach helpful, attractive, and possibly indispensable.

Herein lies the possibility of competitive advantage for an IBG. Having untethered the mind from the limiting paradigms of conventional performance – including vulnerability to mood swings – the leader of Team Me can present a confident and desirable package to any prospective customer, client or employer. This will be a potent combination of a consistently positive attitude, skills enhanced by the wider experience gained through other business activities, and a sense of mission that transcends the task in hand. The competitive advantage of the IBG for the employer, client or customer, is thus embodied in the title itself. *One of the defining characteristics of a generator is that it keeps going when all other power sources fail.*

The other rewarding result of consistent personal development is that if a client or employer is too myopic to see these advantages, and decides to terminate the relationship, Team Me will have the confidence to see the situation as a superb opportunity to find a more appreciative home for his or her outstanding talents.

As Mae West said, 'A good man is hard to find'. IBGs who are committed to personal development, and are enjoying their growth, will be good men – and women – for employers, clients, and customers, to find. They will be confident, good to work with, action-orientated, and effective in whatever they are asked to bring to the party. They will be looking to make things bigger and better. They will not think they can. They will know they can. And they'll be right.

NINE

Confidence and Action

THIS CHAPTER DEALS with some specific issues, and points of action, that spin out from personal development and positive thinking, that have not been covered in the previous chapters. It then looks at how our pioneers, Felicity, Norman and Simon are getting on, as the joys, and challenges, of being an IBG begin to crystallise.

Before continuing, for those who may still harbour doubts as to the importance and effectiveness of the subconscious, and have not had the opportunity of trying the 'I am and strong and worthy' experiment, now might be the time to try it. A picture is worth a thousand words. Doing is better than showing, and experience broadens the mind. What is there to lose?

The Enhancers and the Poisoners

History and religion are often perceived in terms of a titanic battle between the forces of good and evil. In personal development teaching this is given a more limited and slightly less value-laden focus, in the need to take action in the continuous fight between positive and negative. The battle is no less real, and the damage inflicted on the losers can be just as devastating. Surrender to negative influences can bring cowardice, hopelessness, dependency and failure. Espousal of positive influences, and the avoidance of negative, on the other hand, can bring growth, achievement, fulfilment and happiness.

To oversimplify to make the point, human beings break down into two categories – the **Enhancers**, and the **Poisoners**. The former seek to make things bigger and better. They are the givers in life, who delight in the success of others. They have an Abundance Mentality. The latter have a Scarcity Mentality. They are tethered thinkers. They are victims, on whom life continually plays harsh tricks, and they are keen to pollute everyone else with the shite in their lives. They complain, they moan, and, above all, *they lack courage to change things for the better*.

Toxic people should be avoided at all costs. Whatever is said to them, they twist it back into a negative interpretation. They reap a perverse sense of satisfaction in bringing anyone who is more positive than they down to their level of pessimism and cynicism. In the same way that children are encouraged to avoid other children who could influence them negatively, so adults are well advised to avoid Poisoners, because the effects can be similarly destructive.

The good news is that the power of association with others works both ways. Associating with positive, uplifting people is, in turn, inspiring and uplifting. The same is true of companies and other organisations. *Good companies and organisations build a culture of excellence*, within which good people associate, and in so doing, help each other to become outstanding. Not-so-good companies, and organisations, similarly attract similar quality people, who associate with each other at their level of ability, competence and enthusiasm. It takes enormous effort, skill and commitment to winch a company or organisation up to a new level. It takes no effort at all to let the poisoners hold sway, and watch it slip down the rankings.

Speak only well of people

It is also important to detoxify your own thoughts – and words. Speak only well of people. Society is already drowning in negative without you adding to it. The television news, the newspapers, much conversation, are full of negative, all of which needs purging or diluting. Smart remarks, put-downs, bad-mouthing, gossip, are all the grist of the daily conversational mill. All of this hurts. The pain is inflicted on both ourselves, and others, and sometimes maims.

Several of the personal development teachers advocate an effective antidote to this would-be-harmless-but-in-fact-harmful conversation. The antidote is this. Imagine you only have four weeks to live. Would you then go around behaving in that way? Would you rather be remembered as someone who was kind, considerate, and built people up, or as someone who was snide, superficial, and deflated others at every opportunity?

The temptation to stay with the poisonous, smart-alec, mockers is huge. It's where the bulk of humanity is – a ready-made comfort zone – outside the tent, pissing in. The first steps to extricate yourself are challenging. In the early days it's hard not to join in, especially if you have heard some amusing anecdote about someone's misfortune, or comeuppance. After a little it becomes easier and easier, and eventually only very occasionally do you fall into the bad old ways.

Look for the good – even in the bad

There are three other areas in the positive/negative debate, and the action that comes out of them, that all the personal development teachers seem to agree on. The first is that however bad an occurrence or situation might be, good will eventually come from it – if you believe it will. An example of this is the death of one of the partners in a couple. Despite the profound sadness of the loss of the loved one, often a remaining spouse who takes a positive view on life as a whole, will, after a period of necessary grieving, grow and flourish in the new-found single state. This does not belittle the dead partner, it just shows that good always does come from bad, if the person concerned is looking for it.

The Chinese word for crisis means 'opportunity riding on a dangerous wind'. This has also been articulated as 'every adversity carries within it the seeds of a greater benefit'. This all sounds a bit homespun, and down-on-the-farm. From personal experience, however, I have found this to be consistently true. The demise of my business was a case in point. I would have loved to go on to build a huge and excellent company, and to have become extremely wealthy. I would have loved to see my partner and my colleagues share in that achievement and wealth. Cobra is flourishing, and I hope it will bring wealth to my former colleagues. For me, however, it was not to be. Out of the ashes has come a learning process for me that has helped me become a more understanding, sympathetic, and fulfilled human being. I had a lot to learn – and still do – but the requirement to supercharge my Comfort Zone Growth has brought huge and lasting satisfactions.

Look for the good – and praise it

The second thing that personal development teachers agree on is that one of the most effective ways of enhancing your own level of positive charge, and at the some time enhancing others', is to praise people for their achievements. However poor you are feeling financially, it costs you nothing to give praise. By praise I mean honest recognition of achievement, however humble. I do not mean flattery or bullshit. Almost every situation has some good in it. If there is a human being responsible for that good, some relevant measure of praise is probably appropriate.

A word on praise. We all love it, but most of us are very poor at receiving it. To be over-modest is to be ungracious. This often embarrasses the praise-giver, and everyone feels deflated, rather than enhanced. 'Thank you. I appreciate that,' is easy to say to someone giving praise, and everyone feels good about it. I first really learned this lesson during the fifth London marathon. I had run in the first four, and had then retired, figuring that there were only so many times you could drag a rugby player's body round a race built for whippets, before serious bits began to drop off.

On the four marathons I had run, when the thousands of supporters along the route had shouted encouragement, I had always tried to grin, or wave back, however rough I had been feeling. Indeed, in the first London marathon, the most moving of them all, because no one knew beforehand whether any spectators at all would turn up, the interaction with the crown was fantastic. We even had to laugh out loud – no mean feat after sixteen miles – when one old dear shouted out, 'Don't worry lads, there's dancing at the end!'

In the fifth race, I was the spectator and, with Lizzie, was doing the shouting. The difference in how you felt as an encourager was incredible between those who responded and those who did not. Those who ignored our shouts of congratulations and good wishes, left us slightly flat. Those who responded – the vast majority – gave a huge lift to our feelings, encouraging us to continue even though we were hoarse. Both sides in the exchange came out winners.

'Is that what you want to happen?'

The third area that personal development teachers agree on is how the articulation of negative thoughts can materially affect outcomes. Saying

'I'll never get a distinction', 'I'm sure the boss doesn't like me', or 'I can never find time for exercise', are *all negative affirmations*. This is Henry Ford's point moved on a stage. You may actually believe that you've a good chance of a distinction, or that the boss actually does like you, but by making the negative affirmations, the possibility of the undesirable outcome happening is greatly enhanced. With the third negative affirmation, you may also know that with a little time leadership you could organise your schedule to make sure regular exercise was achievable. The negative affirmation makes it unlikely that reorganisation will take place.

These self-deprecating throw-aways are dangerous. They sound innocent enough, but they become self-fulfilling prophesies in no time at all, because the subconscious processes them as the truth. This is all the more so when they are joined by the inner negative Chatterbox. Both forms of negative affirmation are persistent and powerful. Consistent action needs to be taken to overcome them. The goal is to say only positive things, to yourself and to others.

In the case of the external negative affirmations, every time you catch yourself voicing a negative thought, pose yourself the question (or your partner can perform the same function, if you are working on it together). 'Do I (you) want that to happen?' Put bluntly in these terms, it is embarrassing how inane many negative affirmations become. 'I can't fill in forms', is an absurd thing to say. Of course you can fill in forms. Saying you can't is silly, and just makes the next form harder to fill in.

In the case of the negative Chatterbox, turn up the volume and frequency of the positive Chatterbox, and make a consistent attempt to drown it out. It's possible, but takes self-discipline and constant vigilance.

The Mastermind Alliance

The Mastermind support group, as we saw earlier, was originated by Andrew Carnegie and Napoleon Hill. There have been many variations since, but the principles are similar. In essence, the Mastermind group draws on the basic premise that two or more minds are better than one.

Whether it is just two people (as in the case of Simon and Fleur Smartbutton, when Peter Pressenter wasn't there), or more (as the case with Carnegie's fifty) the important element is that the group should be harmonious. There are two basic functions that a Mastermind group performs. The first is as an opportunity to brainstorm ideas. In brainstorming sessions, the mind can fly free, and no value judgements are applied. Multiple subconsciouses can be tapped into, thinking is untethered, and big, iconoclastic ideas can be envisaged. These ideas are later subjected to the icy stare of logic, but many survive, warm, with a life of their own.

The second function – and benefit – of the mastermind alliance is of positive association, and support. *For IBGs – especially fledgling IBGs – this can be the difference between surviving, with pain, and flourishing, with enjoyment.* Meeting other people who are supportive, understanding, encouraging, who can point you in new directions, and supply helpful introductions, is sustaining and uplifting. It keeps you going when things are slow, and it produces new ideas and new leads.

Feeling part of a team is even more important when the prop of the full-time job has fallen away. It provides stamina when your own resources might be flagging. Canadian geese, flying in a 'V' formation, are constantly changing the leading flyer, because that is where the pressure is. As a result, tests have shown that they can fly 72 per cent further than they could on their own. The intelligent IBG makes sure the Independent in the title is tempered with positive associations, to make sure he, or she, gains the effectiveness of team performance where it is possible, and appropriate.

My Mastermind groups – not that I recognised them to be such at the time – tended to be with friends or ex-colleagues, on a one-on-one basis. I was lucky that some of the major suppliers to us at Cobra continued to be supportive, even though I was no longer involved in the business. The managing director of Reebok took me out to lunch and gave me a whole string of useful advice. Two of the points I remember being of particular relevance. The first was that whatever I planned, it would take at least six months longer than I thought it would to come to fruition. This turned out to be true on more than one occasion, and knowing it in advance helped the evolution of that necessary quality in an IBG's armoury – *patience*.

The other piece of advice he offered was that even though I wasn't looking for a job, I should talk to a couple of top head hunters – introductions to which he supplied – just to keep me plugged into the system. This was useful advice from several points of view. It made me produce a curriculum vitae – which hadn't been touched for fifteen years. It made me focus on what I had to offer, and think about how to sell it in an interview. It also produced a useful tip from one of the head hunters – that networks were important, and that you should never leave a meeting without asking the person you are talking to for a name of someone who might be able to help further. This turned out to be extremely helpful. The simple question, 'Can you suggest someone else who might be able to help?' nearly always has the person you are talking to volunteering the names of a couple of people – with introductions – who will be worth talking to.

The advice was useful from one further, fundamental, point of view. My very short experience of the head hunters confirmed my view – if any confirmation were required – that the last thing I wanted was a job. In those early days as an IBG, there were times when the looming financial pressures indicated that for my family's long-term security a 'proper job' might have to be considered at some future point. These discussions with head hunters – and the one interview I went through with – confirmed with considerable power that a job was something to be avoided at all costs.

As I sat talking to these perfectly pleasant people, black clouds closed in around me. It all became clear. Losing Cobra I could see as failing – but failing to succeed somewhere else later. Taking a job would have been admission that I was not up to making a go of it on my own, and thus would have been close to signing on for social security. While at other times in my life a job would have been a blessing at a time of no income, a job at that time in my personal odyssey through life would have been the equivalent of sinking into the dependency culture.

Active listening – a key life skill

This is a huge and important subject, as it gets to the heart of human communication. The core of it is St Augustine's telling dictum, '*Seek to understand, before you seek to be understood.*' Most of us have our radios turned up to full volume on 'transmit', and have the 'receive' button turned down very low. We like talking more than we like listening.

Research studies tell us that 10 per cent of communication is verbal, 30 per cent is non-verbal sounds, and 60 per cent is body language. Part of the reason for this is that people aren't listening to the words, because they are too busy talking themselves or, if not talking, preparing what they are going to say as soon as they get the chance to start talking again. To be an effective listener, you have to make sure you are *interested* in what the person has to say.

We are not talking here of a quick active listening course, which will tend to have as its pattern: 'I look you full in the face, and pay enough attention so I can summarise the gist of what you are saying. I can then get on with manipulating you better.' We are talking, rather, of really *listening* to what the other person has to say. Listening, in Stephen Covey's memorable phrase, with the third ear – the heart. This is not without dangers. It means that if we hear, and understand, the other person's point of view, we may have to shift our own ground to accommodate the new insight.

This is a further facet of Comfort Zone Growth. If you know someone has diametrically opposed views, especially on an important issue, the act of really listening to their beliefs and their *feelings* takes some courage. The comfort zone has to be enlarged to accommodate it. You are putting yourself at some risk, because by really coming to understand the other person's position, you are forced to accommodate it in a far more threatening way than if you were merely looking deep into his or her eyes, and waiting for a break in the monologue, ready to counter with your monologue.

The reason why active listening is important as a life skill – and especially for IBGs – is that people who make the effort to listen with their whole presence – totally plugged in to the speaker – are far more likely to be trusted than those who don't. It also leads to good feelings between people as a result. Beyond this *the fact that you have the self confidence to listen in learning, rather than preaching, mode shows you are a strong person, yet open minded and influenceable.*

Such open-hearted confidence is an attractive trait in anyone. This is a further reason that employers, clients and customers, will all prefer to deal with IBGs, where possible, rather than anything else that might be on offer.

Time leadership – necessary because there's not enough of it about

For many people, being busy is part of their comfort zone. It proves to themselves that they are in demand, that they are important. Not to be busy would leave them vulnerable and exposed. It is also a convenient screen behind which to hide from the important issues – like family challenges – that require quantity and quality time to address and resolve.

Time leadership – a concept that originates from Stephen Covey – aims at achieving the right *balance in our lives,* rather than looking to prioritise a list of to-do tasks. Balance covers work, family, exercise, recreation, and even community work, in the sense of putting something back in. It aims to use time effectively, rather than efficiently. Four quadrants of time are identified, to aid in getting an insight into the right balance. These are: things to be done that are Important and Urgent, things that are Important but Not Urgent, things that are Urgent but Not Important, and things that are Not Important and Not Urgent. Most people spend far too much time in the last two quadrants, because it's the comfortable place to be. You feel important, because you're busy, busy, and as a result you can avoid tackling those big, important, but *difficult* issues that you know you should be addressing but can wait till next week.

Achieving the balance is not easy. It is particularly difficult for women. The reason for this is a huge proportion of the tasks done by women – especially women with children – are both important and urgent. A crying child, a problem at school – being there when needed – are all important and urgent. This is in addition to time demands as an IBG, or in her employment. This will become an increasing challenge as women take over the world.

Within ten to twenty years women will be running most sectors of the economy. School exam results show that they are already better educated. They have far better people skills than men (and as service industries take over from manufacturing, these will become more and more at a premium). They are more used to coping with entering and leaving the workforce, as they have babies. They are used to coping with time pressures, and to having considerably less leisure time than men. As a result, they are better at balancing the use of what time they do have. For the same reasons, they will make very good IBGs.

A quick word on the intuitive people skills of women. Back in the 1970s I was the director in charge of account management for an international advertising agency. One of my responsibilities was recruitment. I had a very good secretary, who would meet interviewees at the lift, and walk them to my office. Between the lift and my office, a distance of no more than thirty or forty yards, she would chat to them. I would then interview them for the next forty-five minutes to an hour. Afterwards we would compare notes. She would invariably have learned as much about the people – and be accurate in her judgement of them – in forty-five seconds, as I had managed to achieve in forty-five minutes.

Procrastination is the thief of time

The words of Edward Young, the eighteenth-century English poet, a noted coiner of epigrams until he was put in the shade somewhat by Alexander Pope, are as true today as when he penned them. Procrastination – whether through fear, idleness or a supposed lack of time – is one of the largest time destroyers of all, *particularly when tasks are important, but not urgent.* Procrastination – from the Latin word *cras,* meaning tomorrow – steals time because time is taken by thinking about the task that should be performed, rather than performing it.

Its effect is doubly negative, as a sense of guilt usually accompanies the act (or lack of act), which is coupled with a lowering in the sense of self-worth caused by the knowledge that the delay in taking action is slovenly and inexcusable. This sense of guilt is heightened when the action put off is in the important category. As we know, *action cures fear. Do it now,* (or, as the Nike slogan commands – Just Do It) gets to the heart of it. It is a call to focus on the self-discipline required to *act.* Being self-disciplined enough to do it now – especially important tasks, whether urgent or non-urgent – makes it possible to move on to the next stage – being pro*active* – leading events, rather than following them.

Back to time leadership in the wider sense. This boils down to: am I doing the right things, rather than am I doing things right? While leadership and balance – creating time for family and exercise, etc. – are the driving principles that we should address when proactively organis-ing our total time, we should not forget that efficiency has a role to play as well. As we saw earlier, watching television – particularly the news – is neither an efficient nor an effective use of time. Also, when you are working, it makes sense to work all the time, rather than dissipating time on trivial tasks, chit-chat and poor organisation (it is estimated that executives spend on average *six weeks* a year trying to retrieve mislaid files, correspondence, and information of all sorts). *Every hour wasted at work is an hour taken from your family.*

For an IBG, the challenges of balance are especially intense, because in the nature of having several income streams there will be many demands on time. The approach I have found most useful is to view the situation from the point of view of *investing, rather than spending, time doing things.* This has two effects. One is that it points you towards income streams that are *time-flexible.* If an alternative or secondary income stream is insufficiently time-flexible then it may have to be changed for one that is. Otherwise, it quickly becomes apparent that time is being poorly invested, because too much pressure means that nothing gets done effectively, and other income streams can suffer as a result.

The second effect of considering time as an investment is that it forces you to take a hard look at the profitability – current and potential – of each area of your activities. Other qualitative considerations are, of course, relevant. How much you enjoy the income stream, what the people are like, how high a percentage of overall income it provides, what other benefits it provides, will all affect your decision on where to invest more time, and where to consider reducing, or eliminating, time investment. Taking the positive view, it's a nice problem to have. If you are having to decide where to invest time, it tends to mean that at least you have created a number of sources of income. This means you are gaining control of your life, and creating choices, even though the income sources may not, as yet, be producing at their optimum level.

The Worry Box – get ready to slam the lid

Because worry can be such an invasive, inhibiting and destructive force, it is worth having more than one method of dealing with it. The acronym for fear, **F**alse **E**xpectations **A**ppearing **R**eal, is accurate for its close relative, worry. As we saw with Homer Simpson, the fears are very often baseless. I include within worry the morbid reliving of past traumas, which can be the most debilitating – and avoidable – of all psychological states.

Taking the latter first, there can be nothing more toxic than reliving past failures or disasters. It is the creation of negative energy at a very high level. It is the living embodiment, in darker tones, of the Burns' wife waiting for the husband who is late home through drinking, 'nursing her wrath to keep it warm'. Nursing our hurt to keep it warm must be one of the most unproductive uses of time and energy available to us as human beings.

Constantly rehearsing the events and feelings of the event – losing a job, a wife, a husband, a parent, being slighted as a lover – is to reinvent the hurt of something that was painful enough when suffered once. To be consistently resuffered amounts something approaching masochism. *It is wallowing in a comfort zone of misery* that abnegates any responsibility to move on, or to take action to rebuild and re-engage.

The constant replaying of the loop of misery and pain must be broken. Assuming a desire to change – as with any addiction (drugs, alcohol etc), there must be a desire on the part of the addict to change, otherwise the chances of success are low. The goal must be to obliterate the pain of the past, and to move on. No little luxurious nursing of wrath from time to time. The wrath must be allowed to grow totally cold – and thus unable to cause any more pain. Here are two methods to apply to solving the problem once and for all.

The first is to imagine your own personal **Worry Box**. This Worry Box is a metre cube, made of extremely thick steel. The lid is so heavy you can only just open it. When fully open, it rests just beyond the upright position. The steel is cold, and highly polished, giving off a slight bluish sheen. A large padlock hangs open, ready for use. The Worry Box stands on the edge of a high cliff – so high, the ground at the bottom is lost in mists.

You make one last, farewell, rehearsal of the hurt you wish to leave behind. This becomes liquified in a foul black solution that you can see in a glass jug in the top right hand corner of your brain. You then take the jug, and pour it into the steel chest. You can here it splashing in the bottom, but nothing escapes. When the jug is completely empty, you put it down, and get hold of the lid of the Worry Box. With some difficulty, you get it past the upright position, and it drops, slamming with a resounding finality.

You secure the padlock, which shuts with a satisfying click. There is no key to reopen it. The black burden you have been carrying around with you for all this time has finally been sealed off, and you are free of its evil influence and powers. As a final act of unburdening, you lever the box over the cliff edge, and see it fall tumbling down, until it is lost from view in the swirling mists below. You can – and must – now restart your life. You *act as if* you are a happy, positive person. Within days you will be one.

A second technique, suggested by Anthony Robbins, can be applied to future worries, as well as past traumas. Whatever the problem that is bothering you – past traumas, present or future concerns – you visualise it intensely on a large poster in front of you. You then place the poster in the forks of a giant catapult. Next, you place a much smaller picture of how you want to be – worry free – in the ammunition holder in the sling of the catapult. You draw the elastic back to full stretch, and then let go. As you do this, you say 'woooosh' out loud, as the smaller picture smashes through the large, negative picture, smashing it to tiny pieces. The positive picture is now in front of you, and that is the new reality. This should be repeated seven or eight times, to confirm the shattering of the old behaviour or thinking process.

Remember these techniques are only supports to the central precept that *you control your feelings*. However bad the external situation is, or may become, you can, like Victor Frankl in the concentration camp, develop a broader vision that not only gives meaning and satisfaction to your life, but takes away most of the unnecessary pain and suffering. You are no longer manipulated by past events that conspired to inhibit your ability to act, and develop. You are sovereign, in control, and on the brink of a bright future.

The benefit of the Worry Box or the catapult is that it helps you control, rather than merely cope with, negative events and situations. Coping strategies are helpful too. Two coping strategies I used during the last days at Cobra – before I knew anything about the more comprehensive and effective methods outlined above – were reading poetry, and outlining worst case scenarios. If I felt a sleepless night – and there were many – or a panic attack threatening, I would read poetry before putting out the light. I read poetry anyway, but I read a great deal more at that time.

I'm not quite sure why it was so effective. It was partly, I suspect, because the timeless voice of Donne or Herbert gave a sense of a larger, more permanent reality – the great flow of events – that put my puny challenges into perspective. It was partly the sheer beauty and ingenuity of the poetry itself. And partly, too, a comforting sense of nostalgia, in taking me back to times at school and university, when I had read the poems for the first time.

After putting out the light, the sense of confidence, and separation from current worries, gained through plugging into these larger, timeless truths, would sometimes begin to seep away. I would then put Plan B into operation. Plan B was to think harder and deeper about ways to reverse the inexorable deterioration in the bottom line at Cobra, and to find new ways of bringing new courage to us all.

When this eventually became circular, I put Plan C into operation. This involved looking at the very worst that could happen. I had personal guarantees on several shops, as well as to the bank. It had been my job to lead, with our property director, a campaign with our more enlightened landlords to reduce the rent burden on our shops. In fact, several responded with imagination and support, allowing us to reduce our total rent bill by almost 20 per cent. The problem was that some of the stores where personal guarantees existed were the stores that would not easily be re-let, and certainly not at the rents we were paying, as the recession had caused a reversal in rental values. We would thus be liable for the rents, including any rental shortfalls, until the end of the leases – twenty plus years away in some cases.

The worst case scenario was therefore personal bankruptcy, including the loss of our house. Even in those dark days, however, I gained reassurance from the list of things I would still have. I would have some money, which would have been Lizzie's part of the house after the landlords and the bank (a joint guarantee) had had their share. I would still have Lizzie, and the girls, my family and my friends. And I would still have had my self-respect, knowing we had done everything possible to save the company. (In fact we brought in a large firm of accountants towards the end to investigate a turnround, and it was gratifying that we won plaudits for the radical actions we had taken to reduce costs – they could find nothing substantial to reduce further.)

I gained reassurance from the fact that the worst case scenario was thus unpleasant and uncomfortable, but could be coped with, if it had to be. I therefore recommend this as one course of action if something dark and negative looms in your future. In practical terms, it means taking a sheet of paper, and ruling a line down the middle. On the left, list the very worst things that could happen. And reassure yourself, with affirmations if necessary, that you can cope with them. On the right hand side, list all your blessings – friends, family, personal qualities, possessions etc. And be profoundly grateful for them.

The next step – whether you use the Worry Box, the catapult, or the worst case lists, is to start making plans for the future. If the worries are to do with family or health, examine the possible options open to you and write them down. The act of writing them down clarifies thinking, and somehow makes them more manageable – because on paper you can see they are part of a more universal experience, and you are not the first, or only, person to whom it has happened. Apply Mind Leadership, and look for ways to widen your perspective, and to add new, and different value to the situation. Remember my father's approach to the last year of his life. If possible, try to involve a friend or family member in a Mastermind group, to brainstorm ideas, and gain support, plus a wider perspective.

If the worries are to do with your job, start planning now to become an IBG. Produce a STOC Check, develop an IBG Action Plan, and a Planning and Evaluation Schedule. From this you can develop you Brand Positioning Statement. You may ultimately decide that you are not yet ready for life as an IBG, but you will have gained two significant benefits from the process. The first is that action cures fear, and the very act of writing down the various stages of defining what you have to offer is in itself an important step in cutting free a mind tethered by worry. The second benefit is that by the end you will have a far clearer view of who you are, and why your talents are special – and desirable to an employer – which will be of enormous help in making sure the next job is the right one.

Dreams and goals turn obstacles into stepping stones

Dreams and goals will become your compass as an IBG. Your dream – whether it is financial freedom, financial security, or surviving well while bringing up a positive and happy family – is where your compass course should be set. Having a dream – or a **Definite Major Purpose**, or a **Burning Desire** – as it has been variously defined, is *fundamental to survival, let alone success, as an IBG.*

Having a goal, which is a step towards the dream, or even the dream itself with an achievement date on, gives focus, direction, purpose and incentive to all activity. All the impediments that lie in the path are immediately reduced in scale and intensity. The ultimate achievement of the goal, and the rewards – financial and psychological – that will go along with it, make the inevitable struggle worthwhile. Without a goal to focus on, the struggle becomes overwhelming, and each obstacle seems individually intimidating and insuperable.

There are thus two major reasons for being goal orientated. The first is that people with goals invariably achieve more than people without goals. They procrastinate less, and they are positively looking for opportunities, because they want to get on with obtaining their goals. A survey of Harvard students in the 1960s discovered that only 3 per cent of students had goals which they had written down. Twenty-five years later the sample was revisited, and it was found that *those 3 per cent accounted for more personal wealth than the other 97 per cent added together.*

The second major reason for being goal orientated is alluded to above. People without goals see only the obstacles. People with goals see only the goals. *Goals untether the mind from doubt,* and release it from the inhibitions of fear and indecision. Focusing on an intensely desired goal enables the lid to be slammed on the Worry Box. Past and future concerns are put aside as all mental energy is concentrated on the attainment of the goal.

Whatever the business books and personal development books say, formulating dreams and goals is far from easy. Most people are not born with a burning desire. They are spasmodic dreamers, and find it difficult to focus consistently on one specific dream that really gives them a surge of adrenaline each time they visualise it. I have to confess to having challenges in this area, even though I have been applying myself to it for some time now. Missions, values, goals, brand positionings I feel comfortable with, but the dream tends to be elusive. When I can define a dream and focus on it, it supercharges my activities dramatically.

This is the reason that it is so important. *The dream puts the emotional booster onto what the brain has defined as the objective.* Goals can be missed, but the dream endures, giving courage when common sense is beginning to throw up question marks and doubts. *The dream essentially defines your intensely personal motivation.* Visions and Mission Statements define what you hope to achieve looking outward to influence for the better and to help *other people*. Company Mission Statements define how a company wishes to be seen by *other people* (the best, the leader, the innovator, etc.).

Dreams look inwards, and *define what you want for you. They are a private identification of your motivational hot button.* We may articulate our dreams in terms of benefits to other people (e.g. bringing up well-balanced and well-educated children) but, deep down, the dream is about us. It is about how we will be appreciated for what we do, what difference we'll make, and how we will be remembered.

If you can't define your dream, it generally means you're either too lazy, too comfortable, or too scared of failure. There is risk in defining something that may not be achieved. It is the dreamers, however, who have been transformational of their surroundings and have thus changed things for others. Napoleon, Martin Luther King, Colonel Sanders, and Bill Gates were (and are, in Bill Gates's case) all, in their different ways, dreamers. They untethered their thoughts, and put everything into the accomplishment of their goal. *To be truly effective, we must all find, define, and pursue a dream. Once you have a dream, the facts don't matter. They are irrelevant, and can be discounted, as you push forward towards the accomplishment of your dream.*

Goal-setting is another skill that needs to be worked on assiduously if you want to become proficient at it, and to benefit from the learning process. The crucial thing about goals is that they should be achievable – at a stretch. To set goals that are either too easily achieved, or are unrealistic, is counterproductive in the extreme. It is obviously beneficial if goals are aligned with dreams, but this is not necessary for this to be the case. If goal-setting is something that you toy with spasmodically, try this exercise.

Write down ten goals that you aim to achieve in the next month. They can be from any area of activity, but they must be achievable, with effort. They could range from taking your partner out for a meal, to beating your son at tennis, to getting home at a reasonable hour from work at least three times a week. As you achieve each goal, tick it off. Your overall goal should be to be able to tick off at least eight of the goals on your list by the end of the month. When you come to evaluate your performance you will be surprised and delighted by what you have achieved.

Glowing with pride, now set yourself not only ten targets for the next month, but ten goals for the next year. These again can cover any area, from an income goal, to starting to learn a new foreign language. Again, tick each one off as you achieve it. Over time, you can develop five- and ten-year goals, *covering all the areas of your life – business, family, physical, social, educational, etc.* This sounds like a great deal of work. It is, but the benefits far outweigh the effort required.

Whatever the area of my life, I find that if I have a goal, I perform better. I focus better, I stretch further, and I enjoy it far more. In a sense, it's like reimposing the framework of school, or university. There are exams to take, sports to join in, all of which give life a focus and direction. Many of us have drifted since those days, educating ourselves randomly, and waiting to see what turns up in many areas of our lives. Setting goals may have the ring of outdated disciplines, but the truth is that these disciplines were right then, and they're right now. The only differences are that *we* now set our goals, so they're more relevant. Because we are in control, we can also have a great deal more fun and satisfaction along the way.

Value and Mission Statements give shape to our thinking and our activities

Mission Statements come in many forms. Some are framed from meaningless platitudes which dance on the surface of the issues, and have no emotional buy-in from those concerned. Others can give those writing them real insight into who they are, why they do things, and what they are trying to achieve with their lives.

This is a huge subject, and requires far more space than is available here to deal with properly. Mission Statements take time to write. They can take hours, days, even months, to get them anything like right. The very act of writing them is of as much value as the finished article. Thinking through the issues, finding out who you are, is a journey. The physical act of writing somehow involves both the subconscious as well as the conscious mind, as you think through, crystallise, rethink, and distil your personal mission in life.

A personal Mission Statement is just one of many. Over time it is worth developing a family Mission Statement. Many people already have organisational Mission Statements. Any Mission Statement involving more than one person – from two to infinity – should involve *everybody* in the process of evolving and refining it. In practical terms this means involving *everyone* in the process in the first place, and then encouraging groups of people, or individuals, to *customise the overall mission statement, to make it relevant to their individual contribution*. As individual's values may differ from corporate values, the Values Hierarchy that precedes the Mission Statement may, as we shall see, have to accommodate a constructive compromise for both corporation and individual to maintain their integrity.

Because many Mission Statements are so meaningless – written by senior executives, without reference to, or involvement from, the organisation – and then stuck on the wall to be greeted with either boredom or derision, most people find them irrelevant. Because they are also very difficult to write – they involve concentration, insight and self awareness – they are frequently the area that gets neglected. 'Objectives, yes. A plan, yes. Brand positioning, OK. But a dream and a Mission Statement? I haven't got time' is the normal response of most people.

IBGs are not most people. *Most of them do not have the infrastructure and culture of a conventional job to do their thinking and establish their values for them.* An IBG, to be successful in the long term, has to develop Brand Me beyond just the values other people can see and appreciate. The central core, which includes both the dream and the mission, needs to be carefully thought about and articulated if Brand Me is going to have any substance when the first reverses are encountered.

Oversimplifying, it could be put this way. *The dream reduces the size of the obstacles, and makes them less daunting, by providing a larger dimension of thinking that comes from having a highly motivating ultimate goal. The mission, on the other hand, confirms the integrity of, and gives substance to, the sense of self-worth that is necessary to deal with those obstacles and challenges in their strength-sapping day-to-day reality. Put even more simply, dreams and mission statements provide the vision and strength to enable you to fulfil your potential, and not be blown off course by the shite as you move towards achieving your goals.*

There is no right or wrong way to write a Mission Statement. It is more important to get something – anything – down on paper, than to agonise over format, and write nothing. A useful starting point is to go back to the principle, employed by several of the personal development teachers, of imagining you only have a month to live. The alternative version is to imagine what you would like a friend to say about you at your funeral. While doing this, it might be salutary to imagine what an enemy might say at your funeral. Not only would it focus the mind on avoiding bad-mouthing and hurting other people, it would induce a reappraisal of current relationships and priorities.

Stephen Covey uses a variation of this with his students, where he asks them to believe that they have only one semester to live, and to behave for one week as if their imminent death were a reality. Many of the students react at a fundamental level. They write to their parents, telling them how much they love and appreciate them. They set about reconciling with relations, or friends, where important relationships have weakened, or fallen apart. The overwhelming feeling is of warmth, and goodwill. Not in a self-serving way, to earn shallow forgiveness for sins of omission or commission, but in a profound, loving way. Such a feeling of positive love makes the daily tittle-tattle that fills most people's lives – the cheap put-downs, and clever, hurtful remarks – both inappropriate and unthinkable.

From trauma to Mission Statement

Thinking about what you stand for, and how you want to be remembered, can be a chastening experience. When I did it, I found that while my image of myself was of someone who was an achiever, in reality I wasn't even at the starting line. I had spent over half my life finding out what it was about, taking the comfortable route, and being generally too self-satisfied.

In my very early days as an IBG, I worked with an investment company, who put me in as acting chief executive to a small company in which they had an uncomfortably high stake, that was not performing as they had hoped it would. Before putting me in, they sent me on an extensive, and expensive, psychological assessment course. Fortunately I came through, successful and unscathed, but I remember the final

interview with the psychologist. He asked me about my inner motivations, and then wanted to know how profoundly I questioned myself. My
answer was that my inner motivations were unclear, and that I didn't
question myself. He was surprised, and kept probing, to no avail.

I thought about the conversation afterwards, and came to the
conclusion that the traumatic change I had been through should have
precipitated a rethink of values and priorities. What had happened was
that the losing Cobra had confirmed my already strong views on the
importance of family, and beyond that I had closed down any questioning of who, or what, I was, or what lessons there were for me in the
experience. By this action, I had subconsciously hoped to avoid any
further shaking of my already shaken tree. On reflection, this had been
an act of cowardice.

While I may have been slow to take up the opportunity to review my
values and life goals – which came later as I became more involved in the
study of personal development as a subject – it did give me some insight
into how people feel when they go through a challenging experience,
such as losing a job, divorce, or serious illness. To the outsider, this
would appear to be a perfect time to reappraise one's life and beliefs. To
the insider, getting through each day is challenge enough, without
breaking down the whole edifice of self, in order to rebuild it more
strongly.

My advice now would be to achieve a constructive halfway house. My
excuse – not a very good one, but valid none the less – is that I had no
preparation in terms of understanding what personal development
teaching could do for me in terms of personal growth. Nor did I have the
tools. Mission Statements I understood, and was committed to. But a
personal Mission Statement was something I had no concept of. The
provision of a tool kit as preparation to face such challenges is part of the
purpose of this book. It is intended as a rough map of some of the
territory of the potential benefits of self development. Insights and
lessons from the common wisdom of teachers over the centuries can help
rebuild or redirect life after trauma.

Raw from the trauma itself may be too soon to reformulate, and
relaunch. You need to live through the pain, accommodating it and
dealing with it using some of the techniques outlined earlier, *but not
denying it*. Denying it will cause more problems later. Move into
constructive mode as early as possible, before the pain has a chance to
establish itself as a comfort zone, excusing the need to take action to
move on.

Values as the lead-in to Mission Statement

The most important part of preparing the speeches that your friends and enemies will deliver over your coffin is to think through what you stand for. What are your values? Which are the most important? Which are the least important?

Establishing a hierarchy of values – as a list which forms part of your mission statement – makes the articulation of the mission statement(s) immeasurably easier. This applies to whatever version you are looking at – personal, business, social, sporting, educational, etc. – or composite, including all aspects of your life. It avoids writing statements that are no more than pious wish-lists, because they do not tie in with basic values.

Let's look at two simple examples of this form of hypocrisy which can undermine the value of the whole process. The first example would be a corporate Mission Statement that talks about respect for employees, and the importance of the core values of family life. If the value hierarchy of the corporation puts shareholder value at the top, followed by staff commitment, there is an obvious case of *misaligned principles*. The value statement calls for staff commitment and shareholder value, which demands early morning, and late evening, meetings, and, possibly, weekend working, whereas the Mission Statement calls for respect for family life. The two demands are totally incompatible. The result will be a hypocritical Mission Statement that sounds good, but that nobody buys into.

The second example is that of a High-flyer, who enjoys his work more than his family. His personal Mission Statement commits him to spending time with his son, and developing a warm and loving relationship with him. His value hierarchy puts income, recognition, and power, at the top of the list, and nurturing and caring at the bottom. The son hasn't read the Mission Statement, so continues to be difficult, mainly because he is still receiving no full-hearted attention from his father, whom he loves. The father's fuse is no longer than it was before he wrote his Mission Statement, because his mind is still at the office, planning the next large deal he is negotiating for the company. The father remains in his fight or flight relationship with the son, and storms out after the first blow-up. Again the values are misaligned, the Mission Statement is hypocritical, and therefore unachievable, and the whole process comes into disrepute.

To avoid the pitfalls of misalignment between values and mission, it is worth committing your value hierarchy to paper, *as part of the Mission*

Statement. Values should be defined by you and be relevant to you. Again there is no right or wrong list of values – the only test is whether they are true for you or not. For a personal Mission Statement values to be included *in order of importance to you* might include:

- integrity
- family
- love
- contribution (to an effort or project)
- giving (time and/or money to others)
- work
- recognition
- building (relationships, enterprises)
- power
- success

The list is by no means exhaustive, and should be added to in order to suit individual needs. Discussing the priority order for *a family value hierarchy, prior to developing* a **family Mission Statement**, can be enormously productive in its own right. No two family members will agree the same order, but the discussion will throw light on many previously dark corners. Such a list of values could include:

- consideration
- independence
- cooperation
- tidiness
- support
- developing talents
- demonstrating interest in others' struggles/accomplishments
- sense of humour
- respecting others' space
- listening before attacking
- not bearing grudges
- responsibility

And so on. You get the picture. These values can develop into a lengthy list, and can flush out some issues that might otherwise never see the light of day.

To see the Value Hierarchies and Mission Statements in action, we will return to the sagas of Felicity, Norman, and Simon, to see how they fit into their lives. Remember, in all this, that there is no one correct way to do it.

Felicity, Norman and Simon ride again

Felicity's fresh start

'I am strong and I am worthy. I am strong and I am worthy. I am strong and I am worthy.' Felicity Freshstart's brother intoned the words, until he had reached ten repetitions. Felicity sprang from her chair, took hold of her brother's wrist, and pushed down hard. Her brother grinned as she made little or no impression on his outstretched arm. 'Right, now say "I am weak and unworthy" ten times,' she said.

'You've got to be joking,' was his reply. 'No, just try it,' Felicity implored. 'OK, but if it doesn't work, I want you to promise to give up reading those daft books with silly titles. They're for people who haven't got proper personalities.' 'Hold your arm up, and get on with it,' said Felicity, gritting her teeth. 'And be serious.' Felicity's brother closed his eyes, and put on the sepulchral voice of a priest addressing the congregation. 'I am weak and unworthy. I am weak and unworthy.' Felicity laughed, despite herself, and punched him lightly. 'Concentrate, you silly brother,' she said, and waited for the incantation to finish.

Felicity – and her brother – knew the moment of truth had arrived. Felicity took hold of his wrist, and pushed down firmly. To her huge relief, the arm went down, and kept going down, despite her brother's strong attempt to resist it. She winked at her brother, and said, 'And which book would you like to try first? There's one here somewhere on renting a personality.'

Felicity was already on a high. She was very excited about going freelance, and in so doing taking the first steps towards starting her own company. In fact, she had acted rather precipitately. She had resigned from Boffins Technology on just the verbal promise of jobs from two production houses. In her last month at the company, her boss had tried to get the most out of her by throwing all the work he could find at her. Being Felicity, she had accepted it all with a smile, and got on with it. This had caused a problem, because it had prevented her from putting out feelers for work (part of her boss's strategy).

She now had a week to go before her last day, and her leaving party. Knowing how important personal growth would be once she was on her own, she had taken to self-development reading with a genuine enthusiasm. Being extremely time-poor in the past few weeks, she had created more time by getting up an hour earlier each morning. She spent fifteen minutes reading of self-development books, twenty minutes or so communing with her subconscious, ten to fifteen minutes studying professional journals and technical books, and finished with ten minutes of affirmations.

She would have spent time in the evenings on this activity, but she had a busy social life, and her mother was ill, necessitating two or three visits a week to her in the local hospital. As her mother began to recover, Felicity reflected on how she had been able to find three evenings a week out of a schedule she had thought was packed, because visiting her mother was both important and urgent. Food for thought for later.

The morning after her leaving party was Felicity's first morning as an IBG. She had a hangover, and what seemed like a yawning chasm was opening up in front of her. No need to get up an hour earlier, as there was no urgency to get to work. Indeed, there was no work. After the pressure of the past few weeks, this new state of having nothing pressing to do left her a feeling of floating on a vaguely threatening sea.

She had breakfast, and then went into an extended programme of reading, thinking, and affirming. She also spent time visualising success in her new role as an Independent Business Generator, specialising in the field of conference organisation. She rang the two companies who had promised her work, to confirm timings. Here she met her first setback. The first company told her that the project had been cancelled, and the second informed her that the job they had had in mind was now postponed for three weeks, and initial planning wouldn't begin until six weeks' time, at the earliest.

This was a challenge for Felicity. Resigning so swiftly, she had had little opportunity to build up her savings, and she knew that after four or five months of even subsistence living, she would be having difficulties meeting the mortgage payments on her flat.

Felicity was prepared for a struggle, as she knew from reading personal growth books that no great enterprise or achievement was ever accomplished without one. She would have hoped that it might not have come quite as soon, but she accepted it none the less. She therefore went about making practical plans to get through this period of delay. She reviewed her situation, and decided on two additional courses of action.

Being a sociable person, and now without the friendly day-to-day environment of her work, she identified the need for some positive association. She therefore rang Irene, a woman she liked and respected, and who had been Marketing Manager at Boffins Technologies, but who was currently taking a break from employment to bring up two young children. Felicity was very frank about the situation, and explained that she would be delighted if Irene would join her in a Mastermind group to steer her through the early period of establishing her business. Irene, in turn, was delighted, because she liked Felicity, and was keen to put her brain back to work in a business context.

Felicity also decided to develop a Mission Statement. She had her Brand Positioning Statement, she was a keen supporter of the concept of Brand Me, but she realised the need *to focus and define a wider, more emotional vision, if she was not going to be blown off course* by the practicalities of keeping a roof over her head, and food on her table. She therefore set to work and decided to confine her Mission Statement to her business, rather than develop a wider one for her as a person. She recognised the importance of a personal statement, but felt the priority was to define why she wanted to build her business. She understood that there is no one right way to write a Mission Statement, so she decided to write something that worked for her. This is what she developed.

Brand Felicity's Values and Mission Statement

Brand Felicity's values, in order of importance, are:

Values Hierarchy
- integrity
- recognition
- building (enterprise/relationships)
- giving (time and support to others)
- reward
- enjoyment
- independence

Mission
My mission is to build a good company that is successful, fun to work for, and everyone knows will deliver the goods.

To fulfil my mission I will:
- ensure all Team Members work with integrity
- delight clients with the quality of our work
- maintain a sense of fun, even under stress
- build a culture of quality, giving, and caring
- ensure that rewards are first created, and then shared fairly

---

In writing this, Felicity learned a great deal about herself, and her motivations. She realised that independence was important, but was not her great burn. This would considerably affect her recruitment once she was successful. She would be looking for people who had the potential to grow into partners, rather than remain as employees.

She also realised that she wanted recognition for building something of quality, rather than something immense (this would satisfy both her need to build with integrity, and to prove to her parents that she was at least as good as her brothers).

Missions tend to be earnest things, teetering on the edge of piety, but for Felicity, fun was still firmly on the agenda. She would therefore remain her own person. Financial success, and fair reward, were important, too. Brand Felicity was not going to become a friendly club, where everyone sponged off good old Felicity.

The most important word of all in the mission statement, the importance of which only dawned slowly on Felicity, was the word *company. In writing her Mission Statement, she had finally made the fundamental move from IBG as freelance producer, to IBG creating a formal framework for other IBGs to work and flourish.*

This became her burn. She was going to build a good company that everyone would recognise as being not only good, but being *hers*. Suddenly, being hard up, with no income, became far less daunting. She knew what she wanted to do, and she was going to do it.

As a result of writing her Mission Statement, her first meeting with Irene had a different tone from the one she had previously anticipated. Rather than going in saying, 'This is where I am, what do you suggest?' she was saying, 'Here's a clear picture of where I'm going, what's the best way to get there?'

The session with Irene – the first of many – was extremely helpful. Irene gently brought Felicity down to earth. Whatever her mission, Felicity still had no income, and little or no work lined up for the future. They therefore worked out a pragmatic programme of activity to accomplish Felicity's goals. They agreed that Felicity would work as a temporary PA/secretary for a bureau for two to three days a week, to bring in some money to cover basic overheads. The remaining days of the week would be taken up with learning her craft better, and systematically developing her business.

She also agreed to take a look at the network marketing business that Irene ran from home. Irene was very clear that, if Felicity did decide to pursue it, the payout, in any substantial sense would be six months to a year down the road. This would fit in well with the normal cycle time to establish a business such as conference organisation from scratch. Incomes from both businesses would come on stream at similar times, allowing Felicity to take less out of Conference Felicitations, if she needed to invest for longer to assure its healthy growth.

She would develop her craft skill by increasing her study of trade publications, going to trade shows, and making follow-up visits to manufacturers and distributors to find out more about their conference equipment. She would develop her business by producing a brochure outlining the services of Conference Felicitations. Irene volunteered to use her marketing experience to produce the brochure, which would then be mailed, with a suitable covering letter, to a target list of potential clients. Felicity would also keep in regular contact with her personal list of potential clients, in order to take advantage of anything that came up.

Felicity felt pleased. Her Mastermind group had produced more than expected. More importantly, her Mission Statement had given her real focus and commitment. Thinking about it, she realised that before writing her Mission Statement, temping for a secretarial bureau would have been a somewhat humiliating admission of partial defeat. Now, with her mission clearly in mind, it was merely a necessary step towards the accomplishment of a worthwhile goal.

Over the next few weeks Felicity faced many challenges. In following up leads (she always asked for a reference, someone else who might be able to help her), she met a few Poisoners. These people always began by congratulating her on her initiative, telling her they were sure she'd make it. They then proceeded to supply reason after reason why she wouldn't. The industry was oversupplied with talent. Companies were taking fewer and fewer risks, and were gravitating to the larger companies with established reputations. Penalty clauses were being demanded, so creditworthiness was vital. And so on. Felicity tried to drown them out with affirmations and visualisations, but occasionally they got to her.

During the next two or three months she widened her knowledge base considerably. She learned a great deal about her new industry, and her knowledge became quite leading edge. She also took up Irene's offer to look at her second income business. After thinking hard about it, she decided to give it a go. She knew that once she became busy running Conference Felicitations she would have very little time, but she recalled how, under intense time pressure, she had found two or three evenings a week to visit her mother in hospital. Remembering this, she was confident she could find the time, if she really wanted to.

On taking up the business, she found she loved it, and was good at it. Even more importantly, she found the positive association – including even more regular contact with Irene – and the personal development books and tapes, extremely helpful. She felt plugged into a wider culture of supportive people a good counterbalance to her solitary splendour as a freelance IBG.

Money was tight, and she had managed to win only one piece of work, which was the project she had been promised. This turned out to be smaller than anticipated, and was very slow to pay Felicity's invoice (a proud moment when it was raised on her new Conference Felicitations letterhead). Despite her affirmations, visualisations, and the consistent action she was taking to generate income, doubts began to creep in. Irene would lift her in the Mastermind meetings, which now took place twice a week. The network marketing business was going well, which was exciting, but that was a secondary income, and Felicity wanted to fulfil her mission to build Conference Felicitations.

Despite having no work on from her intended primary income stream, Felicity resisted attempts by the secretarial bureau to increase her availability with them. She kept following up leads, and working out, with Irene's help, new ways of putting her name in front of potential clients.

One day, when she was feeling particularly low, the phone rang. Before she picked it up she pressed the palm of her hand with her thumb. *This triggered the response that she had anchored there, for situations just like this.* The positive feelings she had programmed into the anchor, from successes earlier in her life, flooded into her. She felt uplifted, and powerful. She answered the phone with confidence, and the traditional Felicity bounce.

It was her old boss at Boffins Technology on the other end of the line. He wanted to take Felicity to lunch, to discuss a proposition with her. Felicity agreed, and a date and time were set. Felicity didn't know what the proposition might be, but she knew that it was almost certain that it would not involve Conference Felicitations. In the week leading up to the lunch meeting, *Felicity made one particular affirmation, and one particular visualisation, three times a day.* The affirmation was: 'I will only accept work or a job that will aid the rapid development of Conference Felicitations.'

The visualisation was that she *acted as if* she were the leader of Conference Felicitations, a company that was already successful in running outstandingly good conferences. She could feel the buzz of activity in the company's friendly offices, she could hear happy clients ringing her to thank her for successful conferences. She could see the company's first Annual Report, showing profits, and a substantial salary for the Chairman, one F. Freshstart.

When the day finally arrived for lunch with her old boss, Felicity prepared meticulously. She began by pouring any last vestiges of doubt or concern about her future into a mental jug. She then poured the contents of the jug into her Worry Box, slammed the lid, and pushed it over the cliff. Released from these worries, she stood in front of the mirror, and repeated ten times, 'I will only accept work or a job that will aid the development of Conference Felicitations.' She then smiled into the mirror repeating the word 'enthusiasm' ten times, at regular intervals during the morning. She visualised herself as the leader of a successful conference company, and reinforced her trigger and anchor for creating an instant empowered and resourceful state.

By reliving past success, and preliving future success, Felicity met her ex-boss for lunch that day as an equal. He was surprised at her buoyant and effervescent state, which did not augur well with his plans. His information was that she had little or no work, and was therefore likely to jump at anything. He asked her how things were going, and Felicity said, with great enthusiasm, 'Brilliantly', because they were. Her network marketing business was going well, and she knew it wouldn't be long before her conference business was doing the same.

They talked with animation of people they knew in common at Boffins Technology, and her ex-boss alluded to possible changes that might take at Boffins Technology. Although much of Felicity's attention was on waiting for her ex-boss to get to the point, she was also good enough at *total listening* to appreciate that changes were going on in the background, and things were not as they had been. Finally, as the dessert was served, her ex-boss came to the point. After a considerable build-up, he offered her a very good job as an executive with Boffins technology, which would include conference organisation within its responsibilities. The salary was almost double what she had been earning when she left.

'No thanks!' she almost shouted. Her affirmations had worked. She had resisted something that would have seriously inhibited the development of Conference Felicitations. Her old boss was astounded. This was not in his plans. Felicity had not finished, however. She had been listening with her inner ear, and knew there was more to this than her ex-boss was saying, and that there might be more to come.

With an audacity that surprised even her, she said, 'But there may be other ways I can help. Tell me about the changes at Boffins.' Her ex-boss breathed hard, closed his eyes, opened them again, and plunged ahead. He told Felicity how Boffins was about to be taken over by a larger, more successful company, and that the future of several departments was under threat. They had been told there would be a period of six months in which evaluations would take place, and performance of individuals and departments would be monitored. His departments were launching two new products, and it was vital that everything went right with those launches. A recent conference to re-launch a product had not gone well (a fact that Felicity was aware of, but had not brought up), and the next two conferences could be make or break. Felicity's intuition told her that this was a time for boldness. She reached into her handbag and took out one her Conference Felicitations cards. She pushed it across the table to her ex-boss, and smiled confidently. He picked it up, and studied it.

'We can sort at least one for you, and if the briefing is good, both of them.'

'A pity you're not there to do the briefing,' replied her ex-boss.

'Exactly,' said Felicity. And winked. Her ex-boss looked hard into her eyes. Finally, he said: 'Damn you, Felicity Freshstart. You've got me over a barrel. It's a huge risk, but I think I'd rather take the risk on you, than the bigger risk on someone new that doesn't understand the company. You can have one project now, and if the preparation looks good, I'll give you the second one in two months' time.'

'Conference Felicitations doesn't come cheap. We're a premium operation, you know.' Felicity smiled as she said it, but she was making an important point. Her boss was about to say words to the effect that Felicity should not push her luck, but there was a new strength about her that he was aware of, which made him hold back.

'I'm sure you'll be competitive. Let's fix a date now for you to come in, and we can discuss the brief.' And so was launched Conference Felicitations. Felicity knew that if she had not *been acting as if she were already successful* her ex-boss would either not have made the offer, or would have probed in difficult areas like what personnel she had, what infrastructure, etc. As it was, she knew she could put together a high-quality team, initially from freelancers like herself, but slowly building up full-time people. These full-time people would, in the main, she decided, be IBGs. IBGs would have a strong sense of their own worth, but would be happy to work for their primary income stream at a company that had clear ideas on quality, contribution, value, as well as being an enjoyable and uplifting place to work.

As soon as she had said goodbye to her ex-boss, and was out of earshot, Felicity let out a huge whoop of delight. She was off and running! Conference Felicitations was really happening. Felicity never really came back down to earth. She organised both conferences for

Boffins Technology, both of which were triumphs. They not only kept her ex-boss and his department in jobs, but they provided the basis on which she was able to build Conference Felicitations.

She faced many challenges after that day, but her dream was being fulfilled. As she grew, the dream grew. It supercharged her activity and led her on to build exactly what it said in her Mission Statement – a good company that was successful, fun to work for, and everyone trusted to deliver the goods.

Norman opts for a new start

Norman had thought long and hard about George Snakeoil, and his elevation to the board of directors. A few months earlier, when he still had a employee mentality, he would have cursed – silently – the gullibility and stupidity of the chairman and managing director. He would then have kept his head down, and let events run their course, until either George Snakeoil was found out, and was forced out of the company, or until the firm's performance deteriorated to such an extent through George's incompetence that the owners were forced to sell, as the market they were in did not allow for any slackening in competitive performance.

Norman was no longer an employee, he was an Independent Business Generator. His whole mindset had moved on, and matured. *He therefore had to be proactive, and lead events.* His analysis of the situation was simple. His problem was not just that George Snakeoil was a director, but that the chairman and the managing director had been shown to have been out of touch with what was going on in the business, and that their judgement had been fundamentally flawed in appointing him. He could thus no longer respect them as managers of the business.

He therefore needed to move on. As a precursor to reviewing his options, he decided to define his Mission Statement. This, he knew, would clarify his thinking, by probing his values hierarchy, and the motivations underpinning his future business career. He made many attempts at defining his values hierarchy, and in doing so realised that accountancy was something he had grown out of. He wanted to progress to running, or help in running, a business. After much thought, and discussion with his wife, the Mission Statement clarified into a plan of action, bringing both elements together.

Norman's Values and Mission Statement

Values Hierarchy
- family
- integrity
- helping others
- independence
- team building
- enjoyment
- learning
- reward

Mission
My mission is to achieve financial security for my family by working with my wife to build a viable business, which in turn will help other individuals and families to create financial security.

Roles that will have a priority in achieving my mission
Boss – my wife and I will be the leaders of the team, and will be proactive, supportive, and dependable
Father – my children will be part of the team, and will be valued for their contributions
Student – I will be assiduous in learning about leadership, retail operations, horticulture, and any other subject that will foster the development of the enterprise.

In preparing for his Mission Statement, Norman had been very glad he had done the initial work on his IBG Action Plan, and his Planning and Evaluation Schedule.

At this point, he is called in by the chairman and managing director for a conversation about his future. Norman replays in his mind the success of the way he had handled the previous meeting, and in no time at all is a Mighty Lion, looking forward to the fray. He walked into the chairman's office with a beaming smile, said, 'Good morning, gentlemen,' and sat down.

It is clear from the conversation that followed that they understood that they have possibly made a hasty decision in appointing George Snakeoil to the board of directors. Unwilling to lose face by admitting a mistake, and also unwilling to lose further face by a second precipitate action in appointing Norman to the board, they have decided to offer Norman the opportunity to develop a franchise operation within Delectable Foods. They are very keen not to lose Norman's talents – particularly if their unadmitted fears about George Snakeoil's abilities are proved to be correct.

Norman, in his Mastermind sessions with his wife, had foreseen this possibility. Again he smiled, enjoying the discomfort of the two men, feeling that they deserve little sympathy, because they have brought it on themselves through a combination of poor judgement and weak management. 'That is a good offer, gentlemen. I accept it with enthusiasm. I have only two conditions. The first is that as this is a new corporate initiative, I report directly to you two gentlemen, as the general manager of the new division. The second is that my new salary reflects the importance of this new initiative to the company.'

The two men were taken aback, but could see the logic of Norman's demands. They exchange glances and nods, and agree to Norman's conditions. Norman receives a 30 per cent salary increase, thanks them, and goes off to start handing over to his second-in-command, and setting up the groundwork of the new operation. Norman is delighted. He rings his wife to tell her that he will be bringing good news home that night.

After supper that evening, Norman and his wife, Iris, begin to lay out their plans. Norman will develop the franchise business for Delectable Foods to the best of his ability. He will thus be honourable in his behaviour to the company, but in the meantime, he will be developing his future as a fully fledged IBG. The extra income will allow him to save for the time when he leaves to set up his own business, which will be the garden products business he will run with his wife.

Setting up and developing the Delectable Foods franchise initiative will be invaluable experience for his own business. The experience he will gain in operating shops, and training and running franchisees will give credibility to his Business Plan for retailing garden products, when he has to present it to potential investors.

Norman sets to with a will, and embarks upon a very steep learning curve. He decides to manage the first shop himself. He does not take a franchise, as he had thought about in the early days of planning, before the elevation of George Snakeoil to board, as this would tie him too closely to the business, and would make leaving to set up his own business more difficult at a later date. He agrees with the chairman and managing director that he will take over the running of an existing, successful shop, setting up all the systems for running it as a franchise, and then use it as a model shop, for demonstration and training purposes, for potential franchisees.

Norman then sets himself *two clear goals*. The first is to have all the systems, training programmes, franchise contracts, etc., up and running, and with two franchisees appointed, within six months. He thus set a target of being able to hand over the operation, as a successful going concern, to someone else, in a tight timetable that would allow the achievement of his second goal: the setting up of Glorious Gardens within the next six-month period. This would mean he would be resigning from Delectable Foods, and running his own business, within a six-month timescale. He knew these were ambitious goals, but he also knew that if he did not set tough targets, he would get too involved in the Delectable Foods' operation, a comfort zone would develop, and inertia would set in, robbing him of his dream of running his own business.

Norman learned a huge amount over the following months about how shops really run. Feeling himself to be a good and fair team leader, he was personally deeply hurt when he caught a member of staff stealing. He understood intellectually that well over half of all shoplifting is done by staff, rather than customers, but it still hurt him when it was one of his own staff who was doing the stealing. He applied the lessons of the personal development book he was reading, and managed to control his feelings. This gave the event some emotional distance, and allowed him to gain a perspective that put it in a less personal context.

He missed his goal – just – of having two franchisees in place at the end of six months. One had just started, and one was in the final period of training, so he had come quite close. The retailing systems were operating well, and so were Norman's coping systems. The ability to control his feelings had developed rapidly after his first incident of discovering an incidence of staff theft. This rapid personal growth was precipitated by the consistent presence of a Poisoner. George Snakeoil was that Poisoner. Not happy at being cut out of the command structure by Norman's insistence at reporting directly to the chairman and managing director, George Snakeoil had consistently taken every opportunity to talk down Norman's operation, with a view to sabotaging it, if at all possible.

As if all the sniping were not bad enough, he repeatedly came into the store – for which he had no responsibility – making negative comments about staff appearance, cleanliness, etc., all of which were untrue, and damaging to staff morale. He would also seek Norman out, and regale him with stories about how his friends had come into the store and received poor service. Norman knew these stories to be untrue (and he knew his Mystery Shopper scores to be much more positive than the average for the group), but in the early days these accusations were hurtful.

Norman dealt with the situation with the *constant affirmation: 'George Snakeoil amuses me. I find everything he says very funny.'* After a month or two of this affirmation, Norman could handle George Snakeoil without getting in the least upset, and indeed being amused by his visits. Whenever George said anything negative – which was whenever he opened his mouth – Norman roared with laughter. 'Good one, George!' he'd smile, and walk away. George found this behaviour very disconcerting and eventually gave up coming into the shop.

Norman then set about laying the groundwork for Glorious Gardens. He decided to extend his Mastermind group to include Henry Bramble, one of the investing bankers in Delectable Foods, with whom Norman had built up a good relationship while he was still handling the overall finances for the company. Henry had always been very supportive of Norman, and he was, Norman knew, a keen gardener. Henry was very interested by the idea, and delighted to be involved at an early stage. Norman, Iris and Henry would meet each Sunday to move the project on.

Norman also researched the subject by talking to his local market gardener, who was situated some ten miles from his home. He began working there only the Saturdays that he was not working at Delectable Foods, to gain insight into the market – how shoppers bought things, and what they were looking for. He also visited market gardeners at a distance, whenever he had a day off. He found them very forthcoming, and helpful. What Norman was looking for was the application of the law developed in 1895 by the Italian economist Alfredo Pareto, that for a given enterprise 20 per cent of the effort produced 80 per cent of the results, and the remaining 80 per cent of the effort produced only 20 per cent of the results.

Norman wanted to stock only the effective 20 per cent in Glorious Gardens, and to avoid most of the remaining 80 per cent. He was looking for core lines, must haves, and KVIs. KVI stands for Known Value Items. These are the lines that customers know the prices of, and the pricing therefore must be competitive on. Customers might know the price of a bag of fertiliser, for example, but not of a garden trowel. Applying classical food retailing techniques, Norman would then be slightly cheaper on the fertiliser, and make the margin up on the trowel.

Norman learned a great deal about the market from his researches, and also found a new partner. The owner of his local garden centre wanted to be a silent partner, supplying expertise and some capital, but leaving Norman to supply the management input. The concept began to crystallise as an edge-of-town, compact offer, majoring on core lines plus an added dimension of specialist foreign plants. Any garden equipment, from small tractors to hammocks, could be ordered from catalogues in the shop. All staff would be keen gardeners.

The Business Plan came together, and with the help of Henry Bramble, investors were sought. At this point Norman's *Value Hierarchy came into play, inhibiting his ability to control the company.* Because the family, and its security, were so important to him, he was emotionally incapable of investing all the equity of his house as collateral for the venture. In this sense he was not a true entrepreneur, in that he was not willing to risk all to fund his enterprise. This meant that the capital he was prepared to risk only bought him 30 per cent of the company. Iris, who agreed with his sense of caution, helped him rationalise this by saying that 30 per cent was far more than most chief executives owned of their companies.

Norman resigned from Delectable Foods, to the dismay of the chairman and the managing director. George Snakeoil's reaction is not recorded. Norman's first shop opened on time, and business was strong. Norman and his wife worked well together, and enjoyed building relationships with their staff and their customers. Then came the first test. They offered the franchise, and the first candidate was a school teacher. He was an avid gardener, who wanted to retire early and run a small business. Glorious Gardens was the answer to his dreams.

Norman had structured the franchise so that the upfront charges for the fascia, training, franchise fees, etc. were quite low, to make it accessible, with a slightly higher franchise royalty to offset this. Their first franchisee, Peter Preacher, undertook the training, and signed up. A site was found, and the second Glorious Gardens duly opened for business. It never took off.

Norman and Iris became very worried. *With everything going so well, Norman had let his affirmations and visualisations lapse.* He was reading personal development books only very infrequently, and when the wheel fell off he found it very difficult to cope. He reverted to type, and the accountant's *Scarcity Mentality took over.* He *worried* that the market was saturated, their own outlet was sheer luck and wouldn't last, the concept was not really a winner, they would have to cancel their holiday, and there was not enough business to go round anyway.

Iris suggested gently that he should get back into the discipline of reading personal development books, listening to tapes, making affirmations and visualising future success. Norman became defensive, and quite testy. Iris, wishing to avoid any further crisis of confidence gave him a lingering hug. Norman began to melt. Iris whispered, 'I just fancied a bit of that Mighty Lion.'

Norman sighed deeply. Iris was right. Where was the Mighty Lion? Conspicuously absent over the past few weeks, was the answer. Norman kissed Iris on the forehead. 'Thank you, darling. You're right. I must go and find him.' Norman retired to his Quiet Place. After twenty-five minutes his subconscious gave him two clear answers. The first was confirmation of Iris's message – take the necessary steps to become a Mighty Lion once more. The second was a course of action to take after he had once more regained a resourceful, empowered state.

Norman began with the Worry Catapult. He mentally painted all his worries, in graphic detail, onto a large poster. He set that between the forks of the catapult. Next he visualised all the good outcomes he hoped for in the current situation. How Peter Preacher's shop would become a dramatic success, and others would then be queuing up for franchises for Glorious Gardens. He shrank this down in size, and placed the small poster into the sling of the catapult. He then saw the sling being drawn further and further back, until it was at the limit of the stretch of the of the powerful strands of rubber.

He let go of the sling in his mind, and said 'Whoooosh' out loud, as the smaller picture smashed through the larger one, leaving it in unrecognisable tatters. He could then see the new situation clearly. Everything was as he had hoped it would be, and things were going well again. He repeated this exercise several times. He then sat back in his chair and reflected. He was surprised to find that he felt enormously restored, and much less burdened than he had before the exercise.

Over the next few days he set to with a will on his programme of reading personal development books, reliving past successes, preliving future successes, making affirmations and listening to tapes. As the days passed, the sparkle came back to his eye, and he regained his appetite for the fight.

And fight it would be. What his subconscious had told him was that the problem was not the concept, or the site, but Peter Preacher. The plan that his Quiet Time had suggested was that he should remove Peter from the equation for a period of time so that he, Norman, could assess the situation. If Peter was the problem, he should then address it in a forceful and direct way (details supplied with the plan).

Norman discussed the plan with Iris, who was delighted to see her husband once more proactive and decisive. Norman went to see Peter after closing time the following Saturday evening. He sat him down, and began to speak. He had visualised the scene endlessly, and had worked out counters to most things that Peter could throw at him. He began gently by outlining the poor sales figures (his case was underlined by the day's takings being particularly dismal), and then went on to outline his plan (the part he was going to reveal to Peter). He told Peter that as franchisors, it was his and Iris's responsibility to make an assessment of the situation, and make recommendations. To do this properly, he would need to take an objective, unencumbered look at the situation. Peter should therefore take a week's holiday from that night, to allow Norman and Iris to run his shop, and to analyse where improvements could be made.

Norman was *acting as if he were running a large, successful franchising operation*, and Peter's shop was a trivial problem that would soon be rectified. He was ready for Peter to become even more defensive than usual, and dig in obstinately. Because Norman was in such an empowered state, he carried all before him. To his amazement, Peter meekly agreed, and left for a week's holiday.

Norman and Iris learned a great deal in that week. To begin with, the few regular customers the shop had, were slow to talk. But relatively quickly a clear picture emerged. Customers did not enjoy coming to the shop because Peter lectured them endlessly on what they should be doing with their gardens, rather than what they wanted to do with them. They also learned from an ex-colleague of Peter's that his early retirement had been of the push, rather than the jump, variety. The reason, once more, was not that Peter was in any way objectionable, but that he just couldn't refrain from giving his opinion, asked for or not. By the end of the week takings were beginning to rise rapidly, because either Norman or Iris – whichever was manning the shop at the time – gave helpful advice, when asked, and converted almost all the customers who came in into sales.

The following Monday morning Norman, with Iris beside him, was in a highly empowered state, awaiting the arrival of Peter Preacher. Peter entered somewhat diffidently, and sat down opposite Norman in the small office. Norman began the meeting – which for both men would be a difficult one – *on a positive note*. 'Peter, can you let me know what is right about this shop, and what positive ideas you have to improve sales?'

This completely cut across the way Peter had been thinking, and it took him some moments to assemble his thoughts. The net result of that assemblage wasn't too impressive, but it served its purpose of allowing Peter to speak his mind before Norman spoke his. There was also the possibility that he could have come up with some ideas that were worth building on.

Norman laid out the plan of action, which was a simple one. The previous week's sales figures were shown to Peter, which showed an increase of 25 per cent in his absence. Norman informed Peter that he and Iris were within their rights in the contract to take back the franchise for non-achievements on minimum turnover levels. They were not going to. On the contrary, they had decided to invest in Peter's future by sending him on an advanced active listening course, in the very near future, and he was to remain in a support role within his own shop, while Norman or Iris took it in turns to build the business for him. Once the business had been established, and his customer handling skills were at the desired level, he would once more take over the shop, and continue to build the business.

Peter was not overjoyed at the offer, but could see that it was both fair, and that it might work. After thinking it over for a few minutes, he agreed, and the process was set in motion.

Norman learned many lessons from this episode. Three emerged as being the most important. The first was that rigorous selection and training of franchisees is more important in retailing where skill in dealing one-to-one with customers is vital (unlike food retailing, Norman's training ground, where people know exactly what they want, and select it for themselves). The second was that it is better to take action earlier, rather than later. Thirdly, *if you let personal growth lapse just when you need it (all the time), you will be like a rabbit caught in the headlights, frozen to the spot, inactive, and extremely vulnerable.*

As Iris snuggled up to Norman that night, she purred softly two words: 'Mighty Lion.' 'Grrrrr,' was his reply.

Simon Smartbutton Struggles

All is not well at Sapiens Knowledge. The first product is slow in being developed. This is chiefly because Peter Pressenter hasn't been pressing Enter often enough, and the technical specifications have had to be done elsewhere. Simon has bombarded Peter with e-mails, faxes and phone calls, but gets either no, or evasive, replies.

Finally, Simon loses patience, and flies out to Australia to attempt to get the Mastermind group going again. Once there, he meets up with Peter, and the position becomes clear. Peter has been sucked back into the life of the High-flyer, and *has lost his dream*. He is working seventy hours a week, and *because he never took up a programme of personal growth has nothing to fall back on when the pressure comes on*.

Simon has separately been looking at network marketing opportunities to develop with Fleur to build a stream of income they will devote entirely to charitable causes. The better ones he has looked at all have one thing in common. They all put significant emphasis on a continuous culture of positive association and self-development. Simon can now see why. *This separate culture provides the lifejacket to keep individuals buoyant when the corporate culture of their core income streams threatens to drown them.*

Peter, he could see, was a drowning man. To make it worse, Peter felt very bad about letting Simon down, and being so evasive. Simon asked Peter directly what he intends to do about Sapiens Knowledge. The answer is not a lot. He has invested £50,000 in the venture, can see it might still work, and therefore wants to become a sleeping partner. Simon pointed out that £50,000 would not have bought a 25 per cent shareholding as a sleeping partner. Peter shrugged, and said simply, 'We are where we are.'

Simon had been assiduously applying personal development principles since the inception of Sapiens Knowledge, and he called them into action now. He controlled his feelings, and his response to the situation. Rather than getting angry, which would have produced no positive effect, he smiled, and said, 'Thank you. I now know where I stand. I will keep you informed of developments.' Simon had been communing with his subconscious in his Quiet Place, and already had several fall-back plans worked out.

The development of Sapiens Knowledge was not the only reason that Simon had been achieving substantial personal growth. A few weeks previously, Fleur had given birth to their second child. The child, Eric, was handicapped, and would require lifelong care.

A year or so earlier, this would have destroyed Simon. Now, faced with the challenge, *he practised Mind Leadership. He untethered his mind, and he looked for the good in the situation*. And there was plenty of good to be found. Both he and Fleur, buoyed by their now positive attitude to life, felt an enormous and growing love for Eric. This love transcended their day-to-day concerns, and led to a fundamental reappraisal of their values and their lives. They articulated this in a family Mission Statement that they worked on during the days prior to Simon leaving for Australia. This family Mission Statement is a slight misnomer, as it is Simon and Fleur's, rather than the whole family's, only because the children are not yet able to contribute in a meaningful way. The Value Hierarchy showed how much their lives had changed.

The Smartbutton family Mission Statement

Value Hierarchy
- family
- helping others
- income
- integrity
- learning
- having fun
- independence

Family Mission
The family mission is to grow in understanding, good humour, and love, and to help others less fortunate than us.

To achieve this we will:
- build several sources of income to fund long-term care for Eric, and specific charitable causes
- create as much time as possible to be with each other

Simon had always been an enthusiastic supporter of Amnesty International, because its cause in supporting the victims of torture and political oppression had always touched him. This deep sympathy with the plight of others had been submerged in the time pressures of being a High-flyer. Now, out of the cauldron of High-flying, these sympathies blossomed once more. The arrival of Eric had given a further cause to rethink his priorities, and the resulting heartfelt Mission Statement he had written with Fleur *had given them both a new purpose in life. This purpose now drove their every action, with the result that they no longer saw the obstacles – only their goal.*

It was the crystallisation of his mission, more than the affirmations or visualisations he had undertaken – important though those were – that had enabled him to deal so calmly with the reneging of Peter Pressenter. He had a larger goal in life – to create Sapiens Knowledge as a cash generator to fund other, more worthwhile causes. Peter's behaviour was neither going to stop him doing that, nor was he going to allow himself the luxury of feeling sorry for himself at being treated so badly.

He returned to the UK to carry on developing Sapiens Knowledge. Unfortunately Peter's unhelpful ditherings had put them three months behind schedule. This turned out to be crucial. One month before the launch date, a large competitor came out with a very similar product, that took the market by storm. Rather than take the huge risk of launching a me-too product from an unknown company – Sapiens Knowledge – Simon decided to develop the second product rapidly, and launch with that instead.

This threw up considerable funding challenges. The original cash funding was based on the assumption that the first product would launch on time, and would generate income. With neither assumption justified by events, the money was running out fast. Simon once more *looked for the good*. The situation provided a strong solution to the question of what to do about Peter Pressenter. A better solution, indeed, than any of the alternative ones that Simon had already devised. Simon e-mailed Peter at home, outlining the facts. He stated that there were two options. Either he, Simon, would put the company into voluntary liquidation. Or he would restructure the company, and ask the original investors for a further investment. Failing that, he would find new investors.

The restructuring would need extra shareholding to be available for current, or new, investors. He therefore offered Peter A$10,000 for 15 per cent of his 25 per cent holding in Sapiens Knowledge. The choice was liquidation, and receive nothing, or accept A$10,000 of Simon's personal money for a reduced shareholding, more in line with his contribution to the company. Two or three days went by, while Peter checked out the situation with the retired lawyer, Dennis Quillpen, whom he knew was the largest single shareholder outside Simon and himself. Simon had kept Dennis up to date on the situation throughout, so he was able to confirm to Peter the accuracy of the analysis.

Peter took the only route open to him. He suspected (correctly) that Simon would have been extremely loath to put the company into liquidation, but he also felt a personal responsibility for not pushing on with his side of the bargain, and refining the product specification, which would have meant the first product would have been the first of its type on the market. He also wanted to stay involved with the project, and a 10 per cent shareholding, if the company took off, would give him a say in the action. He therefore accepted Simon's terms, and the company was restructured.

By reorganising the scheduling of product launches, and temporarily taking no salary himself, Simon was able to refinance the company by only selling 5 per cent of the shareholding he had repurchased from Peter, leaving 55 per cent overall for Simon. So good – incontestable control of the company – had come from bad – near failure, through Peter's behaviour and market events beyond their control.

The next few months were tough for Simon and Fleur. Sapiens Knowledge was slow producing its new launch product, and when it did come onto the market its performance was distinctly average. The negative Chatterbox began to pop up inside them with increasing frequency. The network marketing business was slow to take off, although both Fleur and Simon enjoyed the personal development side of it – the books, tapes and meetings. They applied the principles of Abundance Thinking. It worked to heart-warming effect. They developed an unshakeable *faith* that the potential of their network marketing business was huge, and that Sapiens Knowledge would strike gold soon.

More important still, their sense of abundance spread to their feelings for their children. Their love for them grew more and more abundant, and the challenges appeared more and more trivial. Repeating their Mission Statement each morning, coupled with visualisations and affirmations, eventually obliterated the Chatterbox. They awoke each morning full of hope, and went to bed each night fulfilled and happy.

Eventually their finances began to improve. The network marketing business began to bring in some interesting money, and the third product that Sapiens Knowledge developed hit the jackpot. Licences were taken up around the world, particularly in Australasia and the Pacific Rim. Even in the dark days, Simon had always spoken well of Peter Pressenter. *He had visualised him changing, sorting his values out*, and committing fully to Sapiens Knowledge as the way to generate both long-term residual income, through the licences and maintenance contracts, and also a far higher quality of life.

One day the call came. A very sheepish Peter was astonished by the genuine warmth of his reception by Simon, who had been expecting the call, because he had been visualising it. The two got together, set out the priorities for the future development of the company, and didn't look back. Simon was soon able to start donating regular sums to the handicapped charity concerned with Eric's condition, and Amnesty International.

Simon and Fleur became beacons to those around them. They were always giving – their time, their services, their good humour, and their money. They became archetypal **Enhancers**, lifting and inspiring people who came into their orbit. Felicity Freshstart, too, had grown. Her growth was from a more defined perspective but, like Simon's, was significant enough to make her almost unrecognisable from person she was before her adventures started. And Norman, the timid accountant, content with preparing papers for semi-competent directors to discuss in board meetings, had grown into a magnificently Mighty Lion (when the occasion demanded).

They had all become successful as Independent Business Generators. Two of them, at least, were beginning to transcend the boundaries of pure business with their personal growth. Will they be content to stop there? Or will they press on, to become Enhancers on another level? Will they have the vision to become Active Social Contributors?

Before I look at what it takes to become an Active Social Contributor, there is one challenge I need to pose. No, you haven't escaped. I'm going to ask you to write a personal Values and Mission Statement. It's not a five-minute job, but it does repay the effort. Understanding where your deepest held values lie on the hierarchy, can give profound insight into your actions and motivations. It is an exercise in going beneath the surface. Like becoming an IBG, or an Active Social Contributor, it's part of a voyage of self-discovery.

The goal of that voyage is to gain Mind Leadership. Mind Leadership gives *control*. Leaders know *who* they are, *where* they are going, and control their responses to whatever challenges are thrown at them along the way. Leaders have *clarity of vision and mission*. They know they have music within them. They have songs to sing. Fulfilling worthwhile goals enables them to play the music and sing the songs that might otherwise remain permanently silent within them.

TEN

Joining the Team Sector

We must give a lot of thought to the future. It's where we are going to live the rest of our lives
Maynard Keynes

IBG's become Active Social Contributors to become more complete human beings

We have looked so far at the Independent Business Generator in the context of the Incomes Revolution, and how he or she will thrive in the new environment. The main steps are clear. The first is to have a precise strategy on developing core, alternative and secondary income streams. The second is to go through the process of taking a STOC Check, defining the most relevant and effective Brand Positioning Statement, and refining the most motivating values and Mission Statement. The third step is to take on board the lessons of personal development and growth, and build integrity, self-worth and resilience. The fourth step is to take consistent and persistent action.

This chapter deals with how the IBG might fit into the wider context of society as a whole. This is important from many aspects. One is that people of integrity and self-worth have a *more developed sense of responsibility*. They also have *more energy, get more done, and are generally looking for ways to express their compassion for human beings who are less blessed, and less motivated, than they are.*

In expressing their humanity in an appropriate, relevant and productive way, they will be contributing to the **Team Sector**. The Team Sector is a more proactive definition of what is also called the Civic Sector, the Third Sector, or the Social Sector. It is not only more proactive as a description, it also more accurate in the sense that it acknowledges that *we are all interdependent, and that both sides benefit from the activities undertaken.*

Just as Lizzie and I received an enormous lifting of our spirits as the marathon runners responded to our shouts of encouragement, so both sides in the interaction within the **Team Sector** will also benefit. This is true, of course, of much of the charity work that is already undertaken. Unfortunately, the word 'charity' is a word that has attracted to itself meanings that can be counterproductive. Sanctimoniousness is one of them.

This holier-than-thou attitude, usually a facet of a marked lack of self-insight and genuine compassion, is definitively summed up by the character of Mrs Jellyby, in Dickens' *Bleak House*. Mrs Jellyby spends her life and energies talking about helping the deprived in Africa. Dickens, the master of characterisation that is exaggerated yet still real, points up her lack of genuine insight and compassion by describing her eyes as seeming to be continually focused on the far distance, 'somewhere in Africa'. While her eyes and her thoughts are set on Africa, her own children cluster about her skirts ill-clad, and cheerfully ignored, even when in great pain and distress.

If we define ourselves as **Team Workers**, we avoid many of these challenges of definition – and accusations of hypocrisy – *because the mindset is changed to one of givers and receivers being in the same team*. The disabled elderly person being bathed, like the struggling marathon runner, gives, in often mute gratitude, as well as takes. *Both are giving, both are receiving, and both, therefore are winning.*

Becoming an ASC may be part of being a Seeker After Truth

Before looking at the Team Sector in more detail, it is worth touching on the area of being, or becoming, a SAT – a Seeker After Truth. This is an area that most people – including myself – find difficult to talk about. It covers two important and fundamental concepts. One is the concept of conscience, and its ability to perceive truth with great accuracy. The other is existence, or non-existence, of a god, or gods, who give meaning and coherence to all our challenges.

We are talking, in essence, of a frame of reference of unalterable principles that should guide our lives. The question which is unanswerable is whether this frame of reference is moral or religious, whether it comes from within us or from outside. I have moved from being an atheist to being an agnostic. My mind is slightly more open than it was. 'By night, an atheist half believes in God' (Edward Young, again), is probably part of this. When we are scared – by death or illness, for ourselves, or others – we sometimes catch ourselves, in Hardy's words, 'Hoping it might be so.'

While it is important that we all keep ourselves open to spirituality, because it is a potential source of enormous strength and comfort, it is not relevant for this discussion. It isn't relevant because it is not conceivable that suddenly the majority of people will become religious, so as a solution it is very limited in application. Furthermore, from what I have seen of some publicly religious people, there can be almost a reverse correlation between professed religious belief, and sensitivity and compassion.

We are therefore talking about the conscience as the receptacle of the guiding principles that could underpin the compassion that in turn could be one of the important drivers of the Team Sector. The conscience, like the subconscious, is a widely validated theory, over time, place, and culture. It strikes a chord for all societies, whether secular or religious, because the sense of good and evil, right and wrong, is a major part of all human beings. Literature, both secular and religious, reflects culture and, as a result, is centrally concerned with it.

Stephen Covey gives a telling example of the presence of conscience, even if in an environment hostile to its very existence. On the occasion in question, he was asked to speak to about 150 students, in cramped, and almost threatening, conditions. The subject chosen was 'The New Morality' – which was shorthand for morality being a changeable feast, which is dictated by circumstances. The so-called situational ethic means that there are no absolute morals or standards. Every situation is different, and it has to be looked at in terms of the people involved, or other factors present. Covey flatly repudiated the proposition, going on to propose that there are a set of unchanging principles that underpin our lives.

There were two students, in the front row, who were particularly clever and articulate, and kept refuting Covey's points with skill, and aggression. The audience was supporting the students, and Covey began to feel surrounded and alone. Finally, in near-desperation, Covey held up his hand, and asked for silence. He then said, 'Each of us knows the truth of these matters in their hearts.' He asked each student there to think – in total silence – for a full minute, and to ask their hearts the question: 'Is this subject the [New Morality], as it is explained here, a true principle, or not?' He then said that if at the end of the minute they still believed it to be true, they could dismiss him, and he would leave.

As the minute slowly ticked away, and Covey looked out over the bowed heads, he sensed a change of mood in the meeting. At the end of the minute, he spoke to the most difficult and persuasive student, and asked, 'In all honesty, my friend, what did you hear?' After a pause, the student replied, 'What I heard was not what I have been saying.' Covey continued with his talk, and found that the students had become less intellectual and defensive, and more open and teachable.

Acknowledging the existence of conscience, and listening to its promptings, is one thing. Obeying them is quite another. This is where the brick-by-brick building of integrity is so important. The building and consolidation of honesty and integrity, as we have seen, is the necessary precursor to a resilient sense of self-worth. Because we have free will, the choice is ours, on a daily basis.

We can either read the personal development books, associate with people of integrity, and grow as individuals day by day. Or we can watch the news, ignore self-development, associate with negative, poisonous people, and remain nearly-people of opaque and uncertain morality. The situational ethic then takes over because the integrity to take responsibility for ourselves and our actions is lacking.

Integrity needs, and develops, courage. Maintaining control of our feelings and our moods is no easy matter. Because it is far from easy, it tends to develop humility and compassion at the same time. Humility flows from the challenges inherent in personal growth, leaving no place for arrogance. Compassion flows through a developing sense of self-worth, bringing with it a deep sympathy with those not yet blessed with such a priceless attribute.

The challenge from neuroscience

Before we look at how conscience leading to compassion could be one powerful motivator behind the more rapid development of the Team Sector, it is worth taking a look at one of the major challenges that is likely to face anyone either taking an initiative, or developing a leadership role in trying, in however small a way, to change things in society.

It is the central proposition of neuroscience that we have little or no choice in how we wear the Coat of Change. It posits, rather, that how we cope with change is preordained by our genes, and is more of a *skin* than a *coat*. We cannot take it off, change its style, or alter it to suit our needs.

Neuroscience, a melding of sociology with biology, seeks to move Darwinian evolution onto a further stage. Rather than saying that just our bodies are the result of a long and slow process of evolution, it states that our minds, too, carry with them the imprints of past experience. Our minds are therefore not blank tablets, waiting to be filled in by experience, but in the words of one of the leading advocates for neuroscience, Edward O. Wilson, a zoologist at Harvard University, 'an exposed negative waiting to be slipped into developer fluid'.

The print is the individual's genetic history, and is thus unchangeable. The genetics of the mind, it is argued, determine things like temperament, role preferences, emotional responses, and levels of aggression. The implications are numerous, and profound, and vary considerably in their acceptability to our sensibilities in their current state of development. The gay gene, for example would indicate that homosexuality is part of natural science, and therefore should carry no undertones of unnaturalness. It is no different from having white skin, or being left handed.

The division of labour between males and females when man was a hunter-gatherer means that attempts by women to usurp the roles of men are fighting the genetic tide. The fact that over 40 per cent of working women are the main breadwinner for their household is just an atypical aberration flying in the face of millions of years of evolution. Men are predetermined to be promiscuous, because millions of years of hunter-gathering poligamy means they are merely doing what their genes have programmed them to do. Murderers kill because their instinct for violence is in their genes. Neuroscientists even predict that it will not be long before brain imaging will allow the early diagnosis of individuals who are what amounts to being hardwired for violence.

If genetics determine our role preferences, temperaments, levels of aggression, it is but a short step to extend their influence into the area of moral choices. In Darwin Mark 2 – where evolution moves from the physical to the mental – *moral choice does not operate any longer in an area of free will, but of one of determinism even more rigorous than that of Freud*. With Freud, it was the haphazard nature of experiences in our early years, and their impact on our formative minds, that determined the shape of our responses in maturity. With neuroscience, there is no serendipity of experience. Our reactive framework is pre-programmed in our genes.

Neuroscience has all the makings of a very serious threat to theories of free will. Freudian theories – which were no more than theories – of behaviour being conditioned by early environment, took over half a century to be discredited. Neuroscience, therefore, which potentially has empirical science backing it, could become much more than a ten-year wonder. Brain imaging techniques – when they are eventually perfected

– are likely to be more persuasive to more people than one man's view – however eminent that man might have been – of what dreams might mean.

The genetic determinism of neuroscience – we are all hardwired to be who we are, and can change nothing – has the potential to undermine a great deal of the message in this book. Leaders are hardwired to be leaders, and the led are destined always to be led. Don't try to achieve personal growth – your brain image shows you're a hopeless case, so don't waste your effort.

The messages emanating from neuroscience are insidious. *The whole message is to retether the mind by implying that self-improvement is a disproved concept still clung onto by pumped-up zealots.* The battle is only just beginning, but it is likely to be a long and extended one.

The claim that we are genetically primed to find certain facial patterns handsome, or sexually attractive, is understandable, and therefore acceptable. But the University of Minesota study of 2,000 twins, under-taken by two evolutionary psychologists, which indicated that an individual's happiness is largely genetically predetermined, gets some-what too close for comfort. The inference that can be drawn from such a study is that whatever efforts are made in terms of influencing the level of positiveness or negativity of response to life's challenges, this is only temporary, and an individual soon settles down, or up, to the level of happiness he or she had hardwired into them at birth.

Developing the genetic negative into a positive

Refuting the developing claims of neuroscience will not be easy. The answer certainly does not lie in a blanket denial of what the new science is discovering. *The real point is how much can we influence in our attitudes and performance?* Once we have established how much, and to what degree, we can adapt our hardwiring, we can then get on with influencing those areas for the better.

Our minds may be genetically hardwired, but at least we have brains that set us apart from other animals. Racehorses have been more expertly bred, more expertly fed, and more technology has been brought in to train them, yet they can't run much faster than they could fifty years ago. Most speed records for horses have remained unchanged for decades. Man, on the other hand, can go through similar advances in training and diet, but because his speed is also driven by aspiration to improve and set new standards, records tumble on a regular basis.

Taking individual cases, many of us lack the physical genetic structure to run the mile in under four minutes, however hard we trained or tried. But from my own experience I know that with training and the right stimulus (in my case, running in staggered races, so people of mixed ability arrived, in theory, at the finish together) my times improved dramatically. I was still nowhere near four minutes, but I ran faster than I ever thought I could run. If I had accepted the genetic stereotype of myself as a slow runner over distance (over ten yards I could stay with sprinters), I would never have achieved the improvements in my times that I did.

The same logic applies to the ability of the mind to improve, only much more so. The mind – or brain, in the language of the neuroscientists, as the mind does not exist as a physical presence – is far more subtle and complex than the body. It stands to reason that it is therefore capable of being influenced to a far greater degree by attitude. Attitude can make us run faster, but ultimately our bodies have a limit as to what they can produce in terms of speed and strength. Genetic pre-programming of the brain may influence our capacity in terms of intelligence, or happiness, but so what? The world is full of intelligent, educated derelicts, so intelligence per se isn't that important. And happiness, in many cases, is an act of will, rather than something rationed at birth.

Victor Frankl demonstrated in the concentration camp that individual will can triumph over the most intransigent objective facts, be they Nazi thugs or, in the new context, unfavourable genes. The successes of Neurolinguistic Programming indicate that it is possible to reprogramme historical, possibly genetically produced, negative self-perceptions and attitudes with considerable, and often (with reinforcement) lasting, success.

So personal growth and development are not so easily trampled upon by the genes that determine our abilities and responses predicated by the neuroscientists. With a fuller knowledge of how our brains function, it may be that we have to work harder to control our responses, feelings, and attitudes. At least more insights into what precise challenges we are fighting in our minds will allow us to target our efforts more accurately.

Neuroscience is likely to provide more excuses to those who would have quit anyway (a self-fulfilling prophesy, if ever there was one!). For the majority, who are determined to take responsibility for not only their lives, but for their attitudes, and for their ability to enhance the lives of others, neuroscience will bring the opportunity to sharpen their skills of Mind Leadership. This quality may have to be redefined as **Brain Leadership**, but it be will just as powerful, and just as necessary, and just as effective as it ever was.

Active Social Contributors are part of a social, not economic, solution

There are many challenges facing modern societies. Economic polarisation, for example, does not only drive a larger and larger gap between rich and poor in terms of money, but in terms of education and health as well. The developing underclass attains lower educational standards, has a poorer diet, is less healthy, and dies younger.

A massive strategic investment in public housing is a possible economic solution. It would have several benefits. At a stroke, it would, for the worst off, improve health, improve employment prospects by increasing mobility and, above all, improve self-respect and self-worth. But we are not dealing here with economic policies (although these must be addressed), but what we, as individuals, can do to influence, in however small a way, the overall health and cohesion of society.

It is up to governments to define economic strategies. It is up to individuals to contribute at whatever level they can to improving society. Corporations, large and small, also have a role to play. Good companies and corporations provide a culture linking individuals by a shared understanding of, and belief in, their values and mission. The best companies and corporations extend this to a proactive role in the community, trying genuinely to put something back into society, above and beyond the provision of employment. Let's take a look at how individual and corporate roles might develop in the Team Sector.

The three overriding motivators behind the Team Sector

The Team Sector is not new. It predates representative government or the modern capitalist system of economics. It is huge, confused, and undervalued. My definition of the Team Sector is *any activity, paid or unpaid, that helps other citizens who are temporarily, or permanently, disadvantaged, or in need of support.* It thus includes frontline *caring* services of all kinds – services where the primary concern is for those cared for, rather than financial gain per se (although this can in many cases be justified as part of the satisfaction in providing the service).

Included therefore would be the fire service, parts of the police force, some teachers, health services (physical and mental), the social services and any organisations or individuals who work with the elderly, the infirm, the homeless, the desperate, the handicapped, the incarcerated, the illiterate, the deprived, the alcohol- or drug-dependent, the carers at their wits' end, and those failing to cope generally. Many of the Buggered group will fit into this category.

Many of these servants of their fellow human beings will be volunteers. If they work for organisations rather than as individuals, those organisations will be funded by the charity sector, central or local government, or any combination of the three.

1. The deep spiritual need to contribute

The first of the motivators behind the current and future importance of the Team Sector is the deep need many people have to be givers – of their time, their money, or their skills – to help others less fortunate than themselves. I have defined it as a spiritual need because, for most people, it is more than a merely rational response to their situation. Active Social Contributors are responding to an inner voice. Whether they believe this voice to be moral or religious in origin is immaterial. They still react to its promptings by acting positively to help other people in a way they feel appropriate.

The friend I mentioned in chapter one who retired early from a large oil company to devote time to helping others is not alone. In his particular case, he works in his local citizens' advice bureau. This is a highly worthwhile, but highly stressful, activity. The people coming in for advice are often close to desperation. They vary from those about to be thrown out of their houses for interruption of mortgage payments, to those wanting to know how to cope, legally, with the fallouts of marital breakdown. Within a few weeks of his starting work in his local office, two other ex-colleagues from the same oil company had started working in the same office!

These people are not latter-day Mrs Jellybys talking the talk, but not walking the walk. They are working at the heart-wrenching coal face of stressful human problems, day in, day out. They are responding to a deep inner need to do something to help others, however personally inconvenient that might be. Active Social Contributors come from all areas of society. From the rich, the poor, the unemployed, the retired, the busy, busy High-flyers – they *all feel the need to contribute, in order to become human.*

ASC's understand that their personal contribution is minute in the face of the overall need. They are under no illusions that their individual actions will change the world. What they do know is that whatever they are doing, for the individual recipients they touch, their contribution can make a difference.

The bottom line is that Active Social Contributors feel better about themselves. Their work within the Team Sector – whether part, or full time, paid or voluntary – gives them self-esteem, a sense of meaning. It can also give them companionship, participation, and a sense of accountability and responsibility.

2. The huge, and growing, need within society for help

Sadly, not everyone feels an overwhelming desire to help his or her fellow man or woman. There are more takers than givers. Takers in the sense that they have serious needs. But also in the sense of those who work hard, take their money, feed their family, but feel no obligation to give anything back.

There are also what I would term the **Honourable Takers**, a category to whom I belonged until relatively recently. These are the people who assuage their social conscience by donating regularly to charities – eminently worthwhile in itself – but do not go the extra mile in regularly putting time, as well as money, into the community. Lizzie has always gone the extra mile in all areas of activity. In Active Social Contributing, she has for years been spending two mornings a week bathing the infirm elderly in their homes. She enjoys it, and claims to get as much out of it as they do. She was formerly a nurse tutor, but enjoys frontline nursing. She even carried on when pregnant, and carried our second child round with her after she was born, much to the delight of the elderly patients.

What makes the work of the Lizzies of this world so important is that the need for their input is growing relentlessly. As the demands on welfare budgets grow, supercharged by the unassuageable demands for more healthcare for more elderly people, and at the same time those welfare budgets are pruned by the pressures of uphill demographics, *it stands to reason that more and more human beings will fall through the cracks.*

Services to the most vulnerable in our society are being withdrawn daily by both national and local government. Because they have no voice, those deprived of the services are unable to articulate their sense of loss. Often, the sense of self-worth is also so low that they accept their lot, and feel they do not have the right to ask. This is compounded by the fact that many services are not offered, but have to be asked for. They are seldom advertised, and if people don't ask for them, they aren't supplied. When services are withdrawn, the handicapped, the elderly, those in poor health, suffer a loss which goes beyond that of the specific service that has been withdrawn. *They lose, also, precious human contacts that form an important part of their quality of life.*

Human contact will become increasingly one of the most important roles of the ASC. Loneliness, in some cases coupled with depression, is becoming a major plague in modern societies. The elderly, and the homeless, are particularly prone to it. Involvement with an ASC, on a regular personal basis, will help to relieve loneliness as well as, by confirming that they are valued as individuals, helping to avoid, or alleviate, depression. This also, of course has wider economic implications, as depression has high financial as well as human costs to society.

The Team Sector is all about win/win. A further dimension of this win/win aspect is the huge benefit of the Team Sector *being a vast and worthwhile absorber of manpower (and womanpower). What is even more exciting about it is that they are activities that can't be replaced by technology.* The caring skills required by Active Social Contributors are not skills that can be replaced by a computer. They are definitively human. Microsoft Windows' Help programme has many items in it. To my simple mind, few are understandable, and even fewer remotely helpful. Listening with the heart certainly isn't one of them.

3. The need for cohesion in society

The 1980s and '90s demonstrated that the command economies of the communist states don't work. From this we can deduce that command societies are unlikely to work either. We will therefore need volunteers to bring about social cohesion.

The divisive forces on society are both horizontal and vertical. The horizontal forces of division are brought about by the de-massification of marketing. The de-massification of marketing is a very large subject in its own right. In essence, it relates to the ability of manufacturers and marketers to produce, highly cost effectively, small runs of products, and to target them at highly defined target audiences. This targeting relates to both the specification of the product or service, and to the medium or media used to convey the marketing message. The very significant increase in the number of product variations stocked by retail outlets is a direct effect of this trend.

While this customisation of marketing may have benefits for both consumers and marketers, there is also a downside. One is the fragmentation of the media – the multiplication of TV channels, magazines, etc. to an almost infinite number of smaller and smaller interest groups. The element of downside in this stems from the fact everyone is now watching, or reading, something different. There is *less and less shared experience* any more. Even within families, family members may watch different programmes in different rooms. In the days of two or three channels, the happenings within popular programmes provided a lingua franca for discussion the next day. Now, apart from the weather, there is little of topical common interest to talk about.

This compounds feelings of fragmentation and separateness already inherent in people living in smaller and smaller units. *Of households in northern Europe 60 per cent now contain either only one or two people.* This freedom of the individual to *be* individual is in many ways desirable, and we should be grateful for it. But not everyone can cope with such fragmentation and isolation. (For many, this alone is a good reason for becoming an IBG, with all the personal growth that goes along with it). This sense of isolation is likely to be supercharged by the growth in home working, which will reduce opportunities for physical contact and association.

If the horizontal forces produce isolation, the vertical forces are likely to produce alienation. The vertical forces of division are those resulting from the polarisation of incomes. *Already there are signs of the very high earners exhibiting the hallmarks of arrogance and greed. This only has to be joined by corruption, and the mixture becomes explosive.*

There are therefore two imperatives. The first is for governments to prevent at all costs a large underclass building up. The second is to prevent the wealthy élite from becoming arrogant and corrupt, thus providing the underclass a genuine reason to be resentful. The latter is no easy task. To achieve it, the government itself must be of unimpeachable probity. Such probity is thus important not merely on moral grounds, but on grounds of civil security: it is but a short step from justified alienation to civil unrest. *It is no exaggeration to say that the future quality of life of many developed societies depends on the level of civic responsibility exhibited by the rulers and the wealthy élites.*

The Team Sector will develop in importance through mutual self-interest

The importance of the wealthy behaving with sensitivity and humanity is underlined by the possibility of living standards overall being at best stable. If, on the other hand, the economic background is one of declining living standards, brought about by uphill demographics, technology replacing jobs, and global competition, then expectations in general may need to be downscaled.

This downscaling of expectations is likely to apply to all points on the income scale, including some within the High-flyers. This is because technology will replace more and more functions of the professions. There will, of course, be huge demand, and huge rewards, for the conceptual élites amongst engineers, accountants, architects, lawyers, and scientists, *but many of the tasks of the workaday professionals will be replaced by machines.* For those marginalised by technology, the reduction in welfare budgets will mean that unemployment benefit will not be a dependable income stream. Times will be tough for the unfortunates who have spent time and money training themselves for professions which no longer need them.

Not only should these people be becoming IBGs *now*, they could form an articulate part of a large group in society whose hopes and expectations have been dashed. If they are already Team Members, they will benefit in several ways. They will benefit from having one or more worthwhile and satisfying outlet for energy that otherwise could be directed both negatively and unproductively. They will also benefit from a sense of perspective of working with people who have a far tougher lot in life than their own.

A further way they will benefit *is to understand that what they are doing is worthwhile from the point of view of social cohesion.* If enough people are contributing actively to others in society, the effect would be for all sectors to get as close as possible to the mutually supportive feelings of a nation at war. If everyone feels they are all in it together, the feelings are very different from different interest groups fighting for their own narrow needs to be satisfied.

At the very lowest level of stark self-interest, the more connections, and the more humane and genuinely motivated those connections are, the less volatile are the receivers. For this reason, *inter*dependence on all levels – social as well as economic – is what the Team Sector is about. Becoming a team player begins to break down, in a subtle but important way, the dependency culture. Because the receivers of help feel more *valued*, they begin to feel more sense of self-worth, and thus a reduced sense of dependency.

Almost as important, those Team Members giving the help, begin to take responsibility for the disadvantaged in society, rather than handing that responsibility over to government, local or national. The attitude of, 'I pay my taxes for welfare – it's not my problem any more' begins to break down. In its place there develops an attitude of, 'We're all in it together, I might as well do my bit to help. I might even enjoy it.'

Civic responsibility is thus leavened by a healthy dose of self-interest. The satisfaction of doing something worthwhile – helping individuals in need – is increased by knowing that social cohesion is being strengthened (protecting yourself and your family), and that you are enjoying the process (probably more than expected). Recognition for being a Team Member (if such recognition were appropriate) is a further potentially powerful motivator. And thinking of those 60 per cent of people in northern Europe living in households with two or fewer people in them, active social contributing gives a potentially very positive antidote to isolation and loneliness.

Who are the core activists in the Team Sector?

The overall core activists in the Team Sector are, of course, national and local government. It is up to these bodies to have a strategic understanding of the role of government funding in the paid sector, as well as to have a clear view on where unpaid bodies, and individuals, fit into the picture. *A comprehensive and coherent overview of what the needs are, followed by a just distribution of taxes to satisfy as many of those needs as possible, will be of the utmost importance, so that both taxpayers and government feel they are part of the same team.*

An Active Social Contributor can be anyone who helps other people. This stretches from part-time or full-time paid experts through to people working in not-for-profit organisations supporting good causes, and on to individuals who give their time and energy willingly to help in some small way other individuals less fortunate than themselves. Some will be in full-time employment elsewhere. Others will be IBGs. Others still will be unemployed, or marginally employed. Givers and receivers are all part of the same team. Both give and both take.

The goal would be to make the paid and unpaid sectors *seamless* in their service of the community. A mum helping out in a small group reading for five-year-olds, a volunteer working as a auxiliary social worker, a volunteer visiting a fit but terrified old person living on a run-down housing estate, are all part of the Team Sector, along with the professional carers.

Whether some of the broad spectrum of activities that contribute to the better functioning of society, and to the greater happiness of individuals within that society, are paid, or unpaid, is likely to vary over time. Priorities within caring will change, and the availability of funds will vary between regions and across funding periods. For the Active Social Contributor, therefore, some flexibility of mind will be necessary.

As long as the primary objective is to help others, and in doing so to improve how we feel about ourselves, this potential loss of what would be an alternative or second income, should be capable of being accommodated. It might not be greeted with undiluted joy, but it is unlikely to produce a greater fluctuation in income than IBGs, at least, are used to dealing with anyway (even in this area we will need to wear the coat of change with comfort).

A further important reason for the voluntary and paid sectors being seamless is that a powerful voluntary input by ASCs will help to prevent the state becoming the employer of last resort. If, for example, a prison warder gave time voluntarily (as an ASC) to guard prisoners during education by outside ASCs, or a policemen visited a run down housing estate (as an ASC) to bring comfort to a terrified elderly victim of crime, this would develop the sector at no cost to the state. Furthermore if the unemployed gave their time voluntarily as ASCs, subsequent change in status, if they found employment, would again not materially affect either the funding of the Team Sector, or of the Social Security budget.

Corporations can fund the Team Sector in time, as well as money

Corporations and companies already fund good causes to a considerable extent. Their funding has parallels in the investment by Active Social Contributors of their time into the community – both have large elements of enlightened self-interest. Companies, like individuals, like to be well regarded by others, and to feel good about themselves. They are, after all, made up of individual human beings. Even shareholders are ultimately – behind the institutions which represent them – human beings.

The debate currently on how future productivity gains, brought about by advances in technology, should be shared between the various stakeholders is intense. Between the extremes of more benefits for shareholders by reducing staff numbers, and more benfits for the staff by reducing staff hours for the same, or more, pay there is possibly a more socially responsible way. Assuming financial institutions come to see the benefits of social stability to the health of their investments, and their potential role in the achievement of that stability, a deal something along the following lines could be struck:

Choice for workers

Either

reduce working week by, say, five hours. No reduction in earnings, but three of the five hours to be invested in Active Social Contributing. A worker would agree with his or her employer the type of work or service, and would be answerable to the employer for the quality of that work or service. The employer would provide a selection of projects for those with no special interests, or ideas of their own. Workers would be free to put in more hours as ASCs, if they chose to do so.

Or

take a shorter working week, but with reduced earnings (say the equivalent of three of the five hours worked less). This money would be a *humanity tax*, and would be invested in a mutually agreed worthwhile cause.

Such action would obviously require business leaders of vision and social responsibility. It would also need shareholders who had the wisdom to understand that society in general, and communities local to company activity in particular, are also stakeholders in any enterprise. Such shareholders and such visionary chief executives exist. All it needs is for Active Social Contributing to be moved higher up the corporate agenda – before it's too late.

Active Social Contributors will find and define
the areas of activity

The field of social contributing is both complex and mature. The welfare state has been going in one form or another for many years in most developed societies. National and local governments have therefore covered most of the large areas, like health and education. The challenge comes from two sources. One is – as we have seen – that uphill demographics mean that fewer people are paying in, and more people are taking out. The second is that welfare demand – for health (more old people living longer, etc.) and for social support of various kinds (more single parents, more, smaller households to support, more crime, etc.) – grows relentlessly, leaving welfare budgets unable to cope.

More and more human beings are therefore falling through the safety net. The need for Active Social Contributors is thus a huge and genuine one. We are not talking make-work projects that are irrelevant or misdirected, but give the contributors a warm glow inside. Active Social Contributors will be *needed*, both for spotting the human requirements, as well as helping to fulfil them.

Ideas for the targeting of resources – particularly currently under-utilised resources – will be welcome, as well as the vision and energy to make things happen. *More flexibility will be required all round. This applies to charities as well as governments.* From personal experience of talking to frontline charities, too many of them have not yet found ways of accommodating well-meaning part-time volunteers (ASCs). Understandably, they prefer professionals for the majority of their work, relying on part-timers for fundraising and and other peripheral activities. They will need to change this approach if they are not to lose a vast reservoir of part-time energy and commitment from ASCs who are looking to join the Team Sector.

One or two ideas, for starters

As seed corn, I would suggest two or three ideas. As ideas, they are random, and not fully thought through. Welfare professionals could probably find holes in them at first glance. Some may already exist. I'd be surprised and disappointed if they didn't. That would be to miss the point. The ideas are suggested merely to illustrate that there are an infinite variety of ways to help people that need help, and that *many of these can help the helpers as well.*

Powering prisoner potential

The growth in crime has driven up the costs of incarcerating prisoners to such an extent that most prisons regimes are too stretched covering the basics of prisoner security and avoiding wide-scale disturbances, to be able to free up time to look at any serious attempt to rehabilitate prisoners. Groups concerned with the rehabilitation of drug users, and the preparation of prisoners for release, are active in prisons, but general run-of-the-mill prisoners have little external stimulus, apart from visits from family and friends.

Prisoners are in prison to atone for offences that are antisocial. They are also human beings with potential to grow and improve. Leaving their minds with no stimulus beyond the association with other criminals has the effect of dramatically increasing the chances of reoffending. Recidivism thus becomes, for many prisoners, a self-fulfilling prophecy.

Assuming that most prisoners are looking for mental stimulation – anything to break the tedium – there would seem to be a void waiting to be filled. Assuming also that the majority of the acting profession, who are out of work at any one time, would welcome the opportunity to hone and refresh their directing and theatrical skills, and to be involved in drama workshops and live drama, there again would seem to be a void waiting to be filled – this time on the outside. Putting the two together would be stimulating for both the actors and the prisoners, and would result in a win/win situation.

Out of work, or retired, teachers, lawyers, counsellors, accountants, etc. – all of whom have skills and knowledge that could be edited to be relevant – could also contribute their time to bringing new insights and understanding to the prisoners. The goal would be to develop the self-awareness, the self-confidence, and ultimately the integrity of the prisoners. Acting skills, lessons in positive thinking – *acting as if* they were honest, socially aware people – would all be an important beginning in the long road of personal development and personal growth.

'But the warders have too much to do anyway. The cost of supervising the extra activities would be unaffordable', I hear the doubters cry. But warders are human beings too. Some of them are very compassionate ones. They, too, can become Active Social Contributors, giving their time free. Most warders would get considerable satisfaction from seeing a man, or a woman, grow in prison into better-balanced, better-intentioned individuals, so that when they come to leave they have some serious chance of staying away from the negative association of criminals, and going on to lead worthwhile, positive lives.

Do-It-Yourself Community Helpline

There are a few zealots who, for reasons I cannot fathom, actually like DIY activity around the house. Lizzie is one of these. When I married her, she was doing up her second house, and owned not one, but two, power drills. She inherited the talent from her mother, who made a lifetime's profession of moving house at frequent intervals to start again on a new challenge in adding value to rundown properties.

Most people – like myself – who undertake home improvements, or mend things that are broken, or leaking, only do so because they cannot afford to pay an expert professional to come in and fix it for them. If my own experience is a guide, I am normally finishing a job before I work out finally how I should have done it in the first place. The problem normally comes when I have to do the job again at a later date, and I have entirely forgotten how I did it on the previous occasion, and have to start the learning process all over again.

The **Do-It-Yourself Community Helpline** is intended for people who are less well off than I am, but have a similar poor understanding and liking for the arts of home improvement. The service would be targeted at people living in substandard accommodation that would be enormously improved – along with their spirits – if some simple improvements were undertaken. These improvements might be made by the occupants, or by ASCs who would be asked in to help that young single mother, elderly, or handicapped person, etc. who needed work done, but was in no position to do it themselves.

A switchboard, funded by DIY manufacturers or retailers, would coordinate requests for information, or for physical help. The calls for information would be routed to retired plumbers, carpenters, electricians, etc. who would be at home, answering the calls, and giving advice. Requests for physical help would be scrutinised by a an on-duty ASC, who would decide, on a set of pre-agreed criteria, whether the applicant qualified for assistance. If the applicant passed the first set of criteria,

ASCs would visit the premises to confirm that it was a deserving case, and that resources should be deployed to start work to fix the problem or improve the living conditions.

There are obvious challenges in the scheme to be overcome – like legal disclaimers on advice, in case it proves to be wrong – but none which could not be overcome. Again the situation could be win/win. The receivers of help either get a problem solved, or the information on how to solve it. Some would even get a material improvement in their living conditions. The givers of help would get the satisfaction of knowing their advice and help was both appreciated, and being put to good effect.

Listening lines

A **Listening Line** would be a number for someone to call if they needed a sympathetic ear, but had no one to turn to. Calls would be answered by Listeners in their homes, but would be routed via a central switchboard, to assure total anonymity at both ends.

Listeners would be the equivalent of secular priests. Their job would be to listen, sympathetically, to people's problems. Currently doctors are taking up much of the burden of listening and counselling let fall by priests in previous generations. Listening Lines would be staffed by a rota of Active Social Contributors who would be given training in the rudimentary skills of counselling.

Unlike citizens' advice bureaux, their job would not be to dispense advice. It would be to listen attentively, and then to refer people on for help from specialist services, if appropriate. Listening is the central role. Listening to anyone who has something they want to pour into an ear that has time to listen. This would include a very broad spectrum – stressed High-flyers, the lonely, the depressed, the concerned, the bereaved, the victims of sexual or criminal violence or abuse – anyone who felt that talking to an objective but sympathetic human being might be helpful in easing the pressure.

Listening Lines would fill an important role in being a small, but significant step before an individual needed the Samaritans. The Samaritans are the Listening Line of last resort. The goal of the Team Players manning the Listening Lines would be to intercede with relief well before someone is seriously considering suicide. A Listener is thus a demanding but satisfying role. Many of the Listeners could be in retirement, but still keen to be Active Social Contributors. They would thus have time, patience, and experience to give – priceless qualities to those in need of someone to talk to. Again, both sides would be winners.

Even the losers win in the Team Sector

So becoming an Active Social Contributor in the Team Sector will be challenging but potentially enormously satisfying. New frameworks and more flexible approaches will be required to meet the new challenges, but the mutual self-interest of both the helpers and the helped will mean that ways will be found. Once full-time, part-time and volunteer workers realise that they are all Active Social Contributors, and are all working in the vitally important Team Sector, their sense of self-worth will begin to grow. The physical, mental, and even spiritual health of great nations will depend on their understanding, encouraging, and developing their Team Sectors.

Felicity, Norman and Simon join the Team Sector

This is our last visit to the lives of our three explorers, who have grown in confidence and maturity as they have learned to wear the Coat of Change. For this visit, we will move the clock forward twenty years.

The Team Sector is developing well. Its early days were scarred by wrangles between the public and the voluntary sectors. Governments – both national and local – fudged issues by under-funding certain areas of welfare. They under-supported the care required for the elderly, hoping Active Social Contributors would step smiling into the gaps they had left. This did not happen, but as good always comes out of bad, the result was positive – in the form of a much more public debate about priorities for the welfare programme.

All concerned knew that there was not enough money to go around. National governments in developed countries eventually got around to acting in concert to tax the enormous productivity gains of the multinational corporations brought about by massive advances in Information Technology. (Well, almost in concert, as one or two smaller countries attempted to go it alone with low tax regimes, in an attempt to become twenty-first-century Hong Kongs).

Even these extra taxes were insufficient to fund the skews in dependency ratios brought about by uphill demographics. In care of the elderly alone the *hours of care now needed was 30 per cent higher – and rising – than twenty years previously.*

An interesting and significant change over the twenty-year period was in the general *attitude towards care workers* – both paid, and volunteer ASCs. As more and more people began to wear the Coat of Change, many of them becoming IBGs in the process, their understanding of the precariousness of income – and indeed life in general – became more pronounced.

Like a wealthy man or woman endowing a hospital that had nursed them back to health, there was *more appreciation in general of people who devoted their skills to the benefit of others.* This was partly helped by the *deeper understanding of the importance and talent required to care well for people,* that was engendered by more and more Active Social Contributors themselves getting involved in the front line of caring. Partly too, it came from *a relishing of the fact that these were skills that could not be replaced by technology.*

Felicity makes Active Social Contributing fun

Felicity is now fifty-five. Slightly plumper, still attractive, and with deeper laugh lines around her eyes, Felicity loves life. Both her conference business, Conference Felicitations, and her network marketing business have prospered. While prospecting for her network marketing business she met a met a divorcee called Geoff, whom she not only recruited to her network, but married some months later.

Conference Felicitations has evolved in a market which had seen some interesting changes. Many of the day-to-day meetings and conferences had been replaced by the spread of video-conferencing equipment in most offices. Personal computers, for home-based, or office-based, workers, and laptops, or pocket diary-sized for workers on the move, all had cameras built in, so audio-visual links for business were becoming universal.

Conference rooms were equipped with multiple cameras and screens, so that meetings between executives at all points of the globe had an almost uncanny quasi-reality. As multiple cameras picked up expressions – all from the common angle of the viewer, it really was very close to being in the same room. The savings in time and money on travel were, of course, enormous.

For perversely human, and therefore understandable reasons, Conference Felicitations prospered as a result of all this mechanisation of human social intercourse. The human chemistry was present in everyday video-conferencing through Personal computers, but at a reduced level. The need for the large company get-togethers that Felicity specialised in became much larger. Positive, physical association intensified in importance as a way of strengthening company cultures in a positive way.

Because Felicity had always majored on the fun, human aspects of the conferences she staged, she was much in demand. Her business grew, she brought in some strong talent to join her, and as they developed, three or four joined her on the board of directors. One emerged as a strong and respected leader, and Felicity was delighted to appoint him chief executive officer, while she took more and more of a back seat.

When Felicity married Geoff she knew it was late (she was approaching forty), but she intended to have children. She needed all the strength of her positive visualisations and affirmations when she discovered that she was unable to do so. She recovered strongly, and became a good second mother to Geoff's three children, when they came for weekends and holidays. Felicity, however, felt the need for more. *Her life was busy, but not complete.* She therefore decided to become an Active Social Contributor – to become a Team Player in the Team Sector.

She examined several charities for children, but finally decided that the biggest need, and the biggest challenge, was in adding to the quality of life of the elderly. She gathered around her a Mastermind group to brainstorm some ideas. They established their values, and went on to define their mission. They decided that their *mission was to bring dignity, and fun, to any elderly who were in danger of losing either, or both, in their lives.* Fun had been an important part of her Mission Statement on founding Conference Felicitations, and she had remained true to it over the years.

They were aware that this was a huge and almost unfulfillable mission, but felt it took them in the right direction. The most important thing was that the size of the idea excited them, and gave them extra energy to go about trying to execute it. They decided to start locally, take it national if it was successful, and then think about going international with it.

Felicity faced the challenge with eager anticipation. She now had financial freedom, both from her income from Conference Felicitations, for whom she now worked two days a week, and her income from her network marketing business. Felicity founded an organisation called Naughty at Ninety, of which she became president. Their strategy was simple. They put all their energies into helping elderly people stay in their homes for as long as possible. This helped them preserve their sense of independence, and gave them dignity. They also created a social life for them that was fun, and sometimes racy.

Keeping elderly people in their homes as long as possible fitted in with the work of several other Active Social Contributor groups, funded both by government, and by charities. The difference about Felicity's organisation was that it attracted funding from large corporations, especially in the video-conferencing industry, and could finance the capital investment necessary to make them interactive. In practical terms this meant installing video conferencing equipment into all the homes of elderly people who were in their catchment area.

Twice a day a friendly ASC would call up elderly friends in their homes to check that they were all right, and to have a short chat – face to face. If there were problems, other services could be alerted. George Orwell's Big Brother became a Fun Friend. The Team Members enjoyed the work, but had to be very disciplined in keeping the chats to a reasonable length, as many of their interlocutors would have been happy to have talked all day. Their exit line was similar each day: 'Must fly now – here's an update on the local news.' At this point there was a short update on local social events, messages from Felicity or her staff and promotions for local services – films, chiropodists, etc., which helped pay for the service. There were also short sessions from local doctors and nurses, giving health tips, dietary advice, and general information on clinics, etc. These in turn were followed by session of gentle exercise, led by local fitness experts.

Some of the social events were quite something. Once a month, Felicity staged a knees-up in a large local hall. There were party games – some quite suggestive (which the participants loved) – as well as conjurors and magicians, plus Scottish, or Square, dancing. The performers, in all cases, were the elderly themselves, or Team Members. Those too infirm to get to the parties were collected and brought by others, or by Team Members. The Team Members were expert at involving the newcomers, and the shy, in the proceedings, so that no one felt left out.

The proceedings were taped by ASCs, some of whom worked at Conference Felicitations. Two or three days later, an edited mini-cassette was sent out to all the homes of those taking part – and to those who had missed the party – to play on their conferencing monitors. Playing the cassette both relived the enjoyment, and heightened the sense of anticipation of the next one. The cassettes were topped and tailed by a few words from Felicity, giving some thoughts on personal development – it's never too late – and positive thinking in particular.

Time passed, and Naughty at Ninety began to spread. Felicity established it as a not-for-profit franchise operation. The reason that it was run commercially (although not for profit) was to allow the original founders of the organisation to maintain tight controls on the operating standards. There is a limit to how home-made videos and events can be before they degenerate into something well-meaning but embarrassing.

It was slow in rolling out for three reasons. The first was that Felicity and her team were adamant that the right quality of management (even if some of them were ASCs), and training, had to be in place before a new territory was licensed. The second was that although video-conferencing equipment was now inexpensive, there was still a capital cost attached to it for the amount of equipment that was required to reach all the homes that wanted it. This money had to be found, even if the manufacturers were supplying systems at heavily subsidised prices.

The third reason for the slowness of the roll-out was that the organisers found that as some of their elderly funsters were forced by failing health, despite all their efforts, to move into residential homes, their sense of loss of the life-support system of Naughty at Ninety was intense. Just when they needed their spirits lifting, and to need to feel that they were still involved in humanity, part of their oxygen supply was cut off, by no longer being able to have their daily chats with the Naughty at Ninety staff, or be involved with the monthly parties.

Felicity and her colleagues at Naughty at Ninety responded positively to the situation. They decided to extend the execution of their Mission Statement to include residential homes. This was a big decision as the implications were significant.

We leave Felicity wrestling with the implications. She is excited about the future, and enjoying every minute of the present. She enjoys her work as an Active Social Contributor even more than she does her work at Conference Felicitations. She is once more at the coal face, leading by example, and interacting with people whom she can infect with her sense of fun. Felicity's father, who had thought her role was to make someone a good wife, is now in his eighties. He tunes in daily to Naughty at Ninety. He is intensely proud of his daughter.

Norman is still a very Active Social Contributor at sixty-six

Norman Newhope has passed the old technical age of retirement. State pensions are now personal, contributory schemes, and have been for several years, so that if Norman had been relying on his state pension scheme for income in retirement – which, fortunately, he wasn't – he could not have chosen when to retire. The timing of retirement is now up to the individual. The earlier retirement is taken, the lower the amount paid in, or credited by the government under the old scheme, the lower the ongoing pension. The later it is taken, the more is paid in, the higher the pension.

Norman, too, has prospered. He has had several setbacks on the way, however. The largest was caused by the collapse in retail property prices as interactive home shopping, particularly in food, really started to take a large share of the market. Manufacturers, having been held to ransom by the increasingly large retailers, began their fightback as interactive equipment in homes became commonplace. By putting their goods through third-party operators specialising in home shopping delivery of food and other groceries, manufacturers had a new route to market. Because there was no need to fund the huge infrastructure of shops, with their property, staff and systems costs, the goods could be delivered to homes more cheaply, and with less hassle.

Retailers fought back, of course, but for most of them, it was a losing battle. Unless they could offer a leisure experience that was enjoyable – which when selling detergents, nappies, or cans of beans was quite challenging – they were in trouble. They provided their own home delivery services, but they were an extra cost on top of high local property costs, so in the long run were not cost effective. Delectable Foods was one of the businesses that did not survive the arrival of home-shopping.

As more and more retailers of chore products – products that customers would rather have delivered, rather than wasting scarce leisure time picking up themselves from stores some distance away – went out of business, retail property prices began to fall. This was good news and bad news for Norman's business. The hundred or so Glorious Gardens already franchised were now paying rents that were too high, and thus uneconomical. Any new competitor coming into the market would be paying considerably lower rent for property, and would therefore be operating on a lower cost base.

The new stores, of course, would themselves have a lower cost base, which would be good for business. He could charge lower prices, and still make more money. The challenge for Norman was that he was running a franchise operation. If the shops had been owned by Glorious Gardens, the new cost base could have been accommodated by averaging the rents across the whole property portfolio. As it was, individual franchisees owned the leases to the individual shops, meaning there was little or no flexibility. Property costs are such a high percentage of overall costs for most retailers, that fiddling about with franchise commissions was irrelevant.

Conversations took place with landlords, and one or two were sympathetic, and took a constructive view by allowing rent concessions until the end of the leases. Others were more pig-headed, with the result that several of Norman's franchisees struggled considerably, and four went bankrupt. This was upsetting for Norman and Iris, who took a personal interest in all their franchisees.

In each case, Norman employed his accountant's training, and as soon as was possible he would reapproach the landlord, who by now finally realised no one was going to pay him the original rent, which was now out of line with the market. Norman agreed a sensible rent, reopened the Glorious Gardens store, and employed the previous franchisee, as manager. As soon as the bankruptcy was discharged, Norman arranged special terms for the manager to become, once more, a franchisee.

One of the four who went bankrupt was Peter Preacher, the troublesome franchisee of Norman and Iris's first franchised outlet. Peter had never really learned to listen. Despite all the coaching and support from Norman and Iris, Peter would listen when things started to go badly, and then stop listening when things started to go well again. Bankruptcy was Peter's watershed. He was shaken to the core. He decided to read the books that Norman had been supplying him with over the months and years, rather than leaving them, unopened, on a bookcase in a spare bedroom. At last he gained some insight into himself, and began to grow as a person. When Norman gave him a second chance in letting him manage his old store until he could discharge his bankruptcy, he took his chance. This time sales grew, and kept growing.

This, in a minor way, was Active Social Contributing, as it saved four families from what could have been even worse distress, and gave them a lifeline to the future. Norman's more formal role as an Active Social Contributor was as a Listener. Listening Lines were staffed from 6 a.m. to midnight, as many of the people needing to talk to a Listener were holding down two, or even three, poorly paid jobs, and having to do shifts with their partners to look after their children. This left them with no time to spare in conventional working hours to unburden themselves of the tensions and stress they were suffering.

Norman enjoyed being a Listener. Though the work was highly demanding in human terms, he always felt uplifted when he was able to help, in however small a way. Listeners worked from home, with calls routed through a central switchboard. Because Listeners had total anonymity, the visual part of the phone link was turned off, so no caller knew to whom they were unburdening themselves.

Norman encountered a very broad range of human challenges as a Listener. On occasion, it took him some way out of his comfort zone, as he listened to experiences that left him profoundly grateful for the relatively sheltered life he had led. Many came from people who were wearing the Coat of Change with great discomfort. Some of these found it hard to shuffle off the employee mentality, even after conventional jobs had given way to *ad hoc* employment.

They found it hard to cope, because they had not made the transition to becoming IBGs. They thus felt themselves to be in the role of an employment supplicant (which they resented), with no control over their income. Working from home was another challenge for some people, especially those with unhappy, or dysfunctional homes. Loneliness was a recurrent problem, as was the encroaching feeling of panic at the inexorable decline into greater and greater debt.

Norman listened, and gave what advice he appropriately could. His goal was gently to reduce the worry level of those who came to him as a Listener, so that no one left the phone call without feeling better than when they had started it. Norman knew that what he was doing was worthwhile, but still, from time to time, felt frustrated at the somewhat passive role of a Listener. He did give good advice where he could, but he knew his central role was to listen, rather than come up with an action plan to change their lives.

One of the recurrent problems set before him was that of poorly educated sons of unemployed fathers. The sons seldom phoned, as that would brought ridicule from their peer group (had they chanced to find out), but the mothers, and sometimes the fathers, poured their hearts out to Norman. Appreciating the problem to be a very challenging one, and international in scale, Norman decided to do something about it. He was already a Team Player through his work as a Listener, but he decided in this case to get glorious Gardens as an organisation involved in the Team Sector.

At the next monthly meeting of the council of franchisees (the leading franchisees in the organisation) he floated the idea of a latter-day apprentice scheme in Glorious Gardens. The scheme would be purely for children with poor academic and family backgrounds, who had never had consistent employment. Norman used the council as a Mastermind group. They were all independent businessmen, and usually came up with the solution to the most intractable of problems. It was in the council that they had thrashed out the details of Norman's initiative to save the franchisees going into liquidation, following the collapse in retail property prices.

The idea of employing teenagers who had never gained employment from backgrounds that had no consistent work ethic did not initially meet universal acclaim at the council. As Norman explained the origin of the idea in more detail, they came to see the bigger picture, and eventually became enthusiastic. They evolved a latter-day apprentice scheme that gave a year's training, followed by a minimum level of guaranteed employment (no one, in any business, apart from owners and core managers, had jobs any more), if specified standards were met. The candidates would come from hard case backgrounds – non-working parents; poor academic performance; no, or poor, record of employment.

The Mastermind group communicated the scheme to the rest of the franchisees, some of whom were less than impressed by the thought of what they saw as employing work-shy, truculent, adolescents, with no ability, or interest in learning. To avoid what could have been an unproductive fiasco, ten of the enthusiastic supporters of the scheme decided to pilot apprenticeships in their own stores, to prove that the scheme could work.

Norman's original store was one of those ten chosen to pilot the scheme. Norman and Iris still worked a day a week on the shop floor, to keep themselves in touch with the customers, and what was happening in the business at the grass roots level. When the apprenticeship was advertised, the result was almost overwhelming. After many interviews, and much soul searching, a young lad called Ken Doe was selected. He had achieved very little at school, had an alcoholic father, who had recently died of an alcohol-related illness, a mother with mental health problems (as a direct result of the father's drinking and behaviour), and three younger siblings, who were still, technically, at school, but seldom turned up for lessons.

There was something about Ken, however, that gave indications that somewhere, deep inside, there was potential, waiting to burst out. Certainly, since his father had died, he had become much more responsible about the home, and had tried much harder to get employment.

When he started, Ken Doe was extremely timid, but with encouragement, and training, he soon developed an attractive self-confidence, and pride in his work. His energy level increased, and within a few months had earned the nickname 'Can Do'. The other nine franchisees on the pilot scheme had a varying level of success, but all declared themselves positive about the longer term outcome.

Some six months after the scheme had been launched, Norman was walking home one night after a late evening session working at his local Glorious Gardens. There was a gentle drizzle, but not enough to make him put up his umbrella. He glanced in a shop window, and in the reflection he caught sight of two or three youths who seemed to be airborne, launching themselves onto his back. He tried to spin round, but it was too late. The leading youth landed on him, forcing him to the ground.

He was forced to lie face down, as they pulled his jacket back, to empty the contents. As he struggled, he could smell the wet of the pavement, and could feel strong hands closing around his throat. His head began to swim, and as he started to lose consciousness, he could hear shouting from across the street: 'Oi! Leave him alone. Don't use the knife. He's all right.' As his mind slipped away from the pressure on his throat, he heard a voice closer to him say, 'Get out of it, Ken, it's nothing to do with you.'

Norman came back to consciousness in the ambulance called by a passer-by who had come across Norman's body on the pavement some minutes later. 'You were lucky, sir,' said the ambulance man. 'They were obviously serious about the attack, but they don't seem to have taken anything.' Norman felt in his pockets. Sure enough all his cards and valuables were there, even his recently replenished cash card.

Norman knew just how lucky he had been. Without the intervention of Ken Doe, who had obviously known the attackers – probably living on the same run-down housing estate – Norman could have been dead by now. He had been stupid enough to try to struggle, and a knife could easily have been used to hasten his unconsciousness. The fact that not only had he escaped with his life, but with all his possessions, was a powerful testimony to Ken's powers of persuasion.

He was, however, badly shaken. For weeks afterwards, he had nightmares, and panic attacks. He worked very hard, with Iris's help, on becoming once more, a Mighty Lion. With visualisations and affirmations, he was soon strong again. It was, however, two weeks before Norman could go back to work. The day before he went back to work, he rang into the local Glorious Gardens, to see how things were going (although Iris had been giving him daily bulletins). The manager replied that everything was fine, apart from the fact that they were concerned about Ken Doe. He seemed to be worried about something, and was far from his normal cheery self.

Norman guessed, correctly, that Ken was worried that Norman might involve him in the affair, and ask him to inform on his friends. The police arriving to interrogate people on his housing estate was the last thing that Ken needed. The assailants would come looking for him, as quickly as you could say 'knife'.

The next day Norman went into Glorious Gardens, and sought out a quiet word with Ken. 'Good morning, Ken,' said Norman. 'Good morning, sir,' said Ken, hardly able to meet his eye. 'Ken, a week or so ago I was the victim of a mugging. I don't suppose you have any idea who my attackers were, do you?' Ken looked concerned. He replied, 'You didn't have anything stolen, did you?'

Norman smiled, and shook his head. He took Ken's hand, and held it firmly in his. He looked into his eyes, and said, 'No I didn't. And thank you, Ken. You're a gentleman.' Ken relaxed visibly. He too smiled. 'Blow that,' he said. 'Thank *you*. You're the gentleman.'

Simon Smartbutton goes to prison as a Team Player

Sapiens Knowledge had grown, and was still flourishing. Peter Press-enter had driven, and was still driving, large sales volumes in the Pacific Rim, using highly effective commission-incentivised independent agents to develop different territories and industry sectors, as new products became available. Peter had hired some very bright managers to develop the core business, and once they had proved themselves, he turned the business over to them. They, in turn, had brought in innovators and experts from different disciplines and parts of the world to develop truly global products and services.

Simon was in semi-retirement, living off the very considerable income generated by the share of the licence income on the products and services, and the dividend income from his shares (Sapiens Knowledge had become a public company some ten years earlier). Fleur's network marketing business had also prospered. She had remained involved in it, even though they could have retired in comfort many years previously had they so wished. The simple reason for staying involved was that she liked the people, the positive environment, and more than anything, she enjoyed seeing people grow as individuals, facing challenges, and overcoming them.

They were both Active Social Contributors. They both worked with the charity that had given them such insight into how to deal with the handicap that their son Eric had been born with, and that had had been so instrumental in transforming their lives for the better. Simon still worked with Amnesty International, and had become a regular visitor and teacher at his local prison. He had also become a Seeker After Truth, though he had still to find a spiritual home where he could feel comfortable. Continually restless in his exploration both of exterior religious forms, and interior spiritual perspectives, Simon had still to find the peace that passeth understanding.

What gave Simon his biggest buzz was his work in the Team Sector in prisons. The prison population had continued to grow, despite more lenient sentencing from the law courts. The underclass that had few hopes of employment had become, in certain areas of the country, alienated and resentful. Crime had become endemic, with drug dependency supercharging an already volatile situation.

Simon liked particularly to work with young adult offenders, where he felt the largest opportunity lay. Young offenders were now recognised as ten- to fifteen-year-olds, and the government had finally woken up to the challenge of very young offenders, instituting constructive rehabilitation schemes in secure surroundings. Rather than release young children back into the community, where they could reoffend with impunity because of their age, these juvenile hard cases were taken away from the backgrounds that were condoning, and, in some cases, encouraging, bad behaviour, and put through high-quality rehabilitation programmes. These programmes were expensive, but gratifyingly effective.

Simon worked with eighteen- to twenty-five-year-olds, most of whom had poor educational standards and little experience of employment of any kind. Knowing the problem to be complex and intractable, Simon decided to attack it on a small scale, but with a Mastermind group from several different disciplines. He was already a visitor of individual prisoners at his local gaol, and decided to use that experience as a jumping-off point. He included in his Mastermind group people with specialist interests, some of whom had not worked in the Team Sector before. One of these was an enlightened senior warder who had originally joined the service to rehabilitate offenders, but through government cutbacks had instead spent his career incarcerating them in as secure a manner as possible.

The warder was joined by the prison chaplain, a man of luminous kindness, understanding and strength, respected by prisoners and prison staff alike. These two were joined by another debutante Team Player, a criminal psychologist whom Simon knew socially, and rated as a man of sympathy and vision. Simon's last member was a member of Fleur's network marketing group. He was a history teacher at a local school (and thus a member of the Team Sector already), and also recognised within the network marketing business as a leading teacher of personal growth skills, in particular the development of a strong sense of self-worth.

Despite their different backgrounds, the group got on well together. Their goal was to devise a teaching programme that was participatory, fun, and would equip the prisoners with some skills, and, *more importantly, some attitudes*, that would be helpful when they had once more to attempt to cope with the challenges of the outside world.

What the group finally came up with was an interesting combination of personal development teaching and basic computer skills. The criminal psychologist had had his reservations about the efficacy of personal growth teaching but, faced with the enthusiasm for it from Simon and the history teacher, had agreed to go along with it. He was to be very impressed by the results.

The thinking behind the computer skills course was simple. The computer (mainly voice-activated now) was the weapon of choice of the affluent Knowledge Workers. To demythologise it, and to remove its fears and strangeness, by making it familiar and friendly, was thus to remove false barriers to future success. It also helped to reduce the absurd belief that still persisted amongst the unskilled, that work was in some way unworthy, even effeminate, if it did not involve physical labour.

Several of the IT innovators and experts at Sapiens Knowledge joined the Team Sector at one remove, by developing some original and stimulating computer games that inmates could play, and learn from at the same time. The skills taught by this method covered literacy and numeracy skills, which were lacking in the inmates, but which they came to absorb in an unobtrusive and enjoyable way, playing the games. The programmes also included data-accessing skills. Computers were by now so user friendly that for most of the time people using them to access information and make transactions were not even aware of the massive facilitating technology whirring away in the background.

Like books twenty or thirty years earlier, computers were universally available, but not in the homes of young men like those incarcerated in the prison in which Simon's initiative was taking place. The seamless convergence of technologies brought great benefits to the affluent, and those in employment, because it took much of the hard work out of many processes and transactions. For the underclass, who produced most of the young men on Simon's training scheme, however, the benefits largely passed them by. Worse, it made them feel more marginalised, and unable to share – legitimately – in the benefits of technology's ability to transform the productivity and effectiveness of daily living.

There were twenty inmates in the inaugural class. They were selected on the grounds that they had volunteered for the course, and were well behaved in general. Simon and the history teacher ran the course, with help and support at appropriate times from the rest of the Mastermind group. The course majored on personal development and encouraging a higher sense of self-worth, with greater familiarity with the benefits of computer technology playing a minor role. Sapiens Knowledge supplied all the technical kit, which was fully interactive with the outside world. There was only one interactive access point, as prison staff were concerned that if each prisoner had personal access during the lessons, the temptation to access pornography and other services during the lessons would be too great for individual prisoners to resist.

The first training session went well, and everybody seemed to enjoy it, including Simon and the history teacher. An intensely shy lad called Karl seemed very much at home in the technology skills part of the teaching, but was the only inmate who seemed unable to relate to the simple personal development skills that were being propounded. He could not meet anyone's eye, and could hardly answer his name. He sat hunched up, with his head lowered. Both Simon and the history teacher saw him as a challenge, and determined to single him out for special attention in subsequent weeks.

About ten days later, the governor asked to see Simon. After enquiring after the progress of the course, he thanked Simon for his generous present, and said that although he and his wife were extremely grateful, such beneficence really wasn't appropriate. Simon was baffled. On enquiring what beneficence he had been responsible for, it transpired that the governor had been sent a magnificent smoked salmon, accompanied by caviar, and his wife had been sent a huge bunch of orchids.

Simon disclaimed all knowledge of the gifts, and asked why the governor thought they were from him. The governor replied that he had checked on the sender's details, and had discovered that they had been ordered by Sapiens Knowledge. Simon was even more baffled. He rang Sapiens Knowledge on his pen phone in the governor's presence. The chief accountant confirmed that the transaction had taken place, but could find no personal authorisation for it. Simon ordered an investigation, and reassured the governor that it wouldn't happen again.

The lesson that week began with a minor breakthrough. As Simon walked through the door, he was greeted by a direct glance from Karl. He wasn't sure but he also thought he detected a hint of a smirk there, but he could have been mistaken. Karl was improving rapidly, but was still singled out for special attention. Advanced Neurolinguistic

Programming techniques were used, and progress was rapid. More frequent eye contact was taking place, and Karl could say his name more clearly. Once more, Karl showed that technology held no terrors for him. Indeed, he seemed to relax palpably when using it.

As usual the session took place in two parts. An hour was spent on self-development, and accessing resources that many of the inmates were surprised to discover they had within them. This was followed by forty-five minutes of technology skills, which was undertaken in small groups, with one of the groups working on the main console with the interactive links to global services, while others either undertook training from Simon and other teachers on specific skills, or played games to improve literacy or numeracy.

Towards the end of the lesson, Simon noticed a great deal of suppressed hilarity from the small group operating the main console, with access to worldwide services. At the centre of the group was Karl, who was the subject of much back-slapping. When the lesson was over, Simon went to the computer and turned on a search mechanism to trace the previous actions of the most recent operator. What he discovered caused him first to gasp, and then to laugh. 'Come and have a look at this,' he called to his colleagues, who were packing up their things.

What the trace showed was an order placed with an escort agency for a young lady of generous dimensions, who was to meet the chief warder outside the prison gates that evening, in order to render him some quite athletic services. They all laughed, because the chief warder was a man of somewhat self-satisfied punctiliousness, who could not be imagined in anything remotely approaching a mode of relaxed playfulness. 'Who paid for the service?' asked the history teacher. Simon searched further, and to his horror, discovered it was Sapiens Knowledge.

Probing deeper, he found that Sapiens Knowledge security systems had been breached, and that his personal authority code had been used to authorise the expenditure. There was a short debate amongst the team as to whether the order should be left to stand, giving them the opportunity to watch the fun from a distance. Reluctantly, they decided that the order to the agency should be cancelled, while an investigation was undertaken into who had done it, and how they had acquired the skill to accomplish such a technically sophisticated feat.

Upon investigation it transpired that Karl's prison sentence was for computer hacking. No theft had been involved, but his activities had caused severe embarrassment to several governments before he had been finally apprehended. The Mastermind group discussed the situation – and their possible responses – at their meeting later that week. After mulling it over, they all felt the activity was mischievous rather than criminal, and that the response should be a positive one. They would talk privately to Karl, to make him realise he had been rumbled, and as recompense for lenient treatment would – as soon as his social confidence was high enough – join the technology teaching team for the lessons.

Karl's response, on receiving the proposition, was a mixture of relief and horror. While he felt totally at home using the technology, the thought of having to teach the skills to others terrified him. He was set a goal of four weeks to achieve the level of resourcefulness that would allow him to be confident enough to at least show how things were done, even if he could not get many words out to support his demonstration.

With some intense coaching, Karl met the deadline. He *acted as if* he was a good teacher and, to his great surprise, he was a good teacher. After two or three weeks he began to enjoy it. His life, along with many others in the twenty-strong group, was transformed. With self-belief there slowly evolved an inner integrity that changed their relationships with those around them, and their view of the world. From victims – in many cases aggressive victims – they began to take control of their lives, and responsibility for their actions.

The project was judged to be a success by all concerned. The governor – who never did find out where the gifts of food and flowers came from – presented it as a case history to other prison governors at his annual conference. The scheme was rolled out – both to other prisons, and on a larger scale within prisons operating the scheme. It also achieved success internationally, even in countries where the Team Sector was less developed. Not only were recidivism rates radically improved, but many more inmates found employment on their release.

What was particularly satisfying for the Mastermind group was the significant increase in support from prison staff. Many joined this part of the Team Sector as volunteers, but after a while it became so popular and widespread that a decision was made by the government to embrace it – primarily as a way to demonstrate to the electorate that they were exploring new and imaginative ways to support their law and order credentials.

This meant that the Active Social Contributors within the prison service who were supporting the initiative changed from being voluntary Team Members to being paid Team Members. Ironically, this was more counter-productive than productive, as the staff involved had enjoyed giving their time free, and felt less satisfied once the rehablitation training became part of their daily work roster.

Simon remained heavily involved in rolling the programmes out, and developing new ones. Karl grew and flourished as an individual, and the sense of humour that had been confined to deeds achievable by interactive technology burgeoned in his social life. He even went on to become an amusing and effective public speaker.

On leaving prison, Karl went to work for Sapiens Knowledge, where he became one of their star technology experts. One Sunday morning, about six weeks after Karl's joining, there was a special delivery to Simon and Fleur's home. Over the breakfast table they opened the beautifully wrapped packages. They contained a magnificent smoked salmon, caviar, and a large bunch of orchids. The note accompanying them read, 'From Karl. With thanks. PS I paid for them with my first pay cheque.'

Epilogue

THE AIM OF this book is to make some suggestions on perspectives and attitudes. Change is all about us. We all know this to be true, but are sometimes slow to take on the implications for us, and the historical context in which we exist. The central message is that there are very solid grounds for hope. Wearing the Coat of Change with courage and confidence means looking at ourselves as humans, not as the individual roles we play of worker, father, daughter, sportsman, musician, etc.

Change – particularly the shift brought about by the Incomes Revolution – means that we are, at the same time, more alone, and in need of individual strength, yet at the same time more interdependent for our mutual survival. Looking at ourselves as humans forces us out of the comfort zones of our familiar individual roles, and confronts us with the challenge of playing a wider, more proactive role in society.

We can convince ourselves we are busy, busy in whatever employment we are currently engaged in, pay token regard to the wider context of society by watching the news, but we are kidding ourselves if we think that will be enough to see us through in the longer term. The wind of change is becoming more frequent, and more capricious. Mini-hurricanes and tornados rip off parts of our roofs, and floods attack the basement. Our trees are shaken, and while some bend, others snap.

The answer is to get into shape to cope with the challenges posed by this menacing change in the social weather pattern. Beyond that, we must look for opportunities arising from the new situation to regain control of our social weather. For opportunities there are. External threat tends to unify through raising the common interest to a level above that of petty differences. The common interest as humans can therefore be raised above these petty differences, to achieve harmony in a society threatened increasingly with disharmony.

I have therefore attempted to provide a toolbox for re-equipping ourselves, both as individuals and within the wider human context, to take on, and benefit from, the threats and opportunities that face us. Like a carpenter's tool belt, the Coat of Change is lined with these tools, not all of which will be necessary at any one time, but may be the appropriate tool for the job as the occasion arises.

Doing tools and thinking tools

These tools are quite specific, and cover two areas – doing and thinking. The doing tools are suggested processes that can be applied to surviving and flourishing in the new environment of work and income. The first tool is the STOC Check (Strengths, Talents, Opportunities and Challenges). The benefit of the STOC Check over a conventional curriculum vitae is that it includes important life skills, like honesty, and a sense of humour. These talents and characteristics are important both in gaining insight into what we have to offer, and in building our sense of self-worth.

The IBG Action Plan is important, because it maps out the strategy for income diversification. It defines, and puts specific action against, the crucially important core, alternative, and secondary income streams. In examining examples of types of diversified income, it is worth looking most closely at network marketing. Franchising is worth considering, but does not pass all the tests of IBG-hood because the key element of independence is in doubt. The IBG Action Plan also establishes the priorities for personal development, and social contribution.

The Planning and Evaluation Schedule has two objectives. Firstly, it puts specific dates against the action committed to in the IBG Action Plan. Secondly, it allocates each action with an Importance and Urgency rating. This gives new perspective and clarity. Actions that are both important and urgent can be addressed first, and judgements can be made on the other elements of the Schedule. The approach thus makes planning both coherent and effective.

The Brand Positioning Statement defines our positioning as an IBG. By distilling our competitive advantage against others in the market, and crystallising our specific benefits, (and adducing support for these benefits), we begin to get some real insight into how to market ourselves.

By living and breathing our Brand Positioning Statement, we can bring more clarity to our roles in our core and alternative income stream employment, and develop our competitive advantage within the same context. We thus make ourselves indispensable, not only through our energy and commitment, but through the specific skills, talents, and abilities we bring to the role we are playing in the organisation.

The Brand Me portfolio is a concept of the real world. Just as Procter and Gamble markets products as diverse as Ariel washing powder, Pringles crisps, Vidal Sassoon hair products and Pampers disposable nappies, we will find ourselves playing different roles in our core, alternative and secondary income activities. This is not a question of incoherence, or corporate schizophrenia, it is merely a flexible and mature response to the different roles we are all called upon to play in the different areas of our lives. The consistency lies in the integrity and personal style we bring to each activity. Team Me extends this concept to involve us all as leaders of our own diverse activities. Once more, integrity across our activities – knowing that we are walking the talk – underpins our confidence and ability to become strong leaders of Team Me.

Probably the most difficult to write is the Values and Mission Statement. This defines who we are, by establishing a hierarchy of values, and commits us to thinking through our central mission in life. Articulating our mission helps us to find the vision and strength to fulfil our potential. As a result, as we move towards achieving our mission we are not blown off course by the shite that inevitably impedes our way throughout the journey. Of all the tools this is the most important.

The Command Centre bridges the gap between doing and thinking tools. It is the doing tool that facilitates thinking. The concepts of the Independent Business Generator, the Mastermind group, and active listening also bridge the gap. The concept of the IBG is a thinking tool in the sense that it encompasses attitude, perspective and self perception, and a doing tool, in the sense that its very concept is a call to action. The focus of thinking tools is that of personal growth. Personal growth allows us to create our own income and our own lives.

Mind Leadership, one of the tools of personal growth, gives us a way of standing back from the battle. It enables us to find a larger dimension to the situation, and to look for new ways of adding value. The core of personal development is developing our integrity, and with it, improving our sense of self-worth. Low self-worth leaves us with tethered thinking. Consciously untethering our minds allows us to regain some insight into

– and access to – the resources that we all have within us, but which are too often suppressed, or disabled.

There are no short cuts to a resilient sense of self-worth. Having an Abundance Mentality, being an Enhancer, rather than a Poisoner, *acting as if* the desired state is already achieved, all help to increase the control our feelings and reactions, by making us more flexible, proactive and positive.

Gaining consistent access to the enormous power of our subconscious minds to give us insight and guidance is a source of significant strength and reassurance. Half an hour in our Quiet Place each day, listening to our subconscious, can reaffirm our commitment to our course of action, as well as giving answers to challenges that face us along the way.

The specific tools of reliving past success and preliving future success – through visualisations and affirmations – help us to *re-enable our resources*. These are daily disciplines, and, like reading personal development books and listening to tapes, need to be undertaken consistently. The mind, like the body, takes time to build up fitness, needs constant exercise to hold onto it, and can lose it with unnerving speed.

Crucial to all self development is *the power of association*. Without association, work on personal growth becomes significantly more challenging. For this reason, either a Mastermind group which meets regularly – not just at the inception of a project – or association within a professional network marketing group, is *crucial for long-term effectiveness*. Association with positive people within a professional network marketing group has a double benefit. One is the support provided by positive, motivated, energised people. The other is that a professional network marketing group has, as its core, personal growth and development. Business growth follows personal growth.

Books, tapes and association, as the tools of personal growth, are just as much tools of the network marketing business, as are products and services. Being part of a *system* of personal development also helps overcome the temptation to reject the culture in the early stages. The culture is different. For a start, it's positive. Some of the books need a positive approach to accommodate their style and presentation, before they yield up their gems. The first two, or even three, books may seem strange and unrewarding. Perseverance brings rewards, however. For it is regular, daily reading of the books that brings consistent personal growth.

A friend (whom I met through network marketing) has set up and runs a very successful business selling proprietary software to enable companies to improve significantly the mental and emotional buy-in of employees to the mission, objectives, and culture of their company. He worked in large companies for twenty years before setting up on his own. He now works from home, combining his new business with his existing network marketing business. His wife works with him in both. He confided recently that without the personal growth brought about through the formal learning programmes of network marketing, he doubts whether he would have survived the first year of his new business.

The great thing about a personal development programme is that it never stops. You are always learning new things, and never stop growing. Indeed, when reverses come, there is a ready-made solution. You select a suitable tape and listen to it, or read the right book, or have positive association with a small Mastermind meeting with close friends or colleagues, or a larger one at a seminar or convention. Very quickly, balance is restored, and the Mighty Lion is once more off, and roaring. Eventually, you get beyond proactive coping, and begin to carry your own good weather – both internal and external – around with you.

My personal experience as an IBG gives hope for others. I now have many friends and colleagues who are, or are in the process of becoming, Independent Business Generators. Almost all of them are agreed that whatever offers of solus employment (i.e. a job) they received, they would not give up the control and independence of being an IBG. One friend who, after two or three successful years as an IBG, accepted the offer of a hugely attractive salary package and returned to full-time corporate employment, is now having serious second thoughts. A classic High-flyer, he spends more time in planes than he does with his family, and despite being European Chief Executive for his company, has no control even over his private time. If the choice is between a dinner party with friends, or a summons to a meeting with a visiting fireman from corporate headquarters, there's only one winner, and it's not the one he would have gone for as an IBG.

I now have managed to build up seven or eight separate income streams, most of them with some sort of residual, or royalty, income. Such an arrangement has many benefits – apart from the obvious one of independence. Possibly the most important benefit is that if a client asks for your presence at a time that is scheduled for a child's sports' day, parents' evening, or even a visit to the theatre with the family, you can say with truth that you are already contracted for that time.

The second is that there is no ceiling to your monthly earnings. You may at times miss your target income for a month or two. But there are few joys like pulverising it, and having some spare cash around to spend.

There are always capital projects – a new computer, a new car – that will swallow the money as soon as it's created, let alone all the other deserving causes – treats for the family, and the countless things that aren't really important, but would be nice to have.

The thought of returning to a situation in which the monthly income was fixed, and could not be exceeded, is deeply unexciting. Unless you are on a huge salary as a High-flyer, having a fixed monthly income means you consistently feel broke. You always spend up to the level of your income, however large it sounds, so when the exceptional costs come in, as they do every month, you are always struggling to pay them. As an IBG, you tend to be more controlled in your core spending – just in case – and to get more joy in spending any serendipitous surplus.

The IBG and the ASC in the Team Sector are leadership roles

Proactive, positive people, sometimes without meaning to, become leaders. The Independent Business Generator is a very special animal. He or she is more assured, more highly skilled (through continual retraining), has a broader view of business (through not being over-dependent on one income stream), is better at interacting with people (listens more, has more self-confidence), is better motivated, more highly energised, and more clear-eyed in general. As a result, IBG's are natural leaders.

Alfredo Pareto, the Italian economist, developed the 80/20 rule in the 1890s. It is an undying truth that 20 per cent of the effort produces 80 per cent of the reward. Leaving aside the minute percentage of companies and organisations that will constitute the core leadership, the other workers will break down into 80 per cent ultimately dispensable, and 20 per cent indispensable. IBGs will constitute most of the 20 per cent of key workers. Some will be asked to join the core leadership. Those that do, will remain IBGs at heart.

The reason that IBGs will be the heart of the most productive 20 per cent is that they will be more effective operators than non-IBGs. IBGs get on with things, have more energy, and need less supervision, leaving managers more time to get on with issues that are important, rather than the urgent. IBG also stands for I'm Bloody Good. Employers will come to see that IBGs bring more to the party, and in doing so, bring more benefits than risks.

The Value and Mission Statement, along with a sense of vision, and a dream, will be crucial to the leadership qualities and long-term strength of IBGs. The 'I' in IBG stands for independent. With multiple income streams, an IBG will not be plugged into the sort of dominant infrastructure and culture that used to exist in the days of career jobs (unless they are members of professional network marketing organisation). Their values and Mission Statement will provide that culture and infrastructure, and avoid misaligned values, by giving them a profound understanding of who they are, and what they stand for.

The Team Sector means harmony; the alternative is cacophony

The step from being an IBG to being an Active Social Contributor is a short but important one. As we have seen, Independent Business Generators control their own weather, but are not immune to outside influences. The demands of a vigorous personal development schedule necessitate the achievement of a deepening personal integrity. Integrity brings with it an embracing of unchanging principles of behaviour that have underpinned religions and civilised societies through the ages. Central amongst these principles is compassion.

There, but for the grace of god, go I. IBG's will have bounced back from enough failures and knocks of various kinds to know exactly how close they have come at times to needing compassion from others. Compassion will therefore be far more readily available than it is today. Having thrown off the Victim Mentality, which has another expression in the dependency culture, a sense of responsibility begins to flower. Expecting the welfare state to look after the growing underclass – or worse still, expecting it to pull itself up by its own bootstraps – becomes no longer acceptable.

The need for the Team Sector to come into more vigorous existence is clear. As the demands on welfare budgets grow, supercharged by the unassuageable demands for more health care for more elderly people, those welfare budgets, just when they need to be increased, will be reduced by the pressures of uphill demographics. More and more human beings will therefore fall through the cracks.

The Team Sector will thus flourish through forces of push and pull. The mutual self-interest will be clear. The Active Social Contributors who become Team Workers will do so because they genuinely want to help, and because they can see the stability of society is threatened if they don't. Social conscience is one element in the motivation, but only one.

Active desire to help others will be the greater part of the motivation. The receivers will, for the most part, respond positively to the help offered, because they, too, do not want to live in a society that is unstable and dangerous, as well as alienating. The more connections there are – and the more humane, genuinely motivated, and numerous those connections are – the less volatile are the receivers.

Defining the Team Sector as any activity, paid or unpaid, that helps other citizens who are temporarily, or permanently, disadvantaged, or in need of support, means that the Team Sector has always been there. It has always been there because human compassion has always been there. It is already huge, constituting paid and unpaid workers in the health and social security services, the fire services, the prison service, etc. What Active Social Contributors will do, in becoming Team Members, is to supercharge the sector – for the individual, and the common, good. They will be happy to work alongside paid professionals, who, in turn, will be happy to work alongside them. They will all be Team Members within the Team Sector.

The important point about defining ourselves as Team Workers, or Team Members, in the Team Sector, is that we avoid many of these challenges of conventional definition – and accusations of hypocrisy – because the mindset is changed to one of givers and receivers being in the same team. The receivers can accept help because they know it is generously and full-heartedly given. The positive uplift of the disabled elderly person receiving a visit, or a prisoner receiving coaching in new skills, sparks a reciprocal positive uplift in the giver. Like the cheering spectator at the marathon who gets a responding wave from the struggling runner, it is positive in both directions. Both are giving, both are receiving, and both, therefore, are winning. Everyone is in the Team Sector. The rich, the poor, the unemployed, the retired, the time-poor High-flyers – they *all feel the need to contribute, possibly in both directions, in order to become human.*

Good companies and corporations will also get involved in the Team Sector. The best companies and corporations try genuinely to put something back into society, above and beyond the provision of employment. Funding time out of productivity gains is a further aspect of the Team Sector being about win/win.

A further dimension of this win/win aspect is the huge benefit provided by the Team Sector being a vast and worthwhile absorber of manpower (and womanpower). This is not to say that the state will be the employer of last resort. Much of this manpower and womanpower will be voluntary. Even more significant is the fact that Team Sector activities can't be replaced by technology. The caring skills required by Team Members are not skills that can be replaced by a computer. Those caring skills – varied and complex as they are – define us as humans.

As Independent Business Generators grow and flourish, and as the Team Sector grows wider, more varied, more coherent, and more demonstrably win/win, individuals will have the opportunity to become more fulfilled as human beings. Their work life will be more rich and varied, and their social life will be more satisfying, because it will expand from taking pleasure with friends, into giving pleasure to others, who will, in turn, become friends.

The methods outlined in this book work. They are proven techniques, and many of them encompass the wisdom of the ages. I personally have validated them in my own life, so I know they are effective, and will work for you too. For most people, as for me, wearing the Coat of Change will feel strange at first. New skills and new talents need to be developed. For all of us, work is required, but the rewards are there to be taken.

The work involves the diligent pursuit of personal growth that will extend our comfort zone, and build our courage until we not only feel at home in the new environment, but discover that it can be liberating. Independence, like freedom, is hugely exciting, particularly if you're deprived of it. The feeling of control that seeps back into your life is uplifting. More so than owning your own company, where there are always other shareholders and staff to consider, and you feel that you are somehow setting a bad example if you are not first to arrive and last to leave each day. As an IBG, you can become truly independent, so that *you spend time where it is most effective as a human being.*

Felicity, Norman, and Simon have shown us the way. They have encountered challenges, but have not only overcome them, they have grown into riper and fuller human beings. Following their example of courage and good humour, we can emulate them, and eventually wear the coat with some style and flair. It will never be a lightweight coat, as the tools attached to the inside need to be carried in constant readiness, but it will be substantial enough to face the winds of change. Wearing it, we will look good. More importantly, we will feel good.

Suggested Reading

The Seven Habits of Highly Effective People, by Stephen R. Covey, Simon and Schuster, 1992. This, and the book that follows, are great books. They are not light reading, and should be taken a chunk at a time. Well worth the effort.

Principle Centred Leadership, also by Stephen R. Covey, Simon and Schuster, 1992.

When Corporations Rule the World, by David C. Korten, Earthscan, 1996. This book is full of fresh insights into the traditional role of capitalist economics and its global effects, particularly in the Third World. If you have even the slightest interest in economics, or poverty, it's a must to read.

The World in 2020, by Hamish McRae, HarperCollins, 1994. Written by an economist with rare insight and humanity.

Word/Exel etc. Simplified series: the 3D Visual Approach to Learning, IDG Books Worldwide Inc, 1995. A wonderful idiot's guide to all you need to know to drive a computer (which isn't much).

Feel the Fear and Do It Anyway, by Susan Jeffers, Random House, 1991. An excellent, and very digestible, book on getting a grip on the underlying insecurities that we all have.

Unlimited Power, by Anthony Robbins, Simon and Schuster, 1986. He modified some of the ideas later, but it's a good introduction to NLP in particular, and especially Robbins' approach to personal development.

Psycho Cybernetics 2000, by Maxwell Maltz, Prentice Hall, 1997. A new edition of a golden oldie of a book, and full of actionable wisdom. The book is better than the title. Well worth a read.

Think and Grow Rich, by Napoleon Hill, The Wilshire Book Company, 1970. Another golden oldie. Remember that it was originally published in 1937.

How to Win Friends and Influence People, by Dale Carnegie, Cedar 1953. A classic for good reason. Everyone should read it, just to say they've done so.

Multi-level Marketing, by Peter Clothier, Kogan Page, 1997. A good insight into network marketing, from a former Trading Standards officer.

Promises to Keep, by Charles Paul Conn, G.P. Putnam and Sons, 1986. A book on Amway, and how it works, by an enthusiastic outsider.

Born to Succeed, by Colin Turner, Element Books, 1996. An excellent communication of the key principles.

Index